MAGNUS OPUM

Better Late Than Never

By Nancy Bernard

© 2010 Nancy E. Bernard

A note on the title: I put a roomful of Latinists on the task of translating Magnus Opum, but they got nowhere. It doesn't parse. Let's pretend it means untold riches.

DEDICATION

To Susan Secor, for introducing me to the love of my life.
And, of course, to Magnus. You gave me new life, new hope and, for the first time in a long time, a future. I can never repay you for all of that.

TABLE OF CONTENTS

Prologue 1
Chapter 1   First Hook 3
Chapter 2   Dog Sightings 5
Chapter 3   Loaner Dog 10
Chapter 4   Meeting the Kids 13
Chapter 5   Keeping My Doggie 18
Chapter 6   Raven, 1963-1971 23
Chapter 7   Dog House 30
Chapter 8   Threat Identification 32
Chapter 9   Competition 36
Chapter 10   Impulse Driving 39
Chapter 11   Jean 42
Chapter 12   Grace 45
Chapter 13   Dog Dumping 46
Chapter 14   House of Poo 48
Chapter 15   First Vet Visit 51
Chapter 16   Big White Goat 56
Chapter 17   Second Vet Visit 61
Chapter 18   Café Society 63
Chapter 19   First Review 67
Chapter 20   Acceptable Classes 69
Chapter 21   Fast Forward 72
Chapter 22   The Vizslas 74

Chapter 23	Park Rules	78
Chapter 24	Itchy and Scratchy	81
Chapter 25	Vespers	83
Chapter 26	Sunday Dinner	85
Chapter 27	Why Me, Really	90
Chapter 28	Great Dane	91
Chapter 29	Takedown	92
Chapter 30	Hammett and Magnus	94
Chapter 31	Amy and Skip	96
Chapter 32	Turkish Boys	101
Chapter 33	Ancient Breed	102
Chapter 34	Civility	106
Chapter 35	Dance Steps	108
Chapter 36	Mary's Gift	110
Chapter 37	Bedtime	114
Chapter 38	The Art Auction	115
Chapter 39	Sushi Dates	117
Chapter 40	Life Happens to Susan S.	121
Chapter 41	Autumn Routine	124
Chapter 42	Dumping People	130
Chapter 43	Spousal Relations	132
Chapter 44	Dan, Dan, Cookie Man	134
Chapter 45	Cyndi	137
Chapter 46	A Little Thing Called The ACL	141

Chapter 47	The Kuvasz List	144
Chapter 48	Does He Shed?	146
Chapter 49	Da Pacem	148
Chapter 50	Easter Week	151
Chapter 51	Of Course It's My Fault	153
Chapter 52	Bones and Bifocals	155
Chapter 53	Dolly	156
Chapter 54	Osteopath	159
Chapter 55	Another California Kuvasz	160
Chapter 56	Poor Old Guy	166
Chapter 57	Hot Spots	167
Chapter 58	Dog People	171
Chapter 59	Tough Guy	172
Chapter 60	Little White Dog	174
Chapter 61	Dog Introductions	176
Chapter 62	Toby	178
Chapter 63	Timmy and TimDad	181
Chapter 64	Assumption	184
Chapter 65	Mrs. James	189
Chapter 66	Stumbling	193
Chapter 67	Tumor	196
Chapter 68	Medical Assistance	198
Chapter 69	A Pointer Gets It	199
Chapter 70	Leash Training	201

Chapter 71	Goats and Donkeys	205
Chapter 72	Dinner with Dutchmen	207
Chapter 73	Bad Days	209
Chapter 74	Bicycle Man	212
Chapter 75	Someone's Out There	213
Chapter 76	Onward	215
Chapter 77	Cookies and Corpses	216
Chapter 78	Magnus's Bloodline	218
Chapter 79	Hammett Fights Back	220
Chapter 80	Anxiety	222
Chapter 81	Thanksgiving	224
Chapter 82	Risky Business	230
Chapter 83	La Luna	235
Chapter 84	Lights and Music	237
Chapter 85	Night Herons	242
Chapter 86	Sorry Season	244
Chapter 87	Cyndi's 2nd Visit	247
Chapter 88	High Technology	251
Chapter 89	The Girls	253
Chapter 90	Back to The Ravine	255
Chapter 91	Hachi	256
Chapter 92	Dog Intelligence	262
Chapter 93	Waterworks of A Different Kind	264
Chapter 94	Visible Kitty	267

Chapter 95	Veterinary Decision	268
Chapter 96	My Hero	269
Chapter 97	Leg Hydraulics	273
Chapter 98	Traffic Management	275
Chapter 99	Great Blue	276
Chapter 100	Bongo Dog	282
Chapter 101	Too Hot	284
Chapter 102	More Bad Judgment	288
Chapter 103	Gaming Nancy	290
Chapter 104	Bad Judgment, Round Three	291
Chapter 105	Antisocial	295
Chapter 106	Gift Season	297
Chapter 107	Cyndi's 3rd Visit	306
Chapter 108	Out and About	311
Chapter 109	Facing Facts	313
Chapter 110	The New Normal	315
Chapter 111	The Price of Love	316
Chapter 112	The Cart in The Park	317
Chapter 113	I'm a Genius	321
Chapter 114	Happy Feet	322
Chapter 115	Goodnight, My Love	324
Gracias	Acknowledgements	328
Appendix A	Magnus Mealz	329
Appendix B	Susan's Champions	332

Prologue

Imagine an elderly Hungarian gentleman from an ancient, noble family, with long, thick, white hair and a still-powerful physique. His posture is proud, his movements are graceful, and his voice is a deep, rich bass.

He assesses people and situations quickly and accurately, and takes on the role of prince or goofball or romantic poet or avenging angel or whatever other character will bring things around to where they need to be.

His code of honor impels him to intercept rude, unfair, or aggressive behavior. He corrects offenders without hesitation, using firm language and strong action. His anger is always righteous, never excessive, and quick to pass.

His sense of justice is leavened with wit. There's a youthful glint in his eye, and a smile plays about his mouth. He can be a tease, he can be earthy, but he's never vulgar or mean. When he's happy, he dances with me. He'll play with me like a little kid, fall into my arms weak with laughter, and rest his head against my chest in utter trust.

Though he is a man of few words—his gestures and expressions communicate his thoughts clearly—when he does speak, his meaning is clear and his language expressive. I have come to respect and trust his intelligence and sense of proportion.

Ours is a relationship of mutual service and support, graciously given and as graciously received. We never tire of each other's company, we never lose the acute awareness of each other's presence, we never lose the ability to step back, forgive, and make up with a kiss when communication goes awry. We're never far from being at play, so that we enjoy our routines as much as our adventures.

He would do anything for me. As long as I treat him with respect—which will be forever—he will give me what I ask, on a silver platter and with a generous garnish of love. As long as he treats me with respect—which will be forever—I will do the same for him.

This is the man who came into my life after many years of disappointment in love. He is considerably older than I am, and has multiple health issues. But he welcomes each downturn as a challenge to overcome. He has the most elastic soul, the most tenacious grip on life and the most appreciation for the small joys of anyone I've ever known or expect to know. He is a wonderful patient who fights back with determination, and kisses my hand in thanks for good care in hard times.

You're laying it on a bit thick, aren't you dear?

The only thing he won't tolerate is pedicures. I'm not to mess with his precious feet.

His name is Magnus. He has a black nose.

CHAPTER 1   FIRST HOOK

I didn't know much about Susan S. except that she'd slipped quietly into a choir I sang with, was a fellow alto, bred some kind of big dog, didn't talk about herself, and made me feel we'd been friends forever in spite of that. She was fun to sing with—a good sight-reader who kept her pitch up—but more importantly, she got along with the other singers easily and equably. That's no mean trick, because they are not what most people would consider normal, and they're all non-normal in their own special ways.

None of my choir mates would object to that statement.

One Sunday she mentioned that she'd brought a dog with her, and asked if I'd like to meet him. I loved dogs, hadn't had one since I was a girl, but was always ready to interfere with other people's dogs. So I said, "Sure. Let's go right now."

We walked to the parking lot under infinite blue skies and mature trees all made over with young leaves. It was Easter season, and the world was new. Susan S. slid the door of her van open, and a big, fluffy, white dog with a hunky head and floppy ears poked his head out, greeted me enthusiastically and jumped down to the pavement. I rubbed his ears and neck and danced around with him a bit. He danced back.

Ah, I love the ladies and the ladies love me. Isn't life grand?

"So, who is this?" I asked.

"This is Magnus."

I said, "His eyes are blue!" A whitish, opaque blue, with no visible pupils. Susan S. said, "Yes. His cornea is discolored, but his vision's all right."

I said, "He looks kind of like a golden retriever."

Susan S. made a moue and said, "He is not a retriever."

"What's his breed again?"

"Hungarian kuvasz."

"How do you spell that?"

She spelled it. She didn't pronounce the z. I promptly decided that the correct pronunciation was kuvaschzt, and she didn't correct me. She's like that—lets you say or do stupid things and just gazes at you. A Hungarian-American friend corrected me a few weeks later. "The z after the s is not pronounced. It's a Hungarian thing. The plural form is kuvaszok."

I thought Magnus was a sweet, gorgeous, fluffy pup, and baby-talked him and fussed over him and romped around with him. I had no idea what—or who—he really was. Susan observed this with an odd half-smile. At the time, I thought the smile was mystical. I now know it was partly disdainful—come on, he's a serious dog—and partly fateful. She knew exactly what she was doing, and it was breaking her heart.

Chapter 2   Dog Sightings

The cute dogs of Prague gave me a bad case of puppy lust. A woman who'd sung with the choir for a while lived there, and invited us to join in an early music festival in September. She also organized a round of Masses for us to sing in Renaissance and Baroque churches around the city, and organized accommodations for us in an old monastery near the castle, in the most picturesque part of town. It was an opportunity not to be missed, but my health was bad, I had lots of work to catch up on, and I never like leaving the cats alone, so I tried to get out of it. The choir director said he needed me badly, and I was so flattered that I decided to go (he knew what he was doing, too). I was well enough to do the rehearsals and masses every day, but not well enough to go on the afternoon tours, so I stayed behind, rested, and took shortish walks around the city.

Dogs were everywhere. Exotic pedigrees, the ubiquitous golden retrievers, mutts, all walking freely beside their owners in the middle of town. The only dogs who were leashed were also muzzled. I asked one lady why she had one dog on leash and the other off. She looked at the muzzled and leashed dog, smiled, and said, "That one can't be trusted." She let me play with the off-leash dog, a fine, strong Schnauzer. It was a warm, sunny day in a small, green, leafy park with old-style cast iron benches along the curving paths. It felt good.

I went to the Medieval Castle and saw dogs milling through the crowds. Stood looking at a Baroque church and saw dogs lounging on the steps. Back and forth across St. Charles Bridge: dogs. Around Wenceslas Square: dogs. Slouching around the monastery: dogs. Through a parade of tour groups: dogs.

On every street I also saw strikingly beautiful, stylish young women, with and without dogs, striding gracefully past heavily burdened grannies in shapeless, mismatched skirts and blouses, who had been robbed of their own youth and beauty, first by Fascists and then by Communists, and who never walked with dogs. The drab older women regarded the jubilant younger women silently, remembering. Even after almost twenty years of recovery, you can still see signs of serial occupation in crumbling walls and faded paint. You can feel a lingering sense of weariness, so inappropriate in this city built for and dedicated to pleasure.

Prague's popularity with tourists is based on the fact that it is one of the few cities in Europe whose historic centers were not devastated by bombing in WWII. It has always been considered the Vienna of the north, and it is still very, very pretty. Not magnificent or glorious or sublime, but pretty. In the best manifestation of prettiness. It is all frosting and gilding and elaborately etched murals and garlands and cherubs. Medieval and Renaissance monuments survive, but the overall effect is wedding-cake Baroque.

Prague was the summer playground of the Hapsburgs, which is why it looks that way.

I also think that's why the city's populace is so good-looking. Firm jawed, clear-eyed, rosy skinned, well built, with shining hair, erect but relaxed carriage, and friendly, gentle manners. I imagine the Hapsburgs were fond of pretty playmates, and imported as many as they could find. That they established a genetic foundation for generations of handsome men and beautiful women. Either that, or Czechs are just genetically gifted.

Czechs today appear to be effortlessly in love with each other, their city, and their lives. The squads—no, battalions—no, army corps—of tour groups appeared to be in love with dumplings, beer, marionettes, garnets and amber. I was in love with dogs. The dog people were delighted that I should be in love with their dogs.

A small brunette woman in a pale yellow business suit walked by with a big, well-kept golden retriever in the Old Town section. Off-leash, of course. They approached a simple circular fountain carved from butter-colored stone. The dog jumped in to play with a half-eaten apple that was floating there. The woman watched with a smile as he jumped out of the fountain with the apple in his mouth and dropped it at her feet. She threw it back in. He bobbed for the apple several more times until she quietly said the word, and the dog went to her heel and followed her away.

This would never be tolerated in America. Someone would have started shouting about filth in the fountain and the dangers to children and not wanting to be splashed when the dog shook out his coat and the dog should be on a leash. Czechs aren't like that. Dogs can go to cafés Dogs can go to restaurants. People can be trusted to train their dogs and handle them responsibly. Everyone welcomed dogs. Every dog was cute. Even the ancient miniature dog of indeterminate breed sitting in an old street musician's accordion case was cute. My choir mates got used to hearing me cry "Cute dog!" and running off to snap a picture. They started giving me cute dog alerts. The cute dogs of Prague.

Back home, I searched "cute dogs" on YouTube. The talking dogs. The skateboarding dogs. The stumbling and rolling puppies. I discovered videos of Carolyn Scott and Rookie, a golden retriever she trained from puppyhood in freestyling, the sport of dancing with dogs. They were so wonderful, so in love, so joyful, that I watched and re-watched that clip over the next few weeks. I still watch it when I need a lift. I show it to friends. It plasters goofy smiles on their faces, even if they're cat people. It aroused an intense desire in me to run out and adopt a worthy soul, but I was worried about the cats. I was afraid Princess Margaret would go outside to live on the fence, or that Dammett Hammett would scratch my eyes out—he's a jealous lover in a brown velvet tuxedo. So I resisted.

That winter my health went on a steady, downward trajectory. I have fibromyalgia, a boring pain and fatigue thing, which is usually manageable, but every once in a while flares up. This time the flareup was a red-hot railroad spike in my shoulder. I tried exercises, stretching, chiropractic, electrical stimulation, ice, heat, and got nothing. No relief. My digestion also went awry. It seemed like everything I ate disagreed with me—it got so I was afraid to eat. I'd try to entice myself by making my favorite dishes and plating them attractively, and then would stare at the food for a while before trying a bite. The food almost hurt in my mouth. I'd choke down a few forkfuls, shove the plate away and give up. So I dropped thirty pounds. They needed dropping, but I don't recommend the technique.

One of the side effects of being sick is that, unless you have devoted friends and family nearby, it's isolating. Most of my friends had dropped away years before, when a flareup crippled me for six months. The few people I was still in touch with this time were turned off by my attitude. It was negative. Sour, critical, and unthinking. My beloved pseudo-niece stopped speaking to me. The man I'd worked for and stuck with through thick and thin for thirteen years had his office manager call to let me know my services were no longer needed. She didn't have to say my performance was under par—I knew it was. My family were no help, being on the east coast.

I don't think anyone knew how sick I was, actually. You learn not to talk about it. You don't want to make pain the focus of your life; you don't want to be a whiner. You cover.

You center into yourself, hide at home, stop trying new experiences, or even doing the things you love to do. The only comfort that remained was the kitties, who encouraged me to spend as much time as possible in bed with them. I got weaker and weaker, and by February was tottering around in tears most of the time.

I didn't go to the doctor, because doctors always said, "It'll go away on its own in six weeks," or "You need to relax."

Ha. You try relaxing with a red-hot spike in your shoulder.

When I finally did go, the doctor took one look at me and offered a cortisone shot, muscle relaxers and anti-inflammatory meds. She told me to take the pills three times a day.

Ahhhhhhh.

The pain went away. But so did the rest of me.

One morning, I woke up puzzling over an odd dream I'd had about policemen in my bedroom. I went downstairs to make tea, and found auto insurance papers all over the counter.

The police in my bedroom were not a dream.

I happened to be wearing a sleazy, clingy, bright red nightgown and imagined displaying myself in it to healthy young men. The sight would not have been inspiring. I hurried upstairs, got properly dressed, and went out to the carport. My car was parked askew. There were fresh scratches on the rear bumper. There was a big dent in the wall of an adjoining carport.

Time to rethink medication strategies.

I cut the meds down to one per day, and then went off them entirely. Keeping a food diary settled the digestive issues (the main culprit was the milk in my morning tea). I went off dairy, started to get my life back, and by March was much improved. At that point all I needed was a dog to get me out of the house, into the fresh air, into the company of human beings, and motivate me to build up my strength. I started thinking more seriously about breeds and discussing them with Susan S.

Chapter 3 — Loaner Dog

Susan S. had problems of her own, so we'd formed a mutual support society and were calling each other several times a week to see if either one of us had bothered to get out of bed or get dressed or accomplish any to-dos. She had nine dogs at the time: half a dozen six-month-old puppies, their dam, and two older dogs.

The dogs were part of her problem. Feeding and dosing and grooming and walking and minding nine dogs didn't leave a lot of time for finding a job, much less selling the pups. My problem was simpler. I wasn't overwhelmed with tasks. I just lacked motivation. A few weeks after meeting the gorgeous dog in the parking lot, she asked if I'd like to borrow one of her seniors to see if the cats could tolerate a dog. I said okay. My heart sank a little at the word "senior," but it was just a test drive, right?

I met Susan S. at the ride-share lot off 280 on Page Mill road. The 280 claims to be the most beautiful highway in America. It may well be. We were facing some rolling foothills, which I think of as sleeping lions: rounded, thinly clad in champagne-colored grasses, sinewed with canyons, and sparsely studded with round-crowned live oaks and lucky horses. Behind us, the wooded slopes of the Santa Cruz mountains rose steeply, thickly studded with multi-million-dollar, geologically and flammalogically precarious homes amid towering Douglas firs, madrone, and fuel-rich chaparral scrub. Susan S. was standing under a live oak by the van when I drove up, and had the cargo door open so the dog she'd introduced me to could catch the breeze.

What's this woman doing here?

She's a tallish, handsome woman with long brown hair that she wears in various old fashioned styles, up or down. She is sturdily built and in her middle age. She can be very hard to read. As you're talking to her, her eyes will go abstracted, or they'll go sharp, or she'll gaze off into the distance. You can hear the wheels turning, but she doesn't share the workings of her mind.

"There you are," she said, with a big, flashy smile. "I just bought him a new leash and collar, and brought enough food to last him for a couple of weeks." She took out a new choke collar and slid it on. "That's a perfect fit. You have to work a little to get it around his ears, which is the way it should be. Take it off when he's in the car or at home. I never want to see that collar on him in the car."

"Why?"

Her eyes went dark. "They can get hung up and die horribly. I've seen it. You don't want to." She was wearing a light yellow blouse, and a long cotton skirt with a pink-and white floral pattern on it. It struck me as oddly femmy clothing for a strong-jawed, opinionated person who was casually wiping drool from her dog's chin with her bare hand.

I didn't think I could do that.

We got into choir-gossip for a while, which is always fun. Then Susan got onto her own strong convictions about Bible-based religion. I'm always interested in this—there are so many ways to read the Bible, and people always bring up something new.

I think I'll just amble off and entertain myself.

"Magnus, come here. NO." Susan said.

"He's just going to find a place to pee," I said.

"Yeah, you pee when and where I tell you to pee," she said, giving Magnus the look. He came back quietly.

It was clear that I was not going to be as macho a dog person as Susan was. Then again, I'd only had one dog, and she was a Labrador, and they're known for their sweet nature and obedience skills. Kuvasz dogs are not known for either of those qualities, but I didn't know that. Yet.

Susan snapped a brand new, bright blue, nylon leash onto Magnus's collar, and handed me the loop at the other end. She got a kick out of watching him disappear into my little Nissan.

"Look! He just fits." She paused, tilted her head and smiled. "Your nice black upholstery…"

As if I cared.

The whole way home, Magnus whined and licked my face, drooled, barked at other dogs. He also barked at bicyclists, motorcycles, men wheeling strollers (?), and people carrying yellow plastic shopping bags (??). His bark was a big basso profundo WOOF. It made me jump and flinch when it went off directly into my ear. It was going off directly in my ear a lot. I tried to calm him, speaking softly and touching his neck.

Who are all these people? Where is she taking me?

When we got back to the condo, I took him for a walk to introduce him to the neighborhood. He walked right beside me, on the yard-side of the sidewalk so he could sniff, see who had been there, when they'd been there, what they'd done, who he could expect to encounter in the future, and how he might expect them to act. I watched him, trying to see into him, but he was placid, not expressing much of anything that I could see. I had no idea who he was or what his life had been before me—as I said, Susan S. is not forthcoming with details—and was trying to fill in the blanks with telepathy. It was nice to focus on figuring out what was going on with someone other than myself. Besides, Magnus's head was much nicer to look at than the inside of my head.

I slipped his leash off to see what he would do. He continued to walk beside me calmly, at heel. After a minute or so, I snapped the leash back on.

He'd had some training.

Chapter 4 — Meeting the Kids

Magnus walked in the front door. Hammett and Margaret recoiled. Then they ran. They stayed outside, peering in from a safe perch on the fence as I let the man explore the condo.

I fed the man and gave him water. The kids wandered back in and watched him warily from indoor high places. Good. At least they were in the house. I let them be, went into the bedroom, got on the floor with Magnus and played with him and petted him and got him all relaxed. The kids followed, keeping an eye on things, and crept in around the walls, under the furniture, and slipped up on to the bed. Then I gently and firmly put my arm around the man's shoulders. I had read that this was a dominance gesture, and had used it successfully on a few out-of-control canines. Magnus was big enough and strong enough that I wanted him to know that I was in charge. He didn't like it much. He squirmed. I stayed calm. He settled. Then I put my chin on top of his head. I had read that this was a stronger dominance gesture. He didn't like it. He squirmed. I stayed calm. He settled.

Ah. Another female who wants to play alpha bitch. I've been dining out on that one all my life.

The kids watched this from the foot of the bed. They clearly didn't think much of what was going on. Usually they are at odds with each other—Hammett devils Margaret something awful—but with a big dog in play, they put up a strong united front.

That united front softened much sooner than I expected. Margaret stopped hiding from Magnus in one day. In three days Hammett and Magnus and I were on the upstairs landing, Hammett sitting at the top of the stairs and staring at Magnus, who was a few feet away. Magnus sighed softly, backed up, and lay down with his head on his paws.

I've since seen clips of young kuvaszok being introduced to their flocks. The puppy lies on its back, exposes its belly, and lets the sheep examine it and poke it with their noses. It's hard to get sheep to be friendly with creatures that are essentially wolves, so the puppy puts on an ostentatious show of submission until the sheep relax.

Hammett hadn't really won. Magnus had simply accepted him as flock, and let him believe that he was in charge.

Actually, Hammett has been in charge since the day he came home. I found him and Margaret in a local shelter that socializes the animals to each other in room-sized cages. My former cat had spent so much time alone—I had basically been coming home only to sleep—that my sole criterion was to find two cats who could get along. The cat who was to become Margaret was lying on her back in a play structure, waving her paws languidly at the one who was to become Hammett, who was playing cat's paw with her. Or so I thought. Later I realized that Hammett was picking on Margaret, and she was wearily fending him off. So much for my good intentions.

The friend who had brought me to the shelter took one look at him and said, "He'll give you years of devilment." I didn't know what she meant. I do now.

Hammett is almost a Burmese—slim and brown, with the apple face of Asian cats. He's extremely handsome. He's not vain, but he knows his looks work in his favor and uses them on everyone, putting on a sweet, demure face and gazing up at you from beneath a shyly lowered brow. The scamp.

Margaret is almost a tabby Maine coon cat, with huge eyes and terrific Cleopatra eye makeup and tufts of white fur in her ears and between her toes. She's more interested in monitoring the state of the food bowl than in socializing. She cries piteously to make me go upstairs so that I can refill the food bowl and shake it to redistribute the contents. Every day, though the bowl is never empty, she makes me go through that ritual. I always sing "shake, shake your bowly" to the old R&B tune when I do this.

On the kids' first night here they got on every surface, smelled every object, poked into every corner, and scoped out potential escape routes. They were about six months old. Hammett found an iron kettle I had filled with thyme from the garden, hopped in it, and claimed it for his litter box.

Margaret got on the sofa. Hammett got on the back of the sofa, tipped a pillow over onto Margaret's back, and jumped down onto it. She tolerated this for some reason, but she really shouldn't have. It set a bad precedent on who'd be on top, figuratively as well as literally. At bedtime, Margaret followed me right upstairs and got under the covers for a snuggle. Hammett stayed downstairs. After a while, I felt sorry for him and went down to the living room, where he was crouching on the couch. I sat next to him. He stretched up toward me, extending a little brown paw to touch my cheek.

Awwww.

The next day he took command. He assaulted Margaret and tried to mount her and chased her relentlessly. I disciplined him for this in ways that would have reduced another cat to utter neurosis. Nothing hurtful, just domineering, such as scruffing him, pinning him to the floor, staring into his eyes, and saying "Baaaaaad boy, Hammett." He'd be good for maybe half an hour before he'd go after Margaret again.

Before you fire off angry letters about kitty abuse, you have to understand that Hammett is a force of nature. I tried to train him to stay off the dining room table for months. I got a squirt gun. He'd jump up on the table and sit right in front of me, giving me that demure look. I'd pick up the squirt gun and say, "You know what I'm gonna do." He'd squinch his head as far into his shoulders as it could go and squeeze his eyes shut. I'd squirt his face. He wouldn't budge. I'd squirt him half a dozen times. He'd jump down. 30 seconds later he'd be on the table again. I'd pick up the squirt gun and say "You know what I'm gonna do." Sometimes he'd try hiding behind a jar of flowers or a stack of books, using the ultra-demure look. He could keep that up all evening. My friend said I should try flying lessons—fling him across the room a few times. That I couldn't do.

I had to respect his persistence and the range of tactics he deployed to thwart my wishes. He always won. But I still thought poor Princess Puffy Pants deserved a bit of peace, so I kept after him when he assaulted her.

All this is to say that I shouldn't have worried about Hammett and Magnus. Hammett's tough. He never lets Magnus in any way intimidate him. He goes nose-to-nose with the big guy and stands his ground.

Margaret doesn't. She has a habit of peeping around corners and ducking out of sight when you notice her. Magnus noticed, and chased her. I shut him in the bathroom for a few minutes. A few days later, she peeped around the bedroom door while I was watching a movie in bed with Hammett. Magnus chased her again, and I shut him in the bathroom again.

Hammett stayed on the bed and watched me do it. He got up and went to the foot of the bed, straining every muscle, raising and lowering his head like an irritated parrot and looking back at me warily. He jumped down and sniffed the bottom of the bathroom door from one side to the other with jerky movements. He jumped back up on the bed, and paced back and forth at the foot of it, keeping an eye on the door.

I let Magnus out. That was the last time he chased a cat—that I know of. But Margaret kept on putting up a big show of apprehension and distrust, sidling past him as he lay dozing, darting away when she got near his head, jumping on the high places when he came in the room. One afternoon my old man was lying across the open sliding door, dozing in the sun. Margaret appeared on the fence, sped along it, dashed down the miniature kitty staircase that leans I built, flashed across the patio, soared over my man's big body with several feet to spare and shot upstairs. He never even opened his eyes.

Cat? What cat? That was just a little breeze.

Chapter 5

"How are Hammett and Margaret taking Magnus?" Susan asked. "Surprisingly well," I said.

"How is he taking them?"

"He's being a perfect gentleman."

"How's he fitting into your life?"

"Pretty well, I think. He obeys me. I can handle just about any part of his body. He lets me groom him. He's kind of rough on the neighbors, though."

"What does that mean?"

"He lunges and barks a lot."

"Keep him on a very short leash. He'll get used to seeing people around the complex."

"He is *really* aggressive with other dogs."

"Huh. That surprises me. What do you do?"

"First, I try to walk at non-peak hours. Second, I try to cross the street when I see a dog approaching. Third, if people insist on coming near, I tell them he's not friendly. If none of the above works, I get down and hold him and speak calmly to him."

She made a face. "I don't know why people think your dog wants to meet all their dogs. That's so rude. Meanwhile, you must be communicating anxiety to him. Try to stay calm—you can't fake it. You have to be in control."

"I think I'm doing that, but I don't know how."

"It's a mental thing. It's hard to describe."

I tried visualizing a mental thing. It didn't work, somehow.

"How old is he, incidentally?"

"He'll be ten in July."

I was completely unconcerned about his age at that point. I was going to deal with whatever came our way. I said, breezily, "He seems much younger. We have a lot of fun."

"You look better, yourself. Your color is good, and your face is smoother. Is he helping you?"

"No end. It's like he gave me a shot of epinephrine. By the end of the first week, he pretty much put his hands on my shoulders, looked in my eyes, and said, 'You are my loverrrrr now.' With a nice European accent."

"He knows a soft touch when he sees one."

I had one more question.

"Has Magnus always peed squatting?"

"I don't know. I suppose he lifts his leg when there's something to lift it against."

"He doesn't. He squats, and kind of waddles along while he pees. It leaves a very characteristic trail…"

After Mass the next week, she took a deep breath, faced me squarely, and said, "Overall, it sounds like things are going well with you two. If you want him, you can keep him."

"I'll think about it."

That was a bald-faced lie. I had fallen for Magnus, and fallen hard. I was infatuated with him, obsessed with him, and we canoodled and cooed at each other like teenagers. We didn't really understand each other, we didn't have a real partnership yet, but in the first flush of love that didn't matter.

It never does. It's all joy and pleasure at that stage. But I tried to act like I was thinking seriously about dog needs and dog care.

"Why do you want to give him to me?"

"I can't give him the care and attention he needs. Plus, I think he's too hard on the puppies."

I started, and looked at her.

"No one's ever gotten hurt," she said quickly, "But I think he'd be happier without them."

I waited a few more days, and then called her. She wasn't home. I left her a message that consisted of two snippets of song. The first was based on the opening phrase of the Agnus, which reads:

Agnus Dei, qui tollis peccata mundi, miserere nobis
(Lamb of God, who takes away the sins of the world,
have mercy on us).
My version was:
Magnus Dei, qui NON tollis peccata mundi, miserere nobis.
The second snippet was:
"Papa don't preach, I'm in trouble deep.
Papa don't preach, I'm keepin' my doggie."
Susan S. called back. She was laughing. She said, "Who else would use a Gregorian chant reference and a Madonna reference in the same message?"

I decided to find out what a kuvasz is. I Googled kuvasz. I called Susan. I said, without so much as a hello, "What on earth made you think that I could handle a kuvasz?" She said, "I can tell you're good with dogs."

Oh, yeah. "Good with dogs." Based on the lunging and barking and threats Magus was handing out, the kuvasz is not just "a dog." They were bred to fight off wolves and bears and to defend farms, and have been employed in that capacity for centuries. Here's a description from the Kuvasz Club of America:

Kuvasz (Ku-vahss)
Livestock Guardian, Hungary

The kuvasz is a very intelligent, assertive dog, combining great strength with quickness and speed that is often unexpected in a dog of its size. A kuvasz is unwavering in its loyalty and devotion to its family, be they people or animals. There is no threat he will not face in protecting those he loves. He is independent in nature, and is discriminating with strangers. He makes his own judgments about who he will consider his acquaintances. This often leads to comments about "aloofness," which seems to add to his noble demeanor.

You must have the time for early obedience training and socialization with the puppy…This socialization and training is an absolute necessity.

Socialization will not train out the kuvasz's innate protectiveness, but it will help him to discriminate between something that is simply new or unusual, and a threat.

Without socialization, the kuvasz will tend to consider all things outside his immediate family and everyday surroundings as potential threats, including infrequent visitors.

My friend Heather loves dogs. I called and told her I'd adopted one, so she immediately made a date to visit us. I left the door open so she could let herself in and have Magnus greet her. He charged the door, barking. She squatted down, held her arms open wide and said, "Atta boy, come ON." He was licking her face by the time I got to the door.

Remember that the kuvasz was bred to act independently to fulfill his purpose. He does not accept things blindly, and that includes whom he should obey. Perhaps, because of this, the kuvasz has a great sense of "justice"…. discipline from those he respects is accepted, if for just reasons. Unfairly applied, it generates resentment. He respects the concept of the Alpha leader(s), but the position must be earned.

It's important to remember that while the kuvasz is a large, strong dog, and strong willed, he is sensitive to neglect or unfair treatment. Tying, beating, teasing, or repeated harsh punishment is unnecessary and deplorable; a kuvasz will ultimately respond to this behavior in an aggressive manner.

A kuvasz that is harshly treated, or beaten, will not remain a trusted companion to you. Just as you were not to him.

My childhood Labrador used to love to play-box and wrestle. I tried it with Magnus—once.

You want some of this?

He nipped my waist lightly.

Lesson 1: Don't box with your kuvasz. Roger that.

I have a particularly nasty memory of mistreating my black Lab, after a family brawl. I was bicycling away from the house as fast as I could go, scared and sobbing, when she ran in front of the bike and overturned me. I swore at her and kicked her until I was overcome with shame and broke into tears and hugged her and begged her forgiveness. She licked my face, and slept with me that night as always. I don't remember what the brawl was about except that I was not at the center of it. But I was always at the center of Raven's heart.

CHAPTER 6   RAVEN, 1963-1971

On my eighth birthday, my father approached me in an unusually gentle, attentive mood and said, "As the youngest child, we think you need to learn responsibility. So your mother and I have decided to give you your own dog. She will not be the family dog: she will be your dog. You will name her, you will train her, and you will take care of her. I'll show you how."

My mother said, "I am not going to pick up messes or feed a dog. If she isn't housebroken soon, and isn't fed on time, and isn't trained, I will take her away from you."

I was mystified. Why would I fail to take care of my own dog? I had spent my life up to then living on hand-me-downs that had gone through three older sisters, and being alternately scorned or ignored as the baby. I wasn't delighted about having something or someone of my very own, and a puppy at that. I was ecstatic.

Dad went outside, and came back in with a beautiful black Labrador puppy. She was just weaned, about two months old. He showed me how to hold her, how to handle her, what could hurt her, and so on. He said she'd love our summers at the lake, because Labradors love to swim. He was as happy and proud as I was.

Dad said, "She's a Labrador retriever. She has a very good pedigree. She wasn't the best dog—she was the runt of the litter—but she's a fine dog. Her father is a field dog, which means he was bred for hunting. Field dogs are bigger, stronger, smarter, and have rougher coats. Her mother is a show dog, so she's smaller, sleeker, and has a silkier coat. Your dog is in between the two. The best of both types."

My sister told me decades later that Daddy had gone out and bought the best dog he could find. We were perennially strapped for cash, so he just skipped the drama and lied about it.

"What's her name?"

Mom said, "Well, since she's a pedigreed dog, you have to pick a name that runs in her family. I have a list of all the family names right here. You can go over them and see what you like."

I went over the list, and consulted Mom, and went over it again, and finally picked Raven and Rascal. My Mom said, "Since she's your dog, you can add your own name. How do you think Nancy's Raven Rascal sounds?"

"Can I do that?"

"Sure. We can call her Raven for short."

"Okay, I like it."

"Now we have to fill in the paperwork, and send it in to register her with The AKC." She helped me with the form and we mailed it in.

I began training Raven. Dad told me how to housebreak her: if she peed inside, bring her to the spot, put her nose in it, and tap her with a rolled-up newspaper. "Don't hit her hard enough to hurt her, just enough to get her attention. Like this." He rapped my arm. "You use a rolled up newspaper so she won't be afraid of your hands. She'll blame the newspaper instead of you. Then you take her outside, right away, and show her where to go."

I don't recall any great effort or difficulty in teaching her this first simple rule. Beyond that, I taught her to come when I whistled, jump up to catch a stick, fetch sticks and drop them gently at my feet, sleep with me, and follow me everywhere I went.

I never neglected her, never forgot to feed her, never got in trouble with her, or otherwise failed in my responsibilities. I think my mother was surprised.

I talked to Raven all the time. I'd tell her what we were going to do, and explain things to her and ask her questions. She'd cock her head and listen, but she never answered. That was fine, I didn't need her to speak. We were going up the steps to the back door one day, when Mom came out and watched me chatting away with my puppy. She said, "She can't understand you, you know."

"She can't?" I was astounded at this. When I talked to Raven, she looked in my eyes and seemed to know exactly what was on my mind. I might say, "Hey Raven, let's go to the orchard," and she'd be right with me. I'd say, "Hop up here," and she'd hop up on the bed. Of course she understood me. What was Mom thinking?

When Raven was a year old, Dad decided it was time to try her skills at hunting. He put on his red hunting jacket, got his gun, and walked Raven down to the marshes to find some ducks. They found some ducks. Dad fired the gun. Raven ran home and hid under my sister's bed. After that, every time she saw Dad get out the red jacket, she hid—which was fine, because in all the decades Dad went out hunting, he never shot anything. Nowadays a guy would just go out in the woods with a camera, but in his generation only sissies went into the woods without guns.

Dad planned to make a killing by breeding and selling Labrador pups. The first time she went into heat, He explained what was going on, and said, "Don't let her outside, because I've found a husband for her, and we don't want other dogs getting at her."

As if I understood any of this.

With four girls and two adults going in and out the door all day and with the effects of the hormones on her, Raven got out. I chased after her. Not a hundred feet from the house, she was already surrounded by males—people weren't into neutering their dogs in those days, and there were no leash laws. One of them was mounting her. She was moaning, and her eyes were shut, and I was afraid. I ran home, and told my mother that a big dog was hurting Raven and trying to pee inside her.

Mom smiled.

"Nancy, they're making babies."

"No they're not. He's hurting her. She's moaning and her eyes are half shut. You can't make babies by peeing, can you?"

"Not exactly. But it's kind of the same."

"Did you do that with Daddy?"

"Yes."

"That's disgusting! I will never do that!"

Mom smiled again.

Dad told me what to expect. Raven would be pregnant; her belly would get big; in about nine weeks, she'd give birth. As her time came near, we fixed up a birthing place in the den: a big cardboard box, lined with old sheets and towels, with food and water bowls nearby so Raven would know it was her place. She understood, and went to it when her labor started. My sisters and I watched the entire birthing, asking questions. As each pup came out, Raven ripped the amniotic sac open, ate it, and licked the new baby clean. Mom told me that when the last puppy was born, Raven would push out something called a placenta and eat it.

Gross.

Mom said it was natural, and it was good for her. She needed the extra vitamins it would give her, and it would make her stronger and better able to feed her babies. As I watched the whole process, it came to seem reasonable and neat.

She had six puppies in that litter. Each one went straight for her teats. They tumbled over each other blindly, vying for position, prodding her with their paws when they finally connected with the nipple. As they grew, I watched them tear her at teats with their sharp baby teeth while she tried to move around the yard. She couldn't get away from them, and they were implacable. I couldn't stand it, couldn't stand the red rips in her flesh, and couldn't understand why her own babies would be so mean.

We managed to find homes for every one when they were weaned just by asking around the neighborhood.

The second time Raven went into heat, I locked her in the basement while we waited for her appointment with another husband. One of the neighborhood kids heard her crying, felt sorry for her, and let her out. She had eight puppies that time.

The third time, we married her off successfully. Dad had four bitches sold before Raven whelped. She had five males. They were too young to wean before we left for camp in June, so I had six dogs to play with that summer.

Camp was a small cottage and bunkhouse on a little point of a big island in Lake Winnipesauke, the biggest lake in New Hampshire. Dad fixed up an old twelve-foot fiberglass boat and put an antique seven-and-a-half horsepower Johnson outboard motor on it for us kids. He gave us a gas account at marina owned by a family friend. He taught us to handle boats and navigate the lake as soon as we could read. At eight, I was already considered competent enough on the water to take the Little Boat anywhere I wanted—whenever I could coerce my sisters into letting me have it.

I honestly tried to sell the puppies. I made posters and took the Little Boat to all the local marinas to post them. But in those days, there were no electric or telephone lines to the island, so people couldn't make inquiries and plans to see the dogs. There was a mail boat, but no letters came about the dogs.

I took all six dogs everywhere except to church and town. We hiked across the hump of the island to a deep, narrow bay with mature trees along the shore, one of which had a heavy rope tied to an upper branch. You had to lean way out from a big rock to grab the end, which was scary, then swing out over the water and let go. The dogs all followed, barking and leaping into the water.

At camp, we swam together for hours. My sisters and I would go out to the ledge twenty yards off the dock to play mermaid-house, putting rocks in our laps so we could sit under water and have tea parties, or walk up and down crevices in the rocks as if they were stairs. The dogs would hang around on the ledge with us or swim with each other. Passing boaters would do double takes when they saw two or three girls and six dogs walking on water.

We took the dogs in the Little Boat and went to the deepest, widest part of the lake to jump out and swim around. We'd get them to tow us through the water (not really, just pretend). Getting them back in the boat was tricky, but we developed a technique that put one girl in the water and one in the boat, pushing and pulling.

We hung out at the weekend barbecues and kept the puppies away from the cocktails people set down on the deck. We slept in a pack.

It was the best summer of my life.

We finally sold the puppies when we went back to Massachusetts and school in the fall. By then they were naturally housebroken, having lived outside all summer. They were well muscled, and their coats glowed. Dad exchanged one for a roll of indoor-outdoor carpet. In the end, he figured out that the experiment had cost a lot more than he'd been able to get for the dogs. We finally had Raven spayed—but not before she whelped another big litter of mutts.

On my first day of high school, I was wearing a dress I'd sewn for myself over the summer—a dark green calico A-line with long sleeves and white collar and cuffs that I was very proud of.

All the students and faculty assembled in the gym for Principal Gray's welcoming address. As he trotted out his annual it's-going-to-be-another-great-year-at-Acton-Boxboro-Regional-High speech, Raven trotted in, scanning the bleachers for me. It took her about 15 seconds to find me. I had to climb down the bleachers and walk her home. I was partly embarrassed, partly happy to show off my new dress, entirely glad to escape the assembly. Kids laughed. My sisters cringed.

Raven knew where my homeroom was, and when I would be there, and a couple of times a week we'd hear her claws clicking along the hall. Of course I'd have to walk her home. Nobody seemed to mind.

Over the course of that year my parents' marriage unraveled, and the family got more and more unstable. Sisters acting out. Nasty fights among them and Mom and Dad. I'd escape with Raven, go out and walk through woods and fields with her. No one noticed our absence. She always brought me back to earth, to nature, to peace. Somewhere in there, I got a case of scarlet fever. Physical and visual hallucinations, fevers, chills, delirium and all that. As I lay in bed one afternoon, still very weak, I heard Raven scratching and whining at the door, but hadn't the will to get up, go downstairs, and open it for her. Everyone else was at work or school.

I never saw her again. I guess she was stolen, since men were building houses in the field next door, and she was a very well bred, polite, affectionate, creature. I hoped she was stolen. But I couldn't help wondering if she'd been crushed by heavy machinery. Over and over, I imagined getting out of bed, going downstairs, letting her in, and taking her back up to bed with me.

She was the core of my life, my rock, my comfort, and my joy. She would never sleep with me again.

She was gone. I cried for weeks.

I'm crying now. There are some losses you never get over. C.S Lewis says we humanize our animals by treating them as members of our families, and that there's no reason to expect that we won't be rejoined with our entire households in heaven. I hope to see Raven in heaven. Must try harder to get there.

CHAPTER 7   DOG HOUSE

So, oh boy, I had a dog again. I went to the pet store and bought a tasteful, taupe-colored, suede-cloth bed in the largest size I could find (too small), stoneware food and water bowls (blue, to match my own dishes), vitamins, glucosamine, grooming brushes, treats, and a 40-pound bag of large-breed kibble from the same brand as the food Susan had given us.

I was already secretly planning to do such a brilliant job of elder care that Magnus would live to 15.

Of course, I had to rearrange the cats' feeding stations. The dry food was upstairs, and wound up on a bookshelf Magnus couldn't reach. The canned food was downstairs, so those dishes went up on the counter. Hammett jumped up to investigate the change. Margaret followed.

I filled Magnus's water bowl and put it on the kitchen floor. Hammett jumped down to drink from it. When Magnus came into the kitchen, Margaret disappeared and Hammett sprang back up on the counter, hung over the edge, and poked at Magnus's fur as he passed by. It took a long time for that big body to pass, so Hammett got to do a lot of satisfying poking.

To give the kids a break, I took my new man with me every time I left the house. This was nice for them, but Magnus quickly decided he wasn't going to be left behind. If I had to go somewhere that didn't welcome dogs, he wound up sitting patiently, guarding the car for an hour or two. I'd go out of my way to find a shady spot, and leave the windows half open (not a security problem with Magnus on duty). But it was hard to listen to him barking as I walked away.

Woman! Don't leave me!

In the afternoon I'd take him walking in the neighborhood, adding a block or two every week as we both got stronger (with all those dogs to care for, Susan S. had only been able to take him out for duties.) Mornings and evenings I'd play with him in the common areas or the parking lot, pretending to be a naughty little lambie. I'd run away bleating and waving my arms, and he'd trot after me, adding little leaps and spins as the mood struck him. I'd let him get ahead of me, then turn and run in the opposite direction as fast as I could. He'd come cantering after me, and stop just short of my toes with a pronounced bow, wiggling with laughter. I'd grab him and rub his neck roughly, and smooth his ears down and kiss him on the snout.

Inside, I'd get on the floor with him, and give the doggie play-bow, and woof him. He'd do the same. We'd end up in a love-heap, with him upside down in my lap, trying to kiss me. Right on the mouth. There hadn't been this much love and joy in my life for a long time. A very long time. The sun was out and the breeze was bringing fresh oxygen to my soul.

Yes, sir, I sill have what it takes.

Even so, Magnus had to sleep on the floor so the kids could have the safe spot on the bed.

Chapter 8 — Threat Identification

The Sunday after I decided to keep Magnus, I asked Susan S. if she'd like to see him after church. She said, "No. I don't want to interfere with his process." I could see that she was holding something back. Tears, most likely.

At home, his process was lovely. Outside, around the complex and on the street, his process was fraught. Magnus was uneasy being around so many people. Apparently he'd never lived in a townhouse. Apparently he hadn't seen a lot of brown people before, either. He did a lot of racial profiling.

One sultry afternoon, when I'd opened the door to catch a breeze, a Latina and her kids walked past the screen door, chatting happily in Spanish. Magnus charged them, barking furiously. I was on it instantly, catching him and restraining him, but the woman was justly terrified. I got a furious lecture about vicious beasts and keeping my door closed.

Returning from a walk one evening, another neighbor was strolling up and down the parking lot for her evening constitutional. She was a very nice, friendly, Chinese-American woman. She was not used to dogs, and when Magnus's huge white form loomed up out of the darkness, she squealed and shied away with her arm over her face. This set him off. He roared and lunged so hard that he almost pulled me off my feet. She was terrified. He has a way of making himself look bigger by puffing up the fur around his neck and shoulders when he goes into action, so her terror was justified. I managed to haul him off and get him inside.

Jesus, my next-door neighbors' son, came around the corner with a basket full of laundry one afternoon. Magnus went on guard and woofed him. Jesus stood still and looked at my guy with respect and understanding. I got between him and Magnus, blocking my man so Jesus could pass.

Jesus and his father, Sergio, came over to fix the door to my shed at one point. Magnus gave them major lip for coming inside, even with me leading them. I had to go out for a few minutes while they were working, so I took out some treats, put them on the patio table, and told Jesus, "If he gives you a hard time, give him these."

"Okay," he said, smiling.

I came back in, and asked if Magnus gave him a hard time.

"Yes," smiling again.

"Did you give him the treats?"

"Yes."

"Did it work?"

"Yes," smiling brilliantly.

When I took Magnus out for his evening duties, we often met a big Polynesian guy with a three-foot-long ponytail who Magnus immediately and consistently identified as a threat. The man was placid, stolid, and undisturbed, but obviously not impressed. I tried telling Magnus the man was okay, but he didn't believe me. I tried putting an arm around the man, which was probably going too far, but Magnus wasn't convinced. He kept it up with this man for several months before he accepted him.

Any people we met on the street tended to be viewed with suspicion. A tall, good-looking man walking toward us said, "Can I pet your dog?" I said, "I dunno. Maybe." I got a good grip on the leash as the man got closer, and Magnus calmly let him reach out and ruffle his fur.

"That went better than I expected," I said.

"He's a good boy," he said. "When he wants to be."

Remember, bicycles, skateboards, motorcycles, people carrying light-colored plastic bags, and men pushing strollers were all suspect. We now added men carrying leaf blowers, men carrying just about anything, noisy children—and all dogs—to the list.

On one of our first walks, we met up with another dog walker, and the other guy asked if I wanted to try a meeting. Magnus had been perfectly calm and hadn't seemed to notice the other dog, so I said okay. As soon as we turned toward them he leaped forward, snarling and snapping like fury incarnate, pulling so hard against the leash that his front legs were off the ground. It was all I could do to hold him back, shouting "Sorry!" over his roars. After that, all dogs were fair game.

When in doubt, assume the worst.

I was surprised. He'd been such a honey at home. Except with the neighbors, but in those instances he was guarding his home and on the street we were in neutral territory.

It's not neutral. It's all disputable ground, sister.

I learned to judge the intelligence of other dog walkers by their reactions to Magnus. The smart ones, especially the smart ones with German shepherds and Rottweilers and chow chows and such, crossed the street a block ahead of us, and shortened their leashes. I learned to do this, too. One guy walking his Lab off leash—on the street—let his dog run straight into Magnus's face, which is extremely uncivilized behavior in any species. When I saw this coming, I hunkered down on the sidewalk with my arms around Magnus, shouting "Not Good!" I was too scared to think of anything else to say. The guy kept on walking toward us and did not call his dog off.

Dog people say getting down on the ground with your dog is a good way to get your face bitten. Dog people say you just ignore the other dog, give the leash a quick sideways jerk to get your dog's attention (it throws him off balance), walk on firmly, or use your hand as a "claw" on the scruff of his neck. Dog people didn't tell me these things until long after I needed to know them.

One afternoon we were walking peaceably past some houses when a couple came out with two dogs on leash, who broke free as soon as they saw Magnus, rushed him, and attacked in concert. I dropped his lead and let him defend himself, which he did, furiously and effectively. No dog landed a bite—and no dog was bitten.

This is an important point. I jokingly call him my wolf-killer, but "killer" is not correct. "Deterrent" is the correct term: kuvasz dogs don't rip out throats unless it's absolutely necessary. They put on a big, ritualized show to demonstrate their killer potential as a kind of bargaining chip. Most dogs buy it. The couple ran forward, grabbed the leashes, dragged their dogs off, and apologized profusely. I was a bit cool with them.

Now I understand why dogs reacted to him so negatively. He was exuding dominance, challenging them to a showdown with his posture. I understand this now because he doesn't do it anymore. At least, not unless he sees a need for it, which is rare.

Knowing that Magnus was elderly and that I would probably have to handle him a lot, I accustomed him to my touch. I got the idea from my first stepfather, who raised Standardbred horses. He always had me handle the young horses when I visited the barn, starting at the head, and gently working around the body and down the legs, picking up the feet and so on. I did the same with Magnus. I gave him full-body massages. I brushed out his long coat and the mats around his ears, gently, making a little progress every night. Pretty soon I could do anything I needed to do (except those pedicures). I trimmed extra-long feathers of fur from his legs and belly and stray curls around his ears to neaten up his lines. I examined his feet and joints. I flexed his legs and his spine, and rubbed his floppy ears and stroked his tail.

I'll give you half an hour to cut that out, lady.

He was definitely enjoying being an only dog. And I wasn't even cooking for him yet.

Chapter 9 Competition

Mom was due to fly out from Rhode Island in May. I hadn't told her about Magnus. I hadn't told her about cutting off my long, henna-red hair (which she'd never approved of). I hadn't told her how much weight I'd lost (she never approved of my size, either). She was waiting outside the San Jose terminal when we drove up, and her eyes and mouth went big and round when she saw us. I pulled to the curb, popped the trunk, and handed in her luggage.

She wasn't interested in the luggage. She said, "Who is this?" immediately opened the door, and reached into the back seat to pet Magnus. "I saw this woman with nice, short, gray hair and a huge white creature in the back seat. I hardly knew it was you."

"This is Magnus. We go everywhere together."

"He's so beautiful. He has blue eyes! What kind of dog is he? Is it hard to keep that coat so white? How much does he weigh? Does he shed?"

He has that effect on people.

Once we were on our way, she said, "Your hair! It's beautiful. How come everyone I love has such great hair?" At home, she kept commenting on how much better I looked in pants, and how she was so glad to see the real Nancy again, and how upset she'd been when I was big and wearing dresses that my father would have said were designed by Omar the Tentmaker. My father would not have fared well in a politically correct era.

Appearances matter a great deal to Mom. She was a beauty in her youth, and is fighting the aging process with every weapon in the beauty arsenal. She exercises every day to a Beach Body video. She takes Beach Body vitamins. She spends at least an hour every morning doing her face and hair. She is always exquisitely dressed. Her colors are soft blues, greens, purples, pinks, cream, and grey.

She's trim and blonde and just over average height. Her movements are quick and definite, her posture erect. She's over eighty now, and still turns heads.

I take after my father.

Mom made an honest effort to fit herself into our routine. On the first walk we took together, I had to rein Magnus in. I said, "I wish I could walk faster. He really wants to go, and it would be good for him."

She said, "You're doing just fine. It's enough that you're out every day. You'll get stronger."

"I'm already way better than I was a couple of months ago."

She started to reply, but Magnus cut between us and tangled her in his leash. She shoved him aside roughly. We went on a few yards, and he tried to force her off the sidewalk again. She pushed back. We went a few more yards. Magnus tried to cut her off from the other side.

Move it, lady. She's mine.

Mom said, angrily, "I want to walk beside you!" and glued herself to my side.

I said, "Magnus hasn't been with me for very long, and he's not secure in his position."

Yes I am. My strategy seems to be working very well.

"I'm your mother!"

"Good luck dominating him."

She sighed furiously. And she didn't give up trying to stay at my side. I kept a straight face.

Magnus managed to stay between us for most of the visit. She finally gave in. "You've found a wonderful man. He's a fine companion, and he'll do you a world of good."

Margaret made herself invisible while Mom was there. Hammett let Mom worship at his shrine, but in an aloof sort of way. Near the end of the visit, as we were watching a movie together in bed, Hammett jumped up, saw Mom, and froze. He crept stiffly across the foot of the bed and came up alongside me on the opposite side from Mom. Then he meatloafed against me with his back to her and his ears flattened against his head. Mom said, "I don't mean to complain, but I don't feel welcome around here."

I said, "You're not. Having to share me with Magnus is bad enough—but with my mother?"

She laughed. "Well, I'm leaving soon enough, and they can have you all to themselves again."

All to themselves—to duke it out over who gets my attention. All my animals have always been very possessive of me. I have never understood why. It couldn't possibly be because I let them walk all over me. Literally, in Hammett's case.

Chapter 10 — Impulse Driving

Having an unsecured, sensate, 90-pound load in the back seat has affected my driving habits—it's like driving around with a goldfish in a bowl. I developed a technique I call Impulse Driving (as in "impulse drive" on *Star Trek*). It means bringing the car slowly up to speed, coasting out of gear as much as possible without inciting road rage in others, and letting momentum carry us gently around curves. It's kind of like driving a boat. After driving an '86 Toyota for almost 20 years, I was surprised how far my new-fangled '96 Nissan would glide without losing speed.

Doing this, plus keeping the tires inflated and the oil fresh, earns me about 40 extra miles per tank. And Magnus doesn't get jostled and tossed. Good things all around.

Mom and I took Magnus for our first road trip together, over the hill to the beach. "Over the hill" in this country—I've thought of California as a country of its own ever since I moved here from New England—means over the coastal mountain range. I like to take the scenic route over Russian Ridge's high, leonine pastures and down through the redwood and Douglas fir forests, to a little Portuguese fishing village, and then on to one or another of the beaches on the miraculously un-commercialized Central California coast.

Magnus stood in the back seat with his head between the front bucket seats and surfed along with the movement of the car over the twisting mountain roads. He drooled all over my right arm, and did a fair amount of whining and moving back and forth and licking.

I was just getting used to this gal, and now she's taking me someplace else? I thought I had her hooked.

I thought I'd gotten myself a drooly dog and was having second thoughts. He was very happy to get out of the car when we reached the beach.

Since it was a weekday, we had the surf to ourselves. The weather was grey and damp and windy, as usual. That's not a bad thing here—sometimes it's nice to get away from brilliant sunshine.

The beach has a large rocky finger that juts into of the surf, at least 30 feet above the strand. It's surrounded by heavy cobblestone shingle, behind which low, crumbly ochre cliffs display clearly marked strata. In the chalky layers full of stones and fossils, you can see that the coast has at various times been under deeper, cooler water. In the mudstone strata, you can see where it was a placid estuary. In the immature sandstone of the upper sediments, you can read recent beaches. Clinging to the top of the cliffs are all manner of grasses, invasive succulents, native wildflowers, and escaped garden plants. This sort of thing fascinates me. Mom and Magnus were indifferent.

We clambered out onto the great rocks, and watched the surf crash and burst and recede around them. Mom and I took pictures of each other with his majesty. We climbed the perilous little path down to the shingle, and eventually reached a sandy stretch. Magnus approached the surf, but only got as far as the faintest film of water.

I'm not fond of getting wet, ma'am, and I consider the surf quite dangerous. But I do appreciate the air and the breeze. And I'm definitely happy that you're not introducing me to someone with a leash in her hand.

He smiled a lot. I smiled a lot. Mom smiled a lot.

After a while, we got in the car and drove north to another beach, a sandier one, and started walking down to the surf. Mom pointed at a No Dogs Allowed sign on the path, and I scanned the beach. It was empty, so we scofflawed, walking up and down as far as we could, enjoying the soft, cool air and the mist and the surge of surf and the little tidal pools with their miniature rip currents. We walked until we got hungry, and then drove to Half Moon Bay for seafood on a little wharf surrounded by sailing and fishing boats. We took the 92 back over the hill—no point in doing the scenic route in the dark. Magnus car-surfed the whole way home, so by the time we got in he was exhausted.

    He doesn't surf and pant and pace in the car anymore. He's gotten used to the back seat on his thick, red-and-gold brocade, fleece-lined blanket. He lounges there, fitting perfectly into the available space, and either naps or looks out the window.

The other day he was looking out the window when a bus passed by, carrying a long poster of photos of actors from some new series on its side. The actors were posed to stare directly out at the onlooker. They were at about the height of the car's window. Magnus lunged and woofed at them with his best ferocity for their presumption in approaching us head on like that.

    Bad manners! Back off!
    I laughed.

CHAPTER 11   JEAN

My best friend Jean and I have a standing date on Saturday nights. In the winter it's usually just dinner. In the summer, we take longish walks. In every season, we talk over whatever has happened over the week, noodling, commiserating, coming up with ex-husband strategies, concerns about her daughters, worries, fears, hopes. Intense discussions.

Magnus kind of changed that.

We were driving to a restaurant in the rain, and Jean was telling me about the latest ex-husband outrage. "He calls me at 10:30, and immediately launches into a story about a fight he had at…"

Hey! Your car is too loud! Simmer down!

"Magnus, settle. SETTLE, Magnus. Wow. That set him off, huh?"

"So some of his co-workers were exchanging emails in Russian, and the guy was stupid enough to…"

German shepherd on the sidewalk! I'm giving you notice!

"Magnus, that's enough. Leave it. Did you see that shepherd? He was giving Magus the evil eye right through the window."

"The Russian guys didn't think anyone would understand what they were writing, so they left their comments in the thread, and…"

Walking around her neighborhood—a new place with new threats for him—I watched him minutely and analyzed his body language aloud, trying to understand what he was perceiving and reacting to, trying to learn to read him so I could be more proactive about avoiding such situations as…

You two dogs come any closer and I'll take you down!

Actually, I don't think the language he was using was that polite, because I had to hold onto the leash with both hands, and brace my legs against his lunging while he slavered and snarled and the other dogs lunged and slavered and snarled, while their owner struggled to hold them in. There was quite a din until they were out of sight.

This woman seriously needs someone to protect her.

"Wow. I have no idea why he did that. It scares me. Do you think he'll ever get over it?"

"How would I know? I've never had an aggressive dog."

"He's so sweet at home... I'm sorry. What were we talking about?"

Jean said, "This is like being with the mother of a small child. You can't have a conversation."

I saw her point. I'd been through not being able to have conversations with girlfriends when their kids were small. I could have said that Jean gave me three hours a week, and that Magnus was giving me his life. I could have reminded her of the times her kids or her ex had superseded my time with her. But I didn't. Between work and family she has more demands on her time and energy than anyone I know. Her time with me is the only break she gets.

There are an almost eerie number of parallels in our lives. We're the same age. We both have roots in New England. We come from similar kinds of families. We met in choir. We moved to California in the same month of the same year. We share books. We share movies. We both struggle with our weight, our moods, and our family conflicts. But there are enough differences to keep things interesting.

She has four daughters. I am childless, and enjoy her girls. She has a preference for clothes that are "neat, but not gaudy"—lots of bright colors, sequins, beads, embroideries, prints, and flowing shapes. I tend to wear simple, tailored clothes in black. Or brown. At a thrift store one afternoon, when she bought a shirt that was patched together from five colorful plaids with flowery embroidery at the yoke, I bought an off-white denim jacket printed with brown and beige foliage. It had some shiny beading and a bit of glittery brown embroidery, which I thought might be a bit much. She convinced me that it was subtle enough to suit my style.

She's the kind of girlfriend who grins and gives you a big hug when she thinks you're looking good. We're both the kind of friend that kicks into gear when the other is in crisis. We plan to buy a house together, and we joke about the things we'll do to it, such as turning the yard into a shrine for the Virgin, complete with a Virgen de Guadalupe painted on the front door, and telling people we're a convent of two, to fend off "what a sweet old couple" comments. Not that we object to gay couples. We just want to be taken for what we are.

What we are—friends—managed to survive the why-can't-we-have-a-conversation stage.

Chapter 12 — Grace

My new man and I continued to study each other, learning to communicate. He followed my every movement and gesture. If I swept my arm in a clockwise circle, he'd circle with it. If I jogged along, he'd trot by my side with his eyes on me. His gaits were light, crisp, and precise—a striding walk, a crisp trot, a rocking canter, a pounding gallop.

It put me in mind of Caroline and Rookie. If Magnus were younger, I'd have tried freestyling with him.

I mentioned this to Susan S. She said a good gait was one of the things she bred for, and I later learned that good gaits are a highly desirable breed characteristic.

He is used to me now, and doesn't give the same kind of high-focus attention anymore, but those first few months were really something. His grace, his responsiveness, and his ability to communicate with movement and gesture were a revelation.

He was a revelation.

I called my sister, too full of Magnus thoughts and Magnus joy to talk about anything else.

"Jesus, Nancy, he's almost ten years old."

"I know. I'm ready to give him the care he needs."

"It's a recipe for heartbreak. He's gonna break your heart."

My sister knew. I didn't want to know. I loved him, and he needed me.

I did know, in my heart. But this was the love God had sent me, and I wasn't turning it away. No one else was willing to see him through.

CHAPTER 13   DOG DUMPING

Susan S. bred Magnus's litter in 1997. When he was weaned, she placed him with a couple in L.A. Two years later, she took him back, had him trained in obedience and show ring skills, and went on the circuit with him and his sister. "In those days, two was when you started working on their championships." She says this casually, as if "Of course he'd get his CH title…"

He got it within a year, at Palm Springs—a popular dog show on a good circuit. After getting his championship he went back to L.A. and Susan neutered him, because she felt his legs were too short and she had other options for extending her line. I think she should have found a nice, long-legged bitch for him. His genes for character and intelligence deserved to be passed on.

I once sent her a link to an article about a woman who sent her dog to Japan to be cloned. My note said, "Since you neutered Magnus, I'm going to have to do this. It only costs $50K."

After he went back to his family with his championship, Susan S. continued to be a part of Magnus's life—she was a co-owner, and he'd always been one of her favorites. "He's a prince," she says. "He has always been a prince." I asked her what that meant. She said, "He was never a wild, crazy dog. Even as a puppy. I don't know. He's just a prince."

She's not always good at putting things into words, but I know what she means. After living with Magnus for all these months, all I can say is, he's a prince. And he's my prince, now.

When he was Susan's prince, she stayed with his family whenever she was in L.A., and always slept with Magnus. Her husband once looked in on the two of them in embrace and said, "You look like sated lovers." She said, "We are."

When he was nine, his owners (a professional couple) decided that Susan (an unemployed and by-then-divorced woman with too many dogs in a rented house) was better equipped to care for him than they were. Susan couldn't tell me what drove their decision. They asked her to take him back. She did, because that's what responsible breeders do when a dog is in danger of being abandoned.

How do people send a dog away when he needs them the most? I don't understand. Mom says that we are responsible for their births, their lives, and their deaths, and that we have a moral obligation to take the best care of them we can. Then again, when she divorced her second husband, she left Teddy the Chesapeake bay retriever (not one of the placid retriever breeds) at her ex's farm. And Teddy was definitely, 100%, her dog. He was with her always, everywhere. She used to leave her luggage on the wharf in Portland, Maine attended only by the dog. The luggage was never disturbed. He was fiercely protective of her. He wouldn't even let me in her house. She said Teddy loved living on the farm, and would be miserable in her new apartment. Maybe she was right.

People give up their dogs all the time, even the rare or fancy breeds—maybe especially the rare or fancy breeds. Susan S. and I speculate that some people see them as status dogs, or choose them for their looks instead of their temperament and when they realize the extent of the responsibility they've taken on, they don't want the dog any more. But that usually happens when the dog is still young.

Maybe this couple's children had grown and gone and they were moving to a condo that didn't allow 90-pound pets, or they were working sixty-hour weeks, or had family or marital troubles or health issues. Who knows? In any case, they gave away a very fine creature. I'm grateful to them, even though it meant missing out on much of the fun part of living with a dog and accepting much of the care and worry. Magnus is worth it.

Chapter 14   House of Poo

When I got back to the car after church, Magnus was in deep doo-doo. Literally—the back seat, his tail, stomach, back, legs, nose and even his ears were smeared with poo. Poo, poo, glorious poo, terrible steaming stinking poo. The car reeked. Magnus looked down, away from me, then looked up again.

I did try to clean this up ma'am, but it's too much for me.

I said, "Oh, you poor boy!"

I stood there for a while contemplating how we were going to handle all that poo, realized we couldn't do anything about it until we got home, got in, rolled all the windows down, opened the sunroof and took off, with Magnus sloshing in poo all the way home and the stench billowing from the car to cast a pall over anyone following us.

He had to do the walk of shame through the complex to the front door. He had to be hosed off outside. He had to go upstairs, be dragged into the bathroom, have his front end hauled into the tub, then his back end, be body-blocked from getting out of the tub, and get sprayed all over with the hand-held shower and scrubbed with a lanoline-based soap (which I fortunately had on hand) for an inordinate amount of time. He sighed.

All right, all right, I'll let you do this, but only because the poo is worse than the water.

After I toweled him off, he ran into the bedroom, gave himself a good shake, turned around, and finally gave me such a big grin that he very nearly got dimples in his cheeks.

Thank you for handling that gracefully. I'm terribly embarrassed about the whole thing.

I went out to clean the backseat with a scrub brush, a big bucket of soapy water, and a stack of old towels. I scrubbed the upholstery and sopped the water up out of it with the towels. The towels came up a solid poo-brown. I rinsed the upholstery and sopped the water out of it again and again until it was more or less not brown. It continued to stink after it dried, so I got a large bottle of rubbing alcohol and soaked the fabric to kill the bacteria that were metabolizing the poo and farting out the gasses that were so nasty even they couldn't tolerate them. That worked well enough for us to be able to drive with the windows closed if we wanted to. Not that we wanted too.

The next morning, the living room floor was smeared and piled with stinking poo. And the morning after that. He had clearly tried to get out before exploding, because the piles of poo—lakes of poo, rivers of poo, oceans of poo—were in front of the slider to the patio. I appreciated the effort, but I threw away the little carpet I'd been using as a doormat. Then I scraped loose poo off the hardwood, scrubbed out the hardened poo, and went back over the floor with clean sponges and oil soap until all traces of poo were gone. I bought a new mat.

He might have gotten into some nasty garbage, but I didn't see how. He hadn't been out of my sight. Maybe the townhouse itself inspired over-the-top pooping, since I'd been through much the same thing—but I was toilet trained, so my weight loss technique didn't soil the floors. I used to walk around singing "Butt-butt-poo, butt-but poo, butt-butt-butt-butt-poo" to the tune of Peter and The Wolf. I started singing butt-butt-poo again.

That's awfully crude, missy.

"It's your butt and your poo this time, honeybun."

It's an affront to my dignity. And it's not helping.

"Well, tell me what will help, then."

Frankly, I don't know.

"Do you think it's my fault?"

Considering the evidence dispassionately, I'd say yes. You've been feeding me.

"Okay. We'll go to Doctor Paul, and have him do some tests."

Fine. But is there any chance we could go soon? Today would be nice, actually. I don't think I can bear putting you through more of these distasteful events.

"I'll call now. But really, I'm more worried about you than about the filth. You must feel terrible."

I don't mind admitting that I do.

CHAPTER 15   FIRST VET VISIT

There were going to be other dogs in the vets' office. We were not exactly done with socialization training, but Magnus must have felt very low because he stayed calm. I kept him close.

I hate these places.

Magnus weighed in at 85 pounds—a little too light for a dog his size. We went into the examining room and waited for Dr. Paul. He's a very thin man in early middle age, a little over six feet tall, and slightly stooped, as if he's bending down to be closer to you. His face is rounded, slightly jowled, café latte brown, with large, brown, kindly eyes and a habitual smile. He works six days a week, twelve hours a day, and has his family come in to help with the practice on Saturdays. He is not out to empty my pockets, but he does take a lot of my time—he takes in emergencies, and we always have to wait.

At length he came in. "Oh, a kuvasz," he said. "We don't see many of those. What brings you in?"

So, you decided to show up.

"Really bad, persistent diarrhea. I'd also like to give him a general check up. I only decided to keep him a few weeks ago, and want to know what I'm dealing with."

"Kuvaszok are generally very healthy dogs. Apart from hip dysplasia, which all big dogs are subject to, their only common problem is allergies."

I was impressed that he was so familiar with the breed, which ranks a low 70th on the AKC's listing of dogs by popularity.

He took blood for testing, examined the fur and skin, showed me that the skin was inflamed, and gave Magnus an allergy shot. I said, "I wondered why he was walking around trying to scratch his belly all the time." He also took some soupy poo samples, but didn't find any bacteria or parasites.

"Overall," Dr. Paul said, "He's in excellent health for a dog his age and size. I'll give you some meds to calm the gut."

I decided to do for Magnus what I'd done for myself in similar circumstances—backed him off to a chicken-and-rice diet. That was not only successful, but wildly popular.

When Susan's starter supply of kibble ran out, I had asked her if she really fed him puppy food. She gave me a how-dumb-can-you-be look and said no. So I bought a 25-pound bag of adult large-breed kibble from the same brand as the bag she'd given me, and gave him two cups in the morning and two cups in the evening, with plenty of water, as instructed.

The next time I saw Susan, I asked if she fed that brand. She gave me another how-dumb-can-you-be look and said, "Nooooooo. Why would you think that?"

"Because you gave me food in one of their bags."

"..."

"Remember when I asked you if you really fed him puppy food?"

"..."

"What do you feed?"

"I can't remember the name. I remember that it's in a purple bag. I can find it in the store, but I can never remember the name."

"Can you take me to the store and show me?"

"I guess so."

That never happened.

The upshot was that I had radically changed Magnus's diet, which explained the diarrhea. I did a bit of research on what dogs can, must, and cannot eat. One of the first things I learned is that corn is high on the "no" list. I looked at the ingredients of the kibble I was feeding. The main ingredient was corn. Lesson 2: Don't feed your Kuvasz what you'd feed a hog or a cow.

I got to thinking that he might do better on homemade food in general. Susan S. said, "You can't cook for the dog. That's crazy. It's too much work. Not to mention the expense."

"He can't live on medication for the rest of his life. Chicken and rice works, so that's the way it's going to be."

Okay. What do dogs eat? In nature, they eat a lot of mice and bunnies. Knowing that the first thing canids eat is the gut of the kill, bunny would include what amounts to chewed up, well-processed greens and seeds and roots. Then there is muscle meat, organ meat, etc. And since Doctor Paul told me dogs need 42 different nutrients, I reasoned that the greatest possible variety of foods should go into the mix. I did lots of Googling about dog diets, learned that half of the ingredients should be protein, a quarter grain and a quarter veg. I eliminated everything that dogs tend to be allergic to, such as corn, and everything that is poisonous to them, such as garlic, onions, chocolate, macadamia nuts, raisins, and extremely large quantities of broccoli.

Why would anyone feed a dog extremely large quantities of broccoli?

I got about 12 pounds of 99-cent chicken at a wholesale club, plus lean ground beef. I got about a pound each of beef liver, gizzards, and tripe at a Mexican market (Anglos don't eat that stuff, I guess). I got several kinds of grains and legumes, and a little of every type of vegetable—greens, roots, string beans, sweet potato, squash, etc.—and a couple of apples.

I simmered the chicken in one pan, the tripe and gizzards in another, cooking at low heat to preserve the vitamins. Took the meat from the bones, and simmered the bones in the broth to add bone minerals. Used the broth to cook the grains and lentils, going very heavy on the broth-to-grain ratio. Chopped the veggies roughly and steamed them all together. Mixed it all up, packed it in cheap food-storage boxes, and had about 30 days worth of Magnus Mealz.

The process took an entire day—an unusually hot one, of course. Magnus lay down just outside the kitchen with his ears on alert and his blue eyes tied to my hands with invisible string. When the batch was done, I gave him his first sample.

My love voodoo is working unusually well with this lady.

Susan S. examined Magnus's teeth a few weeks into the new regime and said, "Ew." I added a corn-free, high-quality commercial kibble back into his diet to help keep his teeth clean.

Now, of course, I realize that he'd have done just fine eating the high-grade kibble alone, but I'd crossed the culinary Rubicon and committed myself. When we run out of stew he looks sadly at plain kibble, sighs, ponders the situation for a good long time, and finally resigns himself to eating it. Or some of it.

At nine P.M. one dog food day, I was taking liver from the frying pan when Magnus woofed so loudly I jumped.

Woman! Hand it over!

I let the moment pass, because you can't let your man boss you too much, then gave him a nice fresh bit of liver when it cooled down.

The kids show up for their share these days. They get it, too.

Incidentally, I tried cooking for them long ago. When Hammett was about two, he jumped on my lap, looked me in the eyes, and peed. I said, "Fine. We'll go to the vet tomorrow." I'd learned the hard way that cats tend to get kidney disease, and when they start urinating in weird places, you need to heed the alarm. My vet did find the dread crystals in Hammett's pee, which were about to grow into stones. He has been on a special diet ever since.

Cooking for cats should be easy—they're pure carnivores. I cooked chicken in every way possible: steamed, simmered, sautéed with butter, sautéed with oil. They would have none of it. I resorted to kidney-diet kibbles and baby food. They like baby food made of babies—lamb and veal. Baby food doesn't have all the nutrients they need, but I've tried every brand and flavor of commercial cat food and they reject all of it.

They do like prosciutto and pâté, but I draw the line at imported deli products. Fortunately, we're well supplied with all-natural food in the form of baby wood rats. Hammett is quite fond of those.

Margaret prefers grasshoppers.

Chapter 16 — Big White Goat

Automotive security has been an ongoing issue. My old Toyota was stolen for the last time a few years ago. This ticked me off—I was going for 20 years on one car, and was just one year short. The car still went down the highway at 70 mph in a straight line, ran reliably, and got good mileage, so if it hadn't been stolen we'd have made 20 easily.

The first time it was stolen was on Christmas Eve in the late 'eighties—I'd cleverly left it parked in Dorchester, Massachusetts, full of suitcases and gifts. It was recovered, heavily vandalized, then was successfully de-vandalized, and served me better than ever afterwards.

It was burglarized three times. First for some web design books in the back seat, while it was parked in San Francisco's SOMA district. Netscape's browser had launched a year or two earlier. I imagined a Gen-Xer with a goatee and black clothes seeing the books, and thinking "Wow—the latest stuff on Web design. Gotta have 'em."

Then, at the condo, it was burglarized for an old cardboard box marked "WADC FILES." I wanted to replace that box with one full of kitty poop, barbed wire, and broken glass, and label it "DESIGNER DRUGS AND JEWELRY."

The third time it was burglarized for the brand new radio I'd had installed to keep me company on my commute to The City (a.k.a. San Francisco).

The final theft was on Easter Eve. I went out to the carport in the morning on the way to Mass, stood looking at the empty space, and wondered dumbly where I'd left the car. It took a while for the truth to sink in. A friend was planning to hear us sing, so I called to beg a ride. By the time I got to the rehearsal room the singers were getting their things together to go up to the church.

The director gave me a filthy look. The singers looked at me pityingly.

I said, "Do you have a spare copy of the Mass?"

"Why?"

"Mine was in the car."

"In the CAR?" he said, stretching his neck forward. "Oh, no."

Everyone sighed. Bill shook his head, and handed me a fresh copy of the music. Another singer's car (and music) had been stolen earlier in the week, and we all wondered what the thieves thought of the 250 or so motets they'd acquired.

Motet is Latin for music with words, usually Psalm verses, Gospel passages, or praise hymns. They're generally written in four parts that weave around each other, and are sung without accompaniment. One assumes they wouldn't be much to the taste of gangbangers.

The Nissan that replaced it has also been broken into three times. Once in The City for no apparent reason, and twice at home, even with a car alarm installed. The fantastic sound system I discovered after I bought the car lasted less than a year before it was ripped out—on Easter Eve.

Christmas Eve, Easter Eve, Easter Eve. Is Jesus trying to tell me something?

Soon after I decided to keep Magnus, I had a date with Kathy and Mike, my oldest friends in California. They've stood by me and stood up for me for years, through auto thefts, bad relationships, tough times at work, and fibro flare-ups. Years ago, we formed a three-person hiking club and went all over the Central Coast in search of adventure. Since I've had to quit hiking, they some of the few friends who still remember to call me and make dates.

Mike is a cheerfully sarcastic guy who is here to get the most out of life in the most decent way possible. He is still married to his first wife and he still loves her. He'd make great Beefeater at the Tower of London. He has a trim beard, a stubborn potbelly, and a confident walk. He's a software developer with a very big brain, but unlike most men of that description, he is not a workaholic. He sets himself a new personal challenge every year and conquers it. Making silver jewelry. Ham radio. Competitive archery. Tooling and dying leather. The banjo. This year, it's the fiddle.

Every Easter, he asks if I'm going to sit up beside my car with a shotgun.

Kathy still blushes over him. I took her to a new boutique downtown that offers lovely, unusual clothes, which, at the time, I couldn't squeeze into. She looked so hot in the outfit she chose that I said, "Oh, boy, when Mike sees you in that you are definitely going to get lucky." She turned pink. "Oh. Actually, that's why I was late."

She's what people call a bird-like woman, as quick and light and deft as Mike is sturdy. She's in the voluntary redhead club, though she doesn't use henna. She pronounces the h in "whether." She enjoys bird watching, hiking, kayaking, beading, textile arts, South Park, and imitating Michael Jackson's crotch-grabbing gesture. She doesn't like to cook. She'll give you the shirt off her back if you need it. She wakes at the crack of dawn and goes to sleep at nine.

Mike's a night owl.

It works for them.

I rang their doorbell. Mike answered. I said, "Hey, Mike, I got a highly intelligent alarm system for the car. Go try to get in it." I stood where I was.

He started moving. When he was 15 feet from the car, a large white form rose up from the front seat and stuck its head out the window.

"I see a big white goat."

"Yeah, you see a goat. Try going closer."

"No way. That is one scary-looking goat."

I walked over to Mike, and we went to the car together. Magnus did his kissing and greeting thing. Some scary goat.

"He's BIG."

"Actually, he's little for the breed. They can go as much as third again larger."

Mike looked at Magnus appreciatively.

"I approve. If you had gotten some little puppy, I wouldn't have approved, but I approve of this fine, big man."

Kathy is not a dog person, but she was a good enough sport and a good enough friend to be nice about it. "I'm sure he'll be good for you. He's just what you need," she said.

At dinner, all I wanted to talk about was Magnus. I was like those 40-year-old yuppies who finally have a baby and discover the miracle of human development. Their child is amazing, really, so smart and cute and advanced. They read all the books about babies and are confident that their expert parenting and the flash cards in the crib will produce a fine, highly intelligent person who will go far in life and be a major benefit to society You look at the developmentally ordinary little poop-producer and say "Yes, he is amazing."

After dinner we walked around the neighborhood with Magnus. "Why is he peeing on everything?" asked Kathy with a grimace.

"He's a male dog. They have to mark their territory," I said.

"He's a good dog," Mike said.

"But he pees on everything," Kathy said.

"He's marking places other dogs have already marked," I said.

She pursed her lips.

Kathy and Mike live in a neighborhood of low, glass-walled, exposed-beam Modernist houses behind fenced courtyards. People either love or hate those houses. The people who buy them love them, and so they are lovingly tended and lovingly landscaped, with mature trees and well-established plantings. It's a nice place to walk.

Magnus pooped in the middle of the street. Kathy hid her mouth behind her hand and said, "Omigod, look at the size of that." When I picked it up with a plastic bag, she said "Eeww. It stinks. I don't think I could do that."

"It's part of the package," I said.

"Hey, listen, I don't touch no cat litter, either. That's why I have the automated litter box. All I have to do is empty the container."

Magnus pooped again. I was out of plastic bags. His big, stinking, steaming pile was right in the middle of someone's driveway. Oops.

"What are you going to do?"

"I have more bags in the car. I'll pick it up on my way home."

The stars were out. Lights were on in people's windows. The air was soft. The breeze was warm. We said goodnight.

"Enjoy your dog."

"I will."

"Yes, good luck with him."

"Thanks for letting me walk him with you."

I did go back and pick up the poop.

Chapter 17 — Second Vet Visit

Two weeks went by after the oceans of poo incident. Magnus and I were getting used to walking around the neighborhood together. I was still too slow for him, but he had stopped pulling on the lead. The weather was getting warmer, which slowed him down, I noticed. I stopped walking him in the heat of the afternoon in favor of mornings and evenings. Then, from one day to the next, he went from perky and alert to slow and dull, walking with his head hanging and his tail down. I turned back after the first block, got him home, and called Dr. Paul.

When he came in the examining room, he asked what brought us back in so soon. I told him. Doctor Paul took one look at Magnus's face, pulled up his ears, and said, "See that? His ears are really dirty, and he certainly has an infection. We'll have to clean that out. I'll take him in the back. It won't take long." He came back to the waiting room in a few minutes. "I'm afraid we're going to have to sedate him," he said. "The infection is so bad that cleaning the ear canal hurts him too much."

"I had no idea. I saw that the fur around his ears was brownish, but figured it was just gross old man stuff."

Dr. Paul smiled and nodded. "We'll have to keep him overnight, but we won't charge you for the hospitalization—he only has to stay because it's already so late."

"Thank you."

You can come get him tomorrow morning, and we'll give you antibiotics. I've given him a shot, but you need to keep him on antibiotics for at least ten days. And you need to keep his ears clean with this stuff," taking a bottle from a shelf. "Just squeeze it into the ear canal, and massage around the ear to work it in. He'll shake his head and shake it out. Once a week."

"Thank you."

Lesson 3: Check your dog's ears. I never checked Raven's ears, but then, she was only eight when I lost her.

I called Susan S. She said, "If it was that bad, he had to have had the infection when I gave him to you. I feel terrible about that. I feel responsible. I'll pay the bill."

She had a check for me the next time I saw her.

Chapter 18

"Why does the dog always have to be with you?" Jean asked, over cups of tea at my dining table.

The dog.

"You know I don't trust him with the kids yet. And they are my first responsibility, right?"

"Yes, they are."

Hammett jumped up on the table. He was brusque with me, demanding attention loudly. Jean said, "He'll never forgive you."

I started to cry, because I knew she was right.

"I shouldn't have said that," Jean said. "You have the perfect dog and the perfect cat. He'll be okay."

We both forgot about Margaret.

It's hard to portion out love fairly when four pairs of eyes want to be the cynosure of yours.

Jean wanted a downtown afternoon. I was upstairs at the computer when she arrived, and since the door was open I called out, "Come on in." I heard her open the door. I heard her take a few steps. Magnus, lying at the top of the stairs, stood up and stared at her with his head raised, chest puffed out, feet foursquare, and ears forward. He took a few steps down the stairs, silently, and resumed his stance.

Not so fast, ma'am.

Jean said, "He won't let me in, Nancy."

I got up, pushed past Magnus, and went down to her. Magnus followed closely, just in case. I thought it was funny.

"I'm not afraid of dogs, but he's intimidating. He has a very powerful presence."

"I'm kind of surprised that he wouldn't let you in. He knows you."

Yeah, and I know she wants you to yourself.

Jean waited downstairs with Magnus in attendance, while I shut down the computer and grabbed my bag. We filed outside, got into my car and drove to Los Altos to walk and window-shop. Magnus walked on leash beside (or between) us. Jean started to go into one of the stores, then stopped and said, "Oh. We can't go in with the dog."

"You can go in. I'll wait out here."

"That's no fun. Let's just walk."

The afternoon was slow and lazy, just a few people out in the shady, tree-lined streets, and just about the right level of activity for Magnus. He was alert, but not going into reaction mode, so Jean and I were able to carry on an actual, uninterrupted conversation.

When we got thirsty, we found a little café with tables on the sidewalk under big old sycamore trees. We tied Magnus to my chair. It was a light chair, and I had a vision of him dragging it into the café, but went inside anyway. When we came out with tea and pastries, the man at the next table was deep in conversation with Magnus.

He was a healthy, prosperous-looking man in early middle age, with short sandy hair, a handsome, tanned face and neat shorts and shirt. He was holding Magnus's face in both hands, gazing into his eyes. "Is this your dog?"

"Yes."

"What's his name?"

"Magnus."

"He's a fine old gent. What kind of dog is he?"

I told him. He told us about his golden retriever, and was clearly a very experienced dog person. He got Magnus to drink water from a cup. I couldn't get Magnus to drink water in public from anything. We spent a pleasant half hour petting my man and talking dogs.

Another man came down the sidewalk with a black and white bulldog who was straining against his leash to get at Magnus. He let his bulldog go right into Magnus's face, even though Magnus was clearly working up a head of steam. I put my arms around my man and glared at the bulldog.

You're alarmed, my dear? I'll handle this.

Our table-neighbor said, in a calm, clear voice, "It's okay, Magnus. There's nothing to worry about."

The bulldog's owner dragged his dog around the corner. Magnus stayed on alert. I said, "I can't believe that guy let his dog run into Magnus's face."

Lesson 4 sank in a few days later: I needed to have taken the nice man's lead. Take calm control of situations—don't feed your anxieties to your kuvasz. That's what the mental thing means.

After a month or so of going downtown once or twice a week, Magnus got used to the cars and pedestrians and noises and restaurant smells and other dogs. And to being approached and gushed over by passers-by.

"You have a beautiful dog."

"What kind of dog is that?"

"Is this a boy or a girl?"

"His eyes are blue!"

"What a nice dog."

"Is that a Newfoundland?"

"Is he a Golden Retriever?"

"What a pretty dog."

"Can I pet your dog?"

"He's so white! How do you keep his coat so clean?"

Every positive contact moved him forward on the socialization trajectory, so I was grateful for the attention. It wasn't long before he greeted all comers politely—or ignored them. He seemed to know who was open to meeting him and who wasn't, because the people he greeted always cooed at him and rubbed him and gazed into his eyes. He started to work this, leaning against peoples' legs and smiling up at them, basking in the attention.

He did still approach nervous people to see what they were nervous about—a nervous sheep generally has reasons for being in that state, and guilty parties tend to be nervous, too—but I just asked him quietly to mind his business. I didn't have to teach him that phrase; he understood it, understood what the situation called for, and walked on by.

It had been just two months.

CHAPTER 19　　　　　　　　　　　　　　　　　FIRST REVIEW

The next Sunday, after Mass, I caught Susan S. in the parking lot making out with Magnus through the car window, which I'd left half-open to keep him cool. (After this, I left it three-quarters open to make things easier for them.)

I said, "You're making out with Magnus."

She said, "Mmmmmmmmm, yes I am."

It was nice to see them like that. She obviously felt he'd gone through his process well enough to enjoy a reunion.

We made a date to meet in Palo Alto for a picnic lunch later on that week.

It was another beautiful day in California. (Don't imagine we take this for granted. We love it.) Susan S. was loving it on a bench in the City Hall plaza wearing another long flowered skirt and pale blouse, with her hair down, flowing in the breeze, and a beatific expression as she watched us walk up. I sat down. Magnus posed on the sidewalk in his alert stance, looking around, on duty.

"He hasn't looked this good since I was showing him," she said. She felt his limbs, and said, "He's muscling up nicely. Good job." We decided to go to Whole Foods for sandwiches and eat outside. Whole Foods was three blocks away. We passed a house with a barking dog. Magnus didn't twitch. Susan beamed and said, "He's become a city dog."

We got our sandwiches and drinks, and sat at some picnic tables under a pergola at the edge of the parking lot. I asked for a sip of her drink. She said, "Ew, no." I said, "You breed dogs that French kiss, and you won't let me drink from your cup?"

She passed me the cup.

Magnus was getting restless, so I told him to sit. He didn't. I told him to lie down. He didn't. I told him to sit. He didn't. Susan said, "Why should he obey you? You've already given him three commands that you haven't enforced."

I can be trained. I enforced.

Chapter 20   Acceptable Classes

We started going to a neighborhood playing field so Magnus could walk on soft grass instead of hard pavement—easier on the joints at any age.

The first time we went was in the early evening, during a softball game. Dogs and kids and noise and people and food everywhere. Too much for my man, so we turned back. I started going there at times of the day when there were just a few dogs and people about. When he got used to the field and the tennis courts and the buildings, I started slipping his leash if there were no dogs in sight—I'd been told that there was a general agreement that dogs could be off leash.

Every time we came onto the field, he would canter for joy in a high, exaggerated, rocking-horse gait with his neck strongly arched. I loved this. We walked around field every day, inspecting every corner. It became his pasture, and its inhabitants became his flock. Within a few weeks he learned to patrol the area calmly at my side. And roll in the grass. And sit in my lap.

One afternoon, he was stretched out on the grass, and I was rubbing him down. A good-looking, middle-aged man in khaki slacks and a blue shirt passed by and said, "That looks about right."

You're telling me, mister.

The first class of people he gave absolute clearance to was children. A month or so along, we went to the field on a Saturday. Three families with all their kids were picnicking and playing soccer together under some young trees on the edge of the grass. They were smiling at us. Magnus approached them slowly, and stopped a few yards away to study them. A pretty girl about nine or ten years old came over and asked if she could pet my dog. Magnus seemed calm, so I sat down, sat him down, put my arms gently around him, and said, "Sure. Do you know how to meet a dog?" She said, "Like this?" and held out her had so he could sniff it.

Within minutes, Magnus was rolling around on his back on the grass surrounded by eight kids who were petting him and laughing and squealing when he tried to lick their little chins. They played with him. He ran around with them. He let them hang on him. He let them touch his head, his back, his tail, his throat, his belly.

I had no idea the little ones could be so sweet. Almost as nice as the ladies.

Since then, every time we go to any park, he has to check out the playground and see if there are any little boys and girls around who need kissing. Bikes became okay. Skateboards became okay. Noisy children became okay, and that was that.

Soon after the breakthrough with children, we were walking around the field toward the tot lot. The tots were out. When they saw us, they ran to the fence, peeked between the rails and said, "Doggie! Doggie!" The teachers told them to keep their arms inside the fence. Magnus went up to the fence and offered to lick faces. "What is he doing?"

"He wants to kiss you. He loves to kiss girls."

Giggles.

"He's so white!"

"What's his name?"

"Magnus."

"Magnus!"

"Magnus!"

"Magnus!"

One tiny girl said, "He looks like a polar bear!"

"Polar bear!"

"Polar bear!"

"Polar bear!"

After a while, since he couldn't lick their faces, he started sniffing around.

"What's he doing?"

"He's reading the smells. Smells are like the newspaper to a dog: they tell him who has been here and what they've done."
"Really?"
With older kids, you can take it farther.
"He's so white!"
"Why do you think the dog is white?"
"I don't know."
"Does he look like any other animals?"
"A Polar bear."
"A sheep."
"These dogs work with sheep."
"So the coat is white so the sheep will think he's one of them?"
"Exactly."
"That's so cool."

CHAPTER 21 FAST FORWARD

We were patrolling the playing field when a pair of Dachshunds suddenly appeared around the corner of an outbuilding, just a few yards away from us. Magnus lunged. (I hadn't seen any dogs, so I had him off leash.) Fortunately, he was right next to me, so I lunged in the same instant and hauled him down. I apologized to the dogs' people profusely, snapped the leash on and walked Magnus home, bossing him and keeping him on a short leash—knowing that I'd been in the wrong.

Why is she being so harsh? Those dogs were running right at her.

He let me get away with that. But he must have thought about threat levels and appropriate responses. A week or so later, some folks playing tennis had their young terrier inside the court with them. He and Magnus studied each other through the fence, and started running up and down together, one safely inside and one safely out. It looked amicable. I asked the woman if she thought her dog would like to play. She said yes and unlatched the gate. The terrier dashed out. He and Magnus made a couple of play bows at each other, and then separated, each to his own devices. I praised my man effusively.

Once Magnus gets an idea, he acts on it. Rapid progress ensued. A few days later we came onto the field after dark, and walked the perimeter. A man was hanging out in the middle of the field, while a smallish, very fast dog ran mad circles around him. Magnus noticed, but since they were 50 yards away from us he stayed calm. When the perimeter walk brought us near the pair, the other dog shot towards us, and sped past Magnus's nose, which would normally merit angry snarking (snapping and barking).

This dog's just silly. I like the man, though.

I greeted the young man, and asked, "What kind of dog is that?"

"A vizsla."

"Oh, right. I couldn't really see her in the dark. Vizslas are Hungarian, aren't they?"

"Yes. What's your dog?"

"Another Hungarian—a kuvasz. We've been working on socialization, and this is the first time he's let a dog charge him. I'm very pleased."

"It's probably because they've had time to check each other out as you walked around the field."

"You don't suppose they recognize each other as fellow Hungarians, do you?"

"Ha! Maybe."

The vizsla continued running in circles around us and dashing into Magnus's face, but he hung patiently about, ultimately lying on the grass while the humans did their wordy thing.

The man said, "Do you ever go down to the high school?"

"No. Why?"

"There's an unofficial vizsla club that meets behind the school. There's a playing field and a mile or so of paved trails with a park at the far end. The vizsla people walk together off leash every evening."

"It's an off-leash park?"

"Unofficially. Off-leashing is tolerated unless the dogs misbehave."

"When do they meet?"

"Around sundown."

"I'll have to try that."

On reflection, maybe Magnus was just being extra-good that night because it had been a dog food day.

Chapter 22   The Vizslas

The next evening, we walked westward onto a wide lawn surrounding the high school's baseball fields as the sun was sinking toward the horizon. The summer solstice was near. Hot golden light suffused the atmosphere, half blinding us. I saw seven or eight human silhouettes gathered under one of the half dozen hundred-year live oaks around the lawn, watching at least a dozen sleek, cedar-brown dogs dashing around so fast they blurred.

The unofficial vizsla club. Pronounced veezh-lah. The z before the s is voiced. It's a Hungarian thing.

The vizsla is a pointer and retriever, bred for gentleness and employed by the aristocratic classes as companions for their children. They look something like small, shiny, auburn greyhounds, but with gentler, prettier faces. They are very sensitive. Magnus immediately adopted them as flock. One elderly male snarked at him, but my man's response was so mild that I let it pass.

He's just feeling crabby. No big deal.

When the vizslas were done running in circles and their owners were done introducing themselves to us, we all walked down the bike path alongside the playing fields. The field of oaks was followed by an avenue of spruce and redwood trees, leading us toward a low hill overgrown with wild oats, the dread foxtail grass, and fading wildflowers, all of which were glowing in the setting sun. Several little copses of shrubby oaks and ash trees clustered around the top of the hill. We climbed up towards them, then down along a rough footpath through parched, rough grasses. Spring is over here by late April, and June is already dry and sere. We rejoined the paved path where more towering oaks filtered the low streaming light and dappled the pack. The path was edged with golden grasses and curved along past a donkey paddock with eucalyptus trees for shade, and then onto a long, sweeping, velvety lawn presided over by towering redwoods to the north and oak and ash trees to the south. Asphalt gave way to decomposed granite winding under the redwoods. Beside the path there was a 25-foot deep ravine, under more great oaks that made a vault of arched branches with impossible geometries. The pack turned off the path at the head of a broad flight of railroad-tie stairs, and dashed down to a little creek that flowed beneath the oaks and watered their roots. Magnus stayed with me, picking his way down neatly in sharp contrast to the flighty, milling vizslas, who leapt down to the creek to drink and splash.

"Is the water safe?"

"We do this all the time, and we've never had a case of giardia." I didn't know what giardia was, but I got the point.

Magnus wouldn't drink in the ravine. He went to the graveled streambed but not to the water. He watched the other dogs. When we climbed back up the bank, he went last to make sure no one was left behind.

Someone has to look out for them.

In the course of the first week, he snarked three dogs. The first two times, I called his name sharply, snapped on the leash, and walked him off the park. The other dog people thought I was being extreme. "It's natural for them to do that," they would say. "They'll work it out."

"He can be aggressive. I have to have zero tolerance."

The third snarking was mild enough that all I did was make him sit in front of the other dogs and listen to the "I'm very disappointed in you" speech.

Must you do this in public?

And that was it. Freedom or dominance? Easy choice. Freedom was its own reward. And my man found better ways to dominate.

Watching him in action with his flock was a study. He was on constant alert, scanning the perimeter, head up and stance firm.

He protected and herded the vizslas. He'd hang back with lollygaggers and make sure they caught up with the pack, go after a dog that wandered into a fenced area and couldn't find its way out, or stand watch when the pack met other dogs. If an unfamiliar dog approached, he'd calmly place himself between it and the pack, go into his stance, and give the dog the eye. Usually the dog backed off. Occasionally one would challenge him. He'd swell out that chest, and bark a command. The stranger would cave in and back off.

After a few weeks of guard duty he relaxed and started playing with his charges. They were too fast for him. He couldn't manage the tight turns they made, and fell a few times, so he soon gave up. He barked instead. I figured he needed to build strength after years of relative inaction, and would eventually be able to do as he pleased.

The summer progressed. One evening, as the sun was setting, the vizsla people gathered around a holding pond that serves as flood control for the creek, throwing toys into the water for their dogs to retrieve. The banks of the pond are about thirty feet deep, and so steep that it's difficult to walk down without slipping. You want spikes on the soles of your shoes. The pond is about an acre in size, and is fringed with reeds, floating vines, and grasses.

We disturbed some small snowy egrets who were trying to fish, standing absolutely still in the reeds near the shore like skinny, hunchbacked men, staring intently at the water, and stabbing it with their long beaks when they spied a juicy frog or fish. We were also disturbing a small flock of mallards, which paddled away under a heavy-timbered bridge to a weedy bend in the shadowy tree-lined creek beyond, quacking in protest. The dogs were having a blast, running and swimming at vizsla speed.

I was standing next to a very pleasant man, who was smiling at the dogs, enjoying the summer twilight, smiling at me. I was smiling, too, in involuntary pleasure at being with these gentle, intelligent people and their pretty little dogs. Everything was glowing in the warm tones of sunset, and the air was slightly misty, emphasizing the glow. I couldn't remember feeling so content. It had been a tough decade, but all that was in the past now.

Magnus went down to the water, and disappeared around the corner. Through the reeds and bushes, I saw his snout go to the water and stay there. He was drinking in private.

We left the pond and strolled back up towards the hill and the fields on a path bordered by grasses and chaparral shrubs—mostly scrub oak and coyote bush and the obligatory poison oak, with one long stretch of tangled blackberry brambles. Young trees loitered behind the shrubs.

The vizsla pack turned off at the top of the hill, and went back down to the playing fields. Magnus and I continued down the hill on another gentle grade with more chaparral plants and young oaks and kept walking until after dark, when the air cooled off and the stars came out and the birds went to sleep and the peepers peeped in the oaks over the creek.

Chapter 23 — Park Rules

Walking off leash was a fantasy of mine: me and my big, beautiful dog working together in perfect harmony. But I also wanted him to be able to be a dog, not a puppet. I wanted him to be able to sniff things and have a pack and explore nature. I wanted him to get the extra exercise of wandering off to explore and collect scents, then trotting to catch up with me.

Strictly speaking, this isn't legal. But the neighborhood has a long tradition of off-leashing. So as long as your dog is under control, the people are welcoming, even the non-dog people. Most of the dog people know their critters, and know how to manage them. The dog people who get tickets are the ones with too many dogs, out-of-control dogs, or aggressive dogs.

Since we've been doing this, only a few people have objected. When I see them, I snap the leash on until they're out of sight. I've even chatted with policemen with Magnus standing beside me, off-leash, as the cops praise and pet him.

When Magnus heads for the playground I call out, "He's safe, but he might kiss your little girl." If the parents look edgy, I take him away. But most parents say, "Look at the big white doggie. Do you want to pet him?" I sit on the ground, put my arms around Magnus, pet him and let him lick my chin. That draws in the little people, and little fingers soon sink into white fur.

Some of the bravest kids are the littlest. Tiny toddlers stagger up to Magnus as fast as they can go, with their arms wide open. This makes Magnus nervous. Maybe he's afraid of hurting them unintentionally. Maybe he's afraid they'll fall down. Maybe he thinks they're aliens.

The kids who flip for him most often and spend the longest time hugging and kissing and petting him are girls between eight and sixteen. "Puppy!" they cry, and descend on my guy. He gets all melty with them and gazes into one pair of eyes after another as he decides which girl to kiss next. He likes to kiss girls. Girls seem to like his kisses. It's not uncommon to see four or five of them hanging on his big old body, giggling and smooching.

Off-leashing has been good for him in many ways. He has learned to walk at my side unless things need investigating. His social skills have become excellent. He gets to do his job—assess the environment, guard me, protect his friends, and so on. But most of all, it makes him happy. And that makes me happy.

I was calling Susan to give her progress reports every time something interesting happened, which in my view was several times a week.

"He has completely gotten over the dog aggression."

"That's what I would expect from him. He's a prince."

"When we're walking with other dogs and a strange dog comes near, he intercepts it and makes sure it's safe."

"Of course. That's his job."

"He can come on a field and have three dogs we don't know run right into his face and keep his cool."

"Okay. That I have to see."

She's hard to impress.

I'm not.

We'd been patrolling the playing field near home, and met up with a little muttsky. It was sweet, and walked along with us. We approached a skinny, elderly fellow I'd often seen walking big German shepherds. He had a new, young, strong dog, and was working with her on obedience, on leash. When we approached, she lunged for Magnus and Muttly, and the old fellow was hard-pressed to hold her in. I said, "Maybe she'll calm down if you let her off?" He nodded and slipped the lead.

She lunged, snarling at Magnus.

You don't belong here.

Yes I do.
Die.
You first.

He swelled and loomed, and went eye to eye with her, unflinching. She backed down. He took a few steps backward.

That's better. You young dogs, you just have to learn.

She then tried to snark the Muttly, but Magnus drove in to cut her off.

That'll do, miss.
Yes, sir. Okay.

I praised Magnus for his sense of duty and proportion. Not to mention effectiveness. Grandfather status notwithstanding, he's The Man, through sheer force of will.

Another time, a woman was strolling across the grass in the playing field with her three young daughters. The littlest girl suddenly dashed away from them, heading for the street. Magnus went straight into action, running at top speed to intercept her. I called him off, not wanting the poor child to be terrified by the polar bear, and he circled back. But I was very pleased to see him doing what he was bred to do.

By this time, we were walking at least two miles every day. My legs were firming up, and my mood was much sunnier. I loved the fresh air, the new acquaintances, watching the sky change with the season, and seeing my man in action. He was looking much better, too. When he came to me in April, his hocks—the bones between the foot and ankle—sloped at a 30° angle because he didn't have the muscle to hold them up. By summer, that angle had straightened out to 60°. I was very proud of myself. And of him.

CHAPTER 24   ITCHY AND SCRATCHY

Magnus had been walking around trying to scratch his belly, falling down, making people think he was having seizures, and so on. This had a negative effect on his lovely gait, not to mention his dignity. He'd also been lying on the ground trying to scratch his entire body by wriggling around.

Dr. Paul said he didn't think it was allergies this time. "See? Remember how red the skin was a few months ago? It's nice and pink and normal now. It might be dry skin. It might be mosquito bites. Are you giving him flea medicine?"

"I haven't been. I definitely know when we have fleas, because they drive me nuts, and we've been clean."

"Have you ever used Advantage®?"

"Yes."

"That works on all kinds of insect bites."

"Okay."

I got the back-of-the-neck flea dope, and used it. No change. The scrabbling and lurching and clawing at himself continued. I called Susan S. and told her about the itchiness. She said "Huh," and went on to other subjects. I'd hoped for more.

A few days later she called me back and said, "Some of Magnus's relatives are on a supplement called Missing Link®. It seems to work for them. You can order it online, in bulk, cheap."

"Where?"

"Oh, I don't know. You expect me to remember those kinds of details?"

My pretty space cadet and tough mama.

Dr. Paul said, "Missing Link is good stuff. We prescribe it here." He didn't seem to mind my buying it elsewhere.

I found a site that sold 10-pound bags for about half the retail cost. I bought it. Magnus stopped trying to scratch his belly as he walked around. If you want to call that an endorsement, go ahead.

Chapter 25   Vespers

Vespers is my favorite service. It's the evening office, a quiet, meditative end to the working day. Just a few singers come for Sunday evenings, and we women have gotten so used to singing together that we breathe and sing as one. It creates an intense feeling of connection and mutuality.

The monastic offices—Matins, Terce, Prime, and so on—are chanted Psalms, prefaced with melodic antiphons and followed by a hymns and other praise verses. For Sunday Vespers, we sing Psalms 109 through 113. I have some favorite lines: the one about bashing heads in the streets, the sinners gnashing their teeth and crying, the mountains dancing like goats, the hills dancing like lambs. The absolutely best text is the antiphon for 113, "Our God, however, does whatever He wills." Of course he does. What kind of God would He be if He couldn't?

Vespers is the only service St. Ann's choir can still sing in St. Ann's Chapel, which the Catholic church sold to a high Episcopal congregation some years ago. It's a modern building with attractive proportions and lines, and modern, expressionistic art for the Stations of the Cross and the stained glass windows. One entire wall is pierced with small square windows with red, blue, and yellow glass. The yellow squares are arranged in the shape of crosses; the red and blue make a background.

I figured that out last year, after singing there for about 9 years.

When the setting sun picks them out, the effect is charming. But the chapel's best feature is its acoustics.

With as few as four singers we can fill the space with beautiful sound. We can hear each other, which helps a lot. We can create the harmonic overtones intended by the composers, who were consciously writing harmonies for acoustically live spaces. In the cottage-Gothic church that took us in after the chapel was sold, the wooden walls and fussy surfaces absorb the sound. We can't hear each other. We don't tune up as well, and we don't blend as well. We can't create the harmonics. It's still music, but it loses the unity and unearthly beauty.

Every Sunday, tired and achy from two or more hours of rehearsing and singing the noon Mass, I want to stay home. Duty brings me out. If I don't go, the Susans—yes, there are three Susans in our small group, and they won't let me make up names for them—have to carry the women's section on their own. I've also learned the tenor lines, so if another alto shows up I can support our sole tenor. So, they need me, and unless I'm feeling particularly unwell, I sing.

But by the end of the office, even if we haven't sung well, I receive the peace that eludes me at Mass and in life. Whether it's the breathing, the unison, the serenity of the service, the vibrations of the harmonic overtones, or grace, this is the place where I most often feel God's blessing.

Magnus waits in the car while we sing. Susan S. sings with us, so after the office I let him out to visit with her. He prances up to her, trots back and forth between her and me, greets the other singers and generally disports himself like a pup.

Both of my women at once. What could be better?

And then we all go to John and Susan A.'s house for a feed.

CHAPTER 26　　　　　　　　　　　　　　　　　　SUNDAY DINNER

Susan A. has been hosting Sunday dinner after Vespers for decades. She has a vast collection of tried and true recipes that accommodate all sorts of dietary restrictions—no raw onions, no hot spices, and so on. Her spaghetti carbonara is superb. Her roasts are perfectly done. Her dumplings are tender, her sauces aromatic, and her salads are sinful.

She wants to have t-shirts printed with the acronym ITOFTS. "I'm too old for this shit." She soldiers on anyway. Susan A. is very good at soldiering on.

Susan and John's house is at the very top of a short, steep hill overlooking America's Most Beautiful Highway. You'd think the traffic noise would be an issue, but somehow it isn't. Maybe it's muffled by the big pines that surround the house, or maybe the sound just doesn't travel upward very well.

On Sunday evenings, what traffic noise you do hear comes from cars crowding into their little parking lot. You walk to the front door along a path that is lined with old Porsches and miscellaneous mechanical and electronic stuff on John's side, under the carport, and cactuses, animal bones from the desert, and cascading vines on Susan's side, by the house. There's a big, heavy door with cast iron hinges that swings open at a touch.

Inside, high ceilings with heavy beams, a glass wall across the living room, and an enormous fieldstone fireplace do their bit for Modern design. Antiques from all over the world, collected by Susan's mother during her travels as an army wife, do their bit for cultural continuity. Some of the paintings are European antiques. Most of them are Susan A.'s work. She paints landscapes of ghost towns, trains and abandoned autos, rock formations, modern cowboys, and desert animals. She paints a clear, bright light. She takes photographs everywhere she goes, and composes pictures from them. She has a fine eye for composition. She says she has no technique. She has technique. At somewhere closer to seventy than sixty, she's beginning to sell.

There's a pale green clavichord that John made years ago. There's an antique chest with primitive scenes and figures picked out in low relief in brass. There's a piece of exercise equipment John uses to stretch his back. There are old, sagging velvet couches with carved wooden frames that are covered with tapestry pillows, velvet pillows, Navaho blankets and fur.

Susan A. keeps two Queensland heelers—wiry little cattle dogs that bounce straight up and down on their hind legs like they're on Pogo sticks when she brings their food. They careen around the house playing chase, sliding across tiles at top speed so nimbly that they never collide with furnishings, people, or each other (unless they want to). The male is Bosco, and the female is Blue. They look like back-bred pound dogs unless you're familiar with the breed. My greetings to this house have always included the phrase, "The dogness of the universe," which Susan A. loves.

She's little and round, with good bones and rosy skin and blond hair gone to gray rolled up in an approximate bun at the nape of her neck. She wears colorful, bohemian, often homemade clothes and heavy turquoise and amber jewelry. She says, "I'm probably nine kinds of heretic," but her faith is profound. So is John's.

I envy them this. John once told me of a friend with high career ambitions. Leaning his body to one side, creasing his face with a broad smile and tilting his head, he said, "As if that's going to get him into heaven."

John looks like a skinny old cowboy, right down to a crooked walk, a long white ponytail, cowboy boots, and jeans. He's actually a consulting engineer in communication systems. For business he wears a suit and tie with the cowboy boots and ponytail.

Food and feeding people are cornerstones of their marriage. There's a magnet on their refrigerator that reads, "Sunday dinner is not just a meal. It's an institution." The first thing he did after they were married was to send her to cooking lessons at a famous restaurant in Berkeley.

These two believe in the monastic virtues: hospitality, feed the hungry, clothe the naked, visit the sick. Susan was delighted when her daughter asked her to make costumes for Burning Man—a California performance arts festival noted for over-indulgence in controlled substances and under-indulgence in attire. She says there aren't many opportunities today to clothe the naked.

They make pilgrimages in spring and fall to Death Valley in their silver Airstream, and in summer to the high Sierra to spend holidays in an A-frame cabin in the forest. They used to camp in the back of their truck all over the state, hunting and cooking in the open.

Susan can skin and dress a deer

I introduced her to Magnus right away, of course, and she was naturally charmed. When I came to dinner, I'd leave Magnus in the car, not trusting him to be nice to her dogs. After about a month of this, she said, "Bring him in. You can't leave him in the car like that."

"I'm afraid he'll hurt your dogs."

"Nonsense. He's a fine old fellow, and my dogs are nice."

Magnus came in, started barking at Blue and Bosco, trotting around the living room with them, following them into the kitchen, greeting the guests and affably getting in everyone's way. I was fairly flabbergasted. Just a few weeks past, Jean and I tried to introduce him to her two dogs, and within seconds he'd had Joe on his back on the ground, yelping in fear.

John, who doesn't much care for the Queenslands, does care for Magnus. He won't admit it, but his eyes go soft when he looks at him, and his hand reaches out when Magnus is near.

During that first dinner, Magnus walked around and around the table, sticking his nose under people's arms, trying to scratch his belly between steps and falling down. Once down, he scratched his belly furiously. Susan said, "He's having a fit."

Bosco has fits. This was not a fit. It was acting out. I said, "He's trying to get my attention." He tried to get my attention right through the salad course, which Susan wants served after the meal.

The salad service is my contribution to dinner. I make it the way Susan wants it made. I dress it and serve it the way she wants it dressed and served. She says I'm the only one who can mete out the portions fairly. John jokes that I always forget to count myself when I'm counting how many servings we need. (Not true. I do count myself. I just miscount everyone else.) I clear the table and stack the dishes when we're done eating. After singing three services—Susan and John and a few others sing Lauds as well as Mass and Vespers—and cooking for twenty, Susan A. is visibly exhausted by the time she sits down to eat.

After dinner, we go into the living room to sing Compline, the psalmodic equivalent of "Now I lay me down to sleep." Magnus gets locked out, since he insists on trying to socialize with the chanting guests or mobbing me. On his first night, when Compline was over, we let the dogs out and I was chatting with one of our friends, when he flopped down on his side, raised his forepaw, looked at me out of the corner of his eye, grinned, and gave a loud WOOF.

Woman! Come here and rub me.

I did, naturally. The others watched with knowing smiles. I was sure that Magnus was just over-excited about being with so many new people and smells and having to share me, so I let him boss me.

Magnus is now a regular guest at Sunday and holiday dinners. He greets everyone calmly, watches me make the salad, gets shooed out of the kitchen by John when he's taking the casserole or roast from the oven, receives eye-snout training from Susan as she tosses him bits of vegetables, and hangs around with Blue.

(Bosco has since passed on.) Since Magnus's head is on a level with the dinner plates, he has to be shut up in the living room during the meal. I bring his Magnus Mealz into the living room and place the bowl on the hearth while everyone takes their places at table, sneak away, and barricade the swinging doors to the dining room with rubber bands.

Benedict Arnold.

When I open it after supper, Magnus is always standing in front of it with his head down and his ears forward, regarding me balefully. I suspect he stands there at attention as soon as I hook the rubber bands over the doorknobs.

After some months, I forgot to shut him up one night, and discovered him lying peaceably on the living room rug with the doors open after dinner.

Why fight it? The dining room floor is hard, cold tiles.

Partial banishments aside, he loves Sunday dinner now. He knows the road there, and stands up in the back seat to start kissing me when we're within half a mile of the house. He also knows the route to the park and the roads near home, and starts kissing me as we reach them. I don't know whether he recognizes the ambient scents, or is very good at turtle geometry, measuring distances and counting turns. Probably the latter, don't you think?

Silly woman. Of course it's the scents. It's also the days of the week and the hours of the day. I know your routine, you creature of habit.

Chapter 27 — Why Me, Really

I still wondered why Susan S. had given me a kuvasz—and done so when he was old enough that he would need knowledgeable care. I had never trained a smart, independent, guardy dog. I had barely trained Raven at all. I had never seen a dog through its final days. She didn't give me an answer I could understand for almost two years.

Susan thinks intuitively. I'm more analytical, and need information I can organize and rationalize. So she called one bright warm day, and I pressed her, asking questions and translating her replies back to her.

"It's the way it always is with these marriages," she said. "I've placed a lot of dogs, and seen what good owners are made of. I knew Magnus, and trusted him. I'd seen him in all kinds of situations. I knew you and your cats, and how you treated them and thought about them. I knew you were absolutely devoted to them, and cared for all their needs. I knew you had more room in your heart. I knew your friends. And I knew I'd see you twice a week, and could step in if it wasn't working. I thought it would be the best situation for him—the puppies really irritated him, and they took so much of my time I couldn't give Magnus the attention he needed. I positively knew it would be good for you.

"When we met in Palo Alto for our first reunion, I was convinced that I'd made the right decision. You were happier than I'd ever seen you. You had a light in your eyes and a spring in your step. He was happier and stronger and handsomer than he'd been in a long time.

"I was happy for both of you. But I cried in the car on the way home. I love that dog."

Chapter 28 — Great Dane

Within a few weeks of off-leashing, Magnus started to ignore other dogs, especially golden retrievers and Labradors, which make up the vast majority of the park's dog population. He recognizes them as safe breeds. I relaxed my vigilance around meeting new dogs.

One sunny Saturday, fresh breezes blowing, green grasses shining, I met a young, half-hippy-half-redneck-looking guy on the field with a young great Dane with a black and white coat. We introduced the boys, who were perfectly civil, and started chatting. The boys walked around a bit, got themselves behind us, and all of a sudden exploded into violence. I spun around in horror as the Dane arched its neck over Magnus's, with Magnus snarling and snapping upward and trying to get out from under with fast lateral moves, but the Dane was younger and faster and I froze because I could barely see what was happening and they were so fast and where would I put my hand in that mêlée when the young guy screamed "Get your dog!" and flung himself on the Dane's back, dragging him to the ground. Magnus immediately quieted.

I felt both a coward and a fool.

Lesson 5: Don't relax your vigilance when meeting new dogs.

Chapter 29 — Takedown

I was showing off for Jean about how well my smart, obedient guy was doing with the off-leashing. It was a Sunday afternoon. The park was crowded with dogs and people on-leashing and off-leashing. I kept having to call Magnus when he got distracted and wandered off.

Magnus, seeing Jean and me deep in conversation, decided to take off down the hill at a fast trot. I had to call him several times before he came back. He took off again. I called. He went from a trot to a canter to a flat-out run, around a corner and out of sight. I said, "He wants to run." Jean said, "Nancy, I hear people screaming."

She thinks I'm deaf. She's crazy.

I ran in panic and found Magnus trotting towards me followed by an irate man of Mediterranean mien. "If I ever see that dog down here again without a leash, I'm calling the police." Clearly, Magnus had taken his dog down. I was so ashamed I couldn't even apologize. I hooked my fingers through the choke collar and led Magnus out of the park.

It was the first and only time I hadn't had a leash with me.

As we were driving home, I saw a young woman on the street walking a little white dog, and saying into her cell phone, "She's okay now, but it was really frightening."

Magnus ran away to get a babe. Yup, he's all boy. But I'd say his courtship technique is flawed.

We did a week of intensive recall training. One of the dog people, a skinny little guy who saunters his Bernese mountain dog (you can't really call what he does "walking") with a nonchalant cigarette on his lip, told me to up the ante on recall. "Give real meat as a reward. Use a very specific and consistent command.

And when you don't really need him to come, say things like, 'This way,' or 'Over here, boy.'"

I started carrying jars of baby food. When Magnus did a successful recall, he got to eat the whole thing. Recall got very, very good very, very fast. One evening, the sun growing dim and stars starting to twinkle, we met a smart young shepherd. The boys took to each other, and started straying off toward the street, so I called Magnus, who turned around and galloped toward me while I opened the baby food. The scent also brought the shepherd over at top speed. They fought over the jar, which I swung overhead while I separated them.

I started carrying freeze-dried liver instead, which was high-value but not so high-value that it started fights.

Magnus essentially needs one repetition to learn something when food is the reward. "Magnus COME" means "Meat? What little white female?"

A few weeks later, Jean and I were out with Magnus again, and he was very intent on the little coppice of oaks on top of the hill. Our route circled it, and Magnus had offered to investigate each time we passed it. I called him off to keep him with us. We continued down to the long, green, oak-bordered playing field where we met a friend and stopped to chat. Magnus kept staring at the coppice, ears up. I asked him to stay with me several times, and then let him go to see what he'd do.

He trotted for a few yards, then launched into a beautiful, powerful, efficient canter, ears forward, tail up, heading directly for the little cluster of trees and shrubs. We watched him go for about 100 yards. Jean started to get nervous, so I gave the "Magnus, COME" command. He wheeled around in a perfect half-circle, and cantered straight up to me. I had the half-inch cube of freeze-dried liver ready.

Jean was impressed.

Me, I took it for granted. We're talking Magnus here.

CHAPTER 30   HAMMETT AND MAGNUS

One night Hammett watched me brush Magnus for half an hour—in certain seasons you can brush out a basketful of fur every day. If you like breathing without choking on airborne strands of kinky 6-inch fur, you are highly motivated to do this.

Hammett normally doesn't let me brush his fur. He gets overexcited and bites and grabs my arms with his paws and claws me. I find this discouraging. But when I finished brushing Magnus that night, Hammett let me brush the dead fur and dander out of his coat until it shone.

Why should he get all the attention?

When I brought Magnus's new, soft bed into the living room, Hammett commandeered it. One morning he was lying on it, propped up on his elbow like an odalisque. Magnus approached him politely, and when the big guy was two feet away, the little guy raised a paw.

My claws—I believe you've met them.

Magnus backed up, sighed, sat down, let his forelegs slide forward until his torso settled on the floor, put his head on his paws and regarded Hammett with resignation.

There were friendlier interactions behind my back. I was at the top of the stairs one day, watching the boys at the front screen door, which swings open easily because I took the latch off (it kept locking me out). Hammett was alternately poking it and looking up at Magnus, whose head was right beside his.

Come on man, you have the body mass, you can open it.
That wouldn't be right.
It would be fun. We could be free.
If she wanted the door open, she'd open it.

Magnus actually shook his head slowly from side to side.

Another time, again from the stairs, I saw Hammett up on his haunches boxing with something. My guess is that it was one end or the other of something big and white.

I got a large box of dog biscuits at the wholesale club. Magnus watched me open it and pack batches of biscuits into old bread bags. He watched as I stored it in a floor-level cupboard. The next morning, I found the cupboard open and one chewed-up bread bag on the floor with half the biscuits gone.

There is no part of Magnus that is small enough to get around the knob or into the crevices between the door and the frame.

I imagine Magnus staring at the cupboard door. Hammett saunters up to join him.

What gives?"

There's really good food in there.

No problem. Here, I'll just give a little flick of the wrist with these claws, and there you go.

Fantastic. I'll open the bag. My, these are tasty.

Let me try some. Waaaaait a minute. Where's the MEAT?

That cupboard has never been opened again.

Chapter 31 — Amy and Skip

Amy came to work as a designer on a magazine I was editing when she was 19. She had just two years of training at Brigham Young University. She was in the Bay Area visiting her boyfriend, and walked into our office unannounced, wearing platform flip-flops, tight jeans, and a short tee. She offered to work for free if the publisher would let her be a designer. Marty was so stunned by her gall that he agreed. "I don't know if it was a mistake, but she's starting tomorrow," he said.

"We'll see," I said, and reserved judgment. He didn't always read people well.

When Marty brought Amy around for introductions, I was in my assistant's cube. Marty said, with a mock-disgusted look, "This is our managing editor, Nancy, and her assistant, Tami. They're inseparable." We had our arms around each other's shoulders at the time, and didn't see anything out of the ordinary in it. Tami was the only person who'd responded to the ad for the job, but even if 100 people had applied I probably would have hired her.

Which explains why I took one look at the tight jeans and the platform flip-flops, judged Amy to be a party girl, and ignored her for six months. She told me years later that she kept trying to break through, but that I was impenetrable. She said, "Then I told you I was Mormon, and I thought you might actually run away from me."

"Was I really that bad?"

"You were worse."

"Then why did you even want to get close to me?"

"I respected your work. I was a fan."

"A fan? Of me?" Who would want to be a fan of me, the fat, sweaty old woman who was losing her mind to menopause?

Hormonal dysfunctionality not being a sufficient deterrent, Amy persisted. I started to pay attention. I started stopping by her cube to look at her work. Her work was better than most designers who have advanced degrees and experience. Her sketchbooks showed an able, confident hand and a lot of wit. She asked for and took advice readily.

Then I found out she liked swing dancing. I'd been on a boss-mandated health kick, and my exercise of choice was Swing. We started going to dances together, Amy and Skip and me, taking turns dancing with each other and with other people. They'd have me laughing at nothing, at anything, at everything. Amy and I played pranks on our co-workers. We held impromptu swing dance lessons and office chair races at stupid hour—about 3:30 in the afternoon, when everyone was trying not to fall asleep and needed some oxygen.

The magazine failed a year or so later. I introduced Amy to her next boss. He thanked me for Amy every time he saw me, and when I went freelance, he and Amy became my best clients.

Their firm's home office is in Minneapolis. Amy and Skip and I flew there together for the annual Christmas party, and stayed at the same hotel.

I was in their room when Skip showed up with a Maltese puppy. The room was a hurricane. Amy was packing, and there were clothes and twenty-something high-tech toys all over the floor and furniture. I said, "You can't have a dog. You're never home!"

Skip said, "We need a doggie."

"You bought a dog on the spur of the moment? Just like that?"

"We've been thinking about it for at least a year."

"You have?"

"Yes."

"But dogs need their pack. Can you be his pack?"

Amy said, "We're home all the time, Nancy. We need a dog. We've been researching dogs for months. I never told you. We didn't want a big dog. We couldn't have a dog that has fur, because Skip is allergic, and Maltese have hair. We've read about puppies and how to take care of them. We're ready for this."

"Okay, but why buy him in Minneapolis?"

"Because they cost $1500 in the Bay Area, and $400 here."

"I'm sorry. I didn't realize you were so serious."

"Thank you. We know what we're doing."

When we got to the airport, we made a kennel out of our suitcases and our bodies, and watched the puppy play. He was the definition of cute. Amy and I went to buy toys for him. We found a store with lots of attractive items. I picked out a stuffed cat that was about the size of the puppy. "Here, buy this. It's about the size of his littermates, and he'll be missing them."

She said, "He won't like that," and practically sneered at me. Well, I deserved that for the you-can't-have-a-dog remarks.

"He'll be missing his littermates. It'll comfort him."

"Oh, okay," she said, and snatched it out of my hands. He destroyed it within weeks, and they've had to keep buying replacements. Then they got a second dog to keep him company, which has made him much happier than stuffed cats.

Magnus likes little white dogs, so we decided to introduce him to the Maltese. I went to Amy and Skip's house, and tried walking in the front door with Magnus, but Jasper went mental, all six pounds of him in full-on defense mode, while Cupcake tried to hide under a table. Magnus held his head out of Jasper's reach, put his ears back, and refused to react as Jasper circled and jumped at him, trying to get a grip on the big dog's throat. Amy said, "Maybe we should try another way."

"Let's introduce them outside, in neutral territory," I said.

"Good idea," said Skip's voice from the kitchen.

Skip picked up Jasper, went to the door, and led us all outside. Cupcake followed us yipping and yapping and jumping and feinting. I took Magnus to the edge of the quiet street, had him sit, and sat down with him. Skip sat with Jasper about ten feet away. Jasper was clearly ready to attack.

That creature has no concept of relative size.

Watching Skip with Jasper was a study in contrast. Skip's well over six feet tall, and built like a load-bearing masonry wall: broad, thick and solid. He has red hair in a short, stylish cut, freckles, broad cheekbones, and a glint in his green eyes. He is more the Patriarch with every year of marriage—more commanding, gentler, more responsible, calmer. But he still plays online war games and perpetrates practical jokes. That glint in his eyes is never going to fade. At that moment, though, he was all Patriarch, settling the little squirming dog calmly and firmly.

Amy and Cupcake stood to the side, watching. When Jasper stopped struggling, we let the boys go and headed back in. Jasper ran inside after Cupcake. Magnus followed them through the house, on into the back yard, and invited them to play, bowing and barking. At this point Jasper did get the concept of relative size, and ran away. Smaller and shyer Cupcake seemed more accepting, but though he stayed close he wouldn't actually play with Magnus.

We decided to take everyone to the dog park, got them leashed up, and went in procession down the street. Those tiny dogs made serious time. One step for Magnus was ten for them, but they kept up easily, their bitty legs pumping.

At the park, they ran around chasing each other and otherwise acting remarkably like dogs for such tiny bits of fluff. Magnus tried to join in. I saw him launch, and saw his hind end collapse. After a few such failures, he gave up, and just watched the young ones. Amy looked at me. "That's so sad," she said.

"He's ten years old. And he's only been walking a quarter of a mile a day—I don't know if he's ever been properly exercised. Now he gets two miles a day, so he'll get stronger. We can lay down muscle at any age, right?"

"Right."

It was sad, though, to see him being left out of the fun. I was glad that he wanted to play at all—it had taken him several months to even make the suggestion. He was getting his youth back, at least in that respect.

Chapter 32 — Turkish Boys

Walking around the school one Saturday, we passed a small group of Mediterranean or Middle-Eastern-looking boys between fifteen and eighteen years old. They visibly started when they saw Magnus, smiled broadly, and made a cluster around him. A tall, lanky boy said, "We have those dogs in our home country."

"What's your home country?"

"Turkey. We call this dog the Akbash."

Another boy said, "They have them in Northern Israel now. Jackals came in and started killing the sheep and goats, so they put some Akbash dogs in with the flocks."

I said, "You wouldn't think that a dog with such a heavy coat would do well in the desert."

"They're in the mountains, where it gets cold."

"It even snows up there," another boy said.

I said, "My dog is actually a Hungarian kuvasz, but I think it's descended from The Akbash."

It isn't. Actually, It may be the other way around, with the kuvasz going from Hungary to Turkey when the former was under Ottoman rule. However, they're so similar that unless you're an expert, it's very difficult to tell an Akbash from a kuvasz.

The Akbash/kuvasz type is so well suited to its job, and the necessary characteristics are expressed so consistently, that there are national breeds of big white livestock guards all around Europe and the Mediterranean. In Hungary, there's a second breed, the Komondor. In Poland, it's the Owczarek Podhalanski. In Czechoslovakia it's the Slavensky Cuvac. In Italy it's the Maremma. In France, it's the Great Pyrenees.

In the park, it's Magnus.

CHAPTER 33   ANCIENT BREED

Kuvaszok are among the oldest documented breeds in the world. The earliest physical evidence of the breed is a fossilized skeleton found in 1978 near Keszthely, in Hungary. It dates to the ninth century, and is remarkable in that the anatomy is almost exactly the same as the modern kuvasz.

Other archaeological evidence is more contradictory.

Someone whom you might call an enthusiast for Hungarian breeds spent 47 years organizing and directing research into their origins. Presumably on a part-time basis, because in addition to being a practicing medical doctor, Dr. Sandor Palafalvy bred puli dogs. He and his colleagues conducted a thorough survey of Sumerian, Sanskrit, Greek, and Latin literature and of archeological findings in the Tigris-Euphrates valley. They believed they found repeated references to the breed in multiple sources, and concluded that the kuvasz was domesticated and developed by nomadic Sumerian herdsmen some 7,000 to 8,000 years ago.

Wonderful. That would make the Magyars, who brought the dogs to Hungary, Iranian refugees.

An English archeologist, Sir H.J. McDonald, believed that the kuvasz arose in the Middle East at a much later date. He found a clay tablet in the city of Ugarit on the coast of what is now Turkey, opposite Cyprus. It is now in the British Museum in London, and we are told that if you can read cuneiform, you'll find the name Ku Assa, or Dog of the Horse, written on it. Presumably the dog of the horse ran with horses and guarded the herds. The dates of the Ugarit finds are either around 1,500 B.C. or 600 B.C., depending on whose chronology you believe.

The Code of Hammurabi, written in the third century B.C., covered all aspects of daily life. According to some researchers it includes a section on the legal status of kuvasz, komondor, and puli dogs, which makes them Iranians again.

Most kuvasz people scoff at this scholarship, and say that the Magyars and their dogs originated in central Asia—possibly Tibet—and that along with their horses and herds, they migrated from Asia to Eastern Europe along trade routes that opened up around 2,000 B.C. across the steppes . Their first stop was thought to have been near the Ural Mountains in Russia. Then they moved along and settled in what's now Ukraine for a while, but they got into trouble with a tough tribe there and decided to find a place that offered less intense competition. Their next stop was in the Carpathian Basin, the heartland of Hungary.

Imagine the terror of the locals when the Magyar hordes thundered by the thousands into their mountain-shadowed riparian valley on fast, strong, horses seconded by huge dogs with sharp fangs and bloodlust on their minds. And big, hungry families.

The locals were probably used to it by then. Successive waves of emigrants from the Steppes—Goths, Huns, Avars, Lombards, and Gepids—fleeing enemies and hoping to find nice, steady Roman jobs, preceded them. Each tribe in its turn was co-opted by the Romans or their successors and hired on as mercenaries. Often to fight off the previous wave of invaders. Or the next one.

By the time the Magyars poured in through a northern pass in the Carpathians around 900 AD, most of the locals were either Slavs or remnants of the other tribes. Some of them survived.

The Magyars then tried getting steady jobs in northern Italy, but the Italians—who were by then mostly German Lombards with a Frankish king—didn't take to them. So the Magyars pillaged and devastated the countryside, captured a bunch of towns, exacted tribute and so on until the Venetians finally stopped them. They then pillaged their way back to the Carpathians to figure out what to do with their remaining Slavs. (Someone had to tend the kuvaszok and the livestock while the

Hungarians carved a hefty empire for themselves out of French and German territories.)

You don't hear much about kuvaszok after that until the 1400s. The horsemen and shepherds simply bred their best dogs to each other out of common sense, and didn't bother with record keeping.

King Matthias Corvinus, who reigned from 1443 to 1490, was also what you might call a kuvasz enthusiast. His devotion to the breed may have been inspired by the fact that Kingship is a hazardous occupation. Has there ever been a royal court that was not attended by intrigue, conspiracy, and betrayal? King Matthias is said to have trusted his kuvaszok more than his guards, and never went anywhere without a brace of them.

A brace of dogs is a pair, typically in harness. If I were Matthias, I'd have had them all off leash. "Um, excuse me for a bit, please, O frightful assassin, while I unharness my assassin-subduers."

When Matthias was especially fond of a nobleman, he would give the man a kuvasz from the royal kennels. He was especially fond of one Count Dracula, locally known as Vlad the Impaler, to whom he also gave his daughter's hand in marriage—after the Count was sprung from prison for excessive impaling, of course. One hopes that the kuvasz he gave Vlad as a wedding gift was more loyal to Matthias's daughter than to her husband. Actually, that may be why King Matt gave them the dog.

When the Ottoman Turks overran the country a few years on, they changed the name of the breed to Kawasz, which means "armed guard of the nobility." A far cry from "half-starved nomadic goat-guard."

Okay, okay, the ancient dogs probably weren't half-starved. They're motivated by food and are born trackers, hunters, and killers. Plus there was still plenty of wildlife around. But noble herd-protector, and not noble noble-protector, is job the kuvasz was born to do, and they went back to the pastures and farms for a few more centuries of no-news-is-good-news. Then we come to the all-news-is-bad-news 20th century.

Kuvaszok are working farms and estates all over Hungary. They love their masters, their masters' herds, and their masters' children. Bad men come with guns, sweeping the fields and forests to kill people, steal food and horses, and generally make a mess of things. The soldiers go out of their way to seek and destroy kuvaszok. They were as efficient in this mode of killing as they were in others.

It's ironic to think that the real Hungarians, the Magyars and their Magyar dogs, were being killed by people we called Huns, but who were actually blonder and came from farther north.

Sometimes farmers and their families hid from the soldiers. They shot their dogs to prevent them from barking and giving away their hiding places. I guess if you have to choose between your dogs and your entire household, you have to choose the latter. Maybe the kuvaszok were as willing to die for their masters in that way as any other.

By the end of WWII, there were just 12 breeding pairs left, with fewer than 30 kuvaszok in the entire country. More people whom you might call kuvasz enthusiasts repopulated the breed, with genetic contributions from kuvasz breeders around the world. Peru, for example. Or Sweden. Even America. Anywhere there are herds and pastures, kuvaszok are in demand.

The California county of San Mateo has a herd of goats that keep public lands mowed and brush-free. They are guarded by kuvaszok. I've heard that no one gets near those goats but the shepherd.

Chapter 34 — Civility

Jean and I decided to eat in downtown Palo Alto one Saturday in June. I brought Magnus out with us. She questioned the wisdom of this. Palo Alto on a Saturday night is a busy place, and every time she had seen him in a busy public place he'd been tense and aggressive. She hadn't seen him in a busy public place for a while. I told her he'd be fine. For me this evening was all about showing her how excellent his manners had become.

We walked up and down the University Avenue, which is lined with restaurants and shops and bookstores and teeming with people and dogs until all hours. Magnus walked past dog after dog without reacting. Jean gave me incredulous glances. When a little terrier lunged at him from under a table, he didn't react, but walked on by. When a car blaring hip-hop with that heart-shaking bass turned onto the street, he did react.

Turn that noise down. Now.

We agreed.

After walking for a while, we decided to have cappuccino at a café in a courtyard off the street, so Magnus wouldn't have so much to deal with. I saw the hind end of a very large, white dog in the courtyard. It was a male great Pyrenees, descendant of the kuvasz, and an equally Alpha breed. This did make us a bit nervous, but I watched the dogs greet each other and each other's people politely and calmly, with no dominance moves on either side. Jean made an exaggerated expression of surprise, shaking her head, making her mouth an O and arching her brows.

When we sat down at our table, she said, "You have done an amazing job with him."

"It's not me, it's him. He learns really fast."

"But you gave him the experiences to learn from."

"Yes, but if he didn't want to learn, I wouldn't have had the skills to make him do anything. It's all Magnus."

"Okay, it's him." Her tone was tetchy. I wondered why.

A few weeks later, Jean had an insight. "I finally understand why the dog is always with you. He's a service dog. You need him for your health."

"Exactly."

"He's good for you."

"He is. I feel so much better than I did a few months ago."

"I'm glad you have him."

"Thank you. That means a lot to me."

Jean finally became Magnus's champion, basking, as she said, in reflected glory. One of her favorite Magnus stories is the one about two little King Charles spaniels we met in the park. They were running around together, playing heedlessly, looking like silky animated dust mops bouncing and spinning along the lawn. They were sibs: a black and white male and an auburn and white female. Their meeting with Magnus was amicable—after a few sniffs the little dogs basically ignored him, and he took up his post to watch over them. We stood and chatted with their Mom while we watched the dogs play.

After a while, I saw Magnus mounting the female, so I went over to stop him. He wasn't mounting her. He was trying to get her out of a hole she was digging under a big oak tree, which was already deep enough to hide the first third of her body.

This is not safe. She could suffocate.

Magnus put his paws around her waist and pulled. No effect. He snouted her backside: poke, poke, poke. No effect. He stood back and gave a deep woof. This had an effect. The little auburn spaniel got out of the hole. Magnus drove her away from it. She kept jumping up and snapping at his neck, complaining, but he held his head high and herded her away in a wide circle to the other side of the field. Her Mom said, "She's always the one who makes trouble," and laughed.

Chapter 35. Dance Steps

In Magnus, Susan S. definitely succeeded in breeding a dog with fine gaits. He was born to dance. He chooses his steps and gestures well, and combines them to expressive effect.

The joy dance is an exaggeratedly high, rolling canter with a deeply arched neck that tucks the head nearly to the chest, ears forward and tail waving gently.

The "oh boy, oh boy, cookies!" dance is a bouncy trot towards the goods with the head slightly raised and tilted, and the tail held out straight behind him.

The great high humor dance is a combination of gaits, pacing, then trotting, wheeling about on his hind legs and going into a few steps of the exaggerated canter. He does this one at some point every day (unless I'm unhappy or he's very, very sick).

The dominance dance is a vibrating posture, with the rear legs extended, the chest puffed out and the head held high. The tail is held straight out and the ears are forward. I generally step in at this point, because the next move is pushing forward and raising his head over the other dog's neck. I only had to see this once to know what it was.

The will to do battle is expressed in a sideways, circling dance with the neck stretched out and curving towards the opponent. The ears are held back, and the eyes slitted. The tail is straight out again. I saw this the time I tried to box with him. It was quite convincing.

The jealousy dance goes on in a tight circle around me when, say, I'm bending over to pat Hammett. It includes snouting available body parts (my butt is a favorite), hip checks, plain old leaning against me, standing on my foot and stretching his neck up against my body in what amounts to a gentle slap. It doesn't work, by the way. It does crack me up, though.

The curiosity dance begins as an erect posture with a cocked head, raised tail, and ears forward, then evolves into a neat trot toward the object under investigation.

Curiosity becomes full alert with a dead straight, fully extended, efficient canter. Magnus fluffs out the mane around his neck and shoulders to increase his apparent size. I've never seen the full alert dance completed, and don't want to. This is when he gets the command that means "meat" and wheels around, runs to me, and stops at my feet.

The it's-time-to-walk dance is a circular route around the living room, flipping up pillows with his nose.

The hello-stranger dance is a slow, light trot that ends in leaning against people's thighs and gazing up into their eyes, tail wagging gently. Repeat for each member of the party. I call this dance working the room.

CHAPTER 36   MARY'S GIFT

Mary sang with the choir for years, and still comes out when she can. She's a small, intense woman of about sixty, with long dark hair, a Town And Country lifestyle, and two Tibetan mastiffs, who she lives for. She says that the kuvasz is probably descended from the breed. I think that kuvasz dogs are much prettier and nicer.

I'm not prejudiced.

When Mary heard that I'd adopted a kuvasz, she had to meet him. She's a serious dog person, knows all the breeds, knows all about training, breed intelligence, breed history, and so on. I was such a lightweight by comparison that I had no idea what she was talking about half the time.

We set up a date at the entrance to the Stanford campus, where a long, palm-tree-lined avenue divides to circle around a grassy, landscaped basin. I had never seen a Tibetan mastiff, and didn't know what to expect.

The word "mastiff" should have been a clue.

Mary opened the slider on her van. Two huge, shaggy-coated, hardy dogs that looked like they could handle anything man or nature might dish out hit the ground. One had a black coat, with paler fur on his throat and underside. The other was tawnier, almost auburn. Both had huge heads, heavy jaws, big paws, and long, soft, square-set ears. They gave me a cursory glance, then focused on my man. Quietly, without any outward reaction, they stood their ground. Magnus stood his ground. Mary said, "Don't bring Magnus any closer. Let them study each other for a while. They're all guardians, and they all live to protect us."

I respected that. I was intimidated. Magnus wasn't intimidated, but next to the mastiffs he looked like a dainty pet. Mary greeted him quietly, saying, "He's a beautiful dog, Nancy. He'll take very,

very good care of you." When the dogs were done sizing each other up and decided to accept each other, we started walking. Mary said, "What's going on with his hips?"

"Well, he's old. He can't launch and wheel around like a younger dog, but he can run in a straight line just fine."

"That's so sad! What does the vet say?"

"Arthritis, or maybe dysplasia."

"Have you taken X-rays?

"No." Why should I expect a ten-year-old dog to be able to play with three-year-old dogs? It seemed to me that one might expect some weakness in a septuagenarian. Mary knew better.

Mary petted Magnus about the neck, looking very sad and concerned. We went on through the campus, around the Romanesque revival cloisters that house offices and classrooms. Past the big, resonant chapel with twilight sparkling on the mosaics above the chapel doors. My big dog and Mary's much bigger dogs were calm and steady, no arguments or discussions among them. They didn't play or pay each other much attention, but just patrolled peaceably.

The next time she came to Vespers, she asked to speak to me alone. We drew aside, and she asked me why I hadn't taken X-rays. I said, "Well, he's not doing so badly. We're both getting stronger all the time."

She said, on the verge of tears, "Nancy, the entire meaning of his existence is in his love for you. If he isn't strong enough to protect you, he'll be miserable. You have to find out what's going on, and see what can be done about it."

I admitted that I couldn't afford it.

She said, now truly in tears, "I will pay for it. I don't have a lot, but I have a little money of my own. It's worth it to me to see him happy."

"I can't accept that, Mary."

"I insist."

"I'll think about it."

Later that week, I dropped in on Susan A. to get her advice. She's known Mary for decades. Susan said, "Take it."

So I did. I called Mary, thanked her for her kind offer, and asked her how I should handle it. She said, "Have the vet make the x-rays and tell me how much it cost you. I'll write you a check.

We did the X-rays. Dr. Paul clipped them up on the light box, and said, "The bones are remarkably clean for a dog his age. Look, there's just a little osteoarthritis there. Otherwise, there's no dysplasia. The spine is strong and straight. I don't see much of anything wrong."

"What do you think it could be? I know he wasn't getting regular exercise for a long time, but we've been walking every day for almost six months, and he has gained a lot of muscle. Is it just old age?"

Dr. Paul held his elbow in one hand, and actually stroked his chin with the other. "It might be neurological," he said.

"How can we find out for sure?"

He turned to face me and said, with a twinkle in his eye, "We could do an MRI."

"How much would that cost?"

"Exactly. And what would we do if we knew?"

As I said, Dr. Paul is not out to pick my (shallow) pockets.

It cost $536. Mary wrote me a check. I was grateful to know that my man was structurally sound.

I called Susan S. and reported.

"You had X-rays taken of his hips? Why?"

"Because he's weak in the hindquarters."

"You know he doesn't have dysplasia. I got his clearance when he was two."

I didn't know that show dogs, who are meant to become breeding stock, have to be cleared for hereditary disorders. How would I? I've never shown a dog or known anyone who did.

Meanwhile, older dogs can develop dysplasia, or other disorders, so maybe Mary's money wasn't wasted.

Not long after the x-rays, Magnus and I were walking by the weedy curve of the creek near the pond, and he decided to go down and get a drink of water. I watched him clamber down the steep clay bank, go around the corner behind some bushes, take his drink, and trot back up. Hmmmm. I saw how we could build up those glutes. Good boy, Magnus.

CHAPTER 37   BEDTIME

Towards the end of that first summer, the kids made the mistake of boycotting the bed during a heat wave, and when Magnus's big sweet face appeared at my feet and rested on the duvet, I crumbled. I patted the bed. He heaved his forelegs up, but couldn't get the hind legs to follow—which didn't surprise me. I got out of bed and hoisted him up. He nestled beside me, stretching his body full length against my side.

We sighed with contentment. We were cozy and comfortable together, beginning to settle into a deeper relationship, sure that we belonged together. He was it for me, and I was it for him.

Poor Hammett lost his Number One status. He eventually came to sleep with us—on the opposite side from Magnus—but Margaret only ventured up for brief passages across the covers to reach the food bowl on the bookshelf beside the bed. She did stay in the room with us, but kept her vigils under the dresser.

Magnus won.

Chapter 38   The Art Auction

Every September, the Art Directors club I belonged to for many years held an art auction. Members—mostly graphic designers—plus well-known illustrators from around the country, donate the art, wineries donate wine, we make food for a big buffet, and we all get drunk and compete to bid on the best pieces. It gets lively. It has always been the best party of the year.

This time there were shadows. We'd lost a good friend in a bad way the year before, and we felt his absence like a missing limb. He'd been the impresario of many a dinner over the years, and had a way of making you feel like you were his best friend.

A lot of the older members stayed away. His long-time lover was there, though. She and I hugged each other and cried for a while. I thought it would cheer her up to meet Magnus, so I took her out in the parking lot and let him out of the car. It cheered her up. Some of our friends standing by the entrance came over to pet and praise him, too. He then did a big, extremely loose poop in the middle of the parking lot. (We were having another bout of House of Poo.) My friends were embarrassed, and laughed. I got out one of the plastic bags I always have with me and scooped. Some young people I didn't know had the foresight to get a bucket of water and sluice down the offending slime.

People inside saw us, and waved us in. I decided to try it, put Magnus on leash and walked around the perimeter of the small auditorium to see how people reacted. They reacted well. I took him off leash and started chatting with old friends, getting glasses of wine, grazing the food tables.

Meanwhile, Magnus worked the room. I watched him Through the folding chairs as he went up and down the rows, greeting people and making sure everything was in order with this big new flock. Hands reached out from all directions to touch the white fur, and he accepted all the petting and praise as his due. A few other people brought their dogs in. The dogs found each other and socialized pleasantly in a little knot of their own, moving around the room, eating bits of meat and bread and cheese that seemed to slip out of people's fingers.

Children started carrying art around to show the audience, and the bidding started. People consulted their catalogs to see if the piece being shown was one they wanted, to check what work was still to come, and tally up what they'd already bought. At every auction there are half a dozen pieces that are very good. When one of the good pieces comes up, the bidding gets hot, the crowd gets loud, and the price shoots up fast. Magnus expressed concern about the shouting and waving of bidding cards and the jumping up and down, but soon figured out that it was all in good fun and relaxed.

Magnus worked the party to the end, spreading attention and affection among the guests, never lingering too long in one place or slighting anyone. You could almost see the white bow tie and cummerbund. It was a nice send-off for the last Miniature Art Auction. The organization has not survived the loss of our friend.

Chapter 39

Sushi Dates

Some years ago, I was driving home after a late appointment, and was too hungry to wait for dinner. I noticed a Sushi restaurant next to the Safeway in my neighborhood. That's not an auspicious location, but I figured they'd have Udon, and that's hard to mess up. I went in and ordered Nabeyaki Udon. It came out steaming in a big iron pot, with a whole poached egg showing among the grilled chicken, carrots, fried tofu, fish cake, broccoli, and a big tempura shrimp on top of the noodles. It smelled so good I fanned it off to cool it down so I could get to it quicker. I got to it. It was the best Udon I'd ever had.

At the Sushi bar, a young, good-looking Sushi chef was chatting to himself, singing, and dancing around. I felt sorry for him. There were no Sushi customers. So, I decided to test the Sushi, and ordered umi—sea urchin. If umi isn't absolutely fresh, it's awful. It stinks and is slimy. If it is good, it's sweet and firm and melts in your mouth. There aren't a lot of people who are willing to order it.

The chef saw the order and said, "Umi! Umi!" and danced around while he wrapped a strip of dried seaweed around a ball of rice, slipped the umi on it and topped it with a tiny raw quail egg.

The umi was sweet and firm and melted in my mouth.

I went back the next week, tried everything the chef suggested, and thought it was the best Sushi I'd ever had. I told my roommate about it.

When I'd advertised the room, I got so many calls and interviewed so many extremely nice, smart, young women that I was overwhelmed. Any one of them would have been terrific, but I chose Hilary, sight unseen, over the phone. She didn't say much, but she laughed in all the right places.

She was a bright spot in my household. She would sit in her room humming little tunes and playing with things. She made me laugh until my stomach hurt. She always said, and still does, that my food doesn't suck. She said I shouldn't vacuum, because of my back, and always did the vacuuming for me, and she continued to do that after she moved out. She climbed in bed with me every night to watch *Star Trek: Voyager* reruns and make sarcastic comments.

"You don't wanna go in there. Nooooo! Don't DO it!"

"He's LYING, you idiot! Can't you SEE that?"

"You GO, Janeway."

"I'm sure Seven of Nine's breasts are real. How could you imply that they're silicone?"

Hilary probably weighs 95 pounds dripping wet. She is small and healthy, not anorexic. She is not remarkably pretty, but men follow her as if they were dogs and she had bones in her pockets. She loves Hammett's tiny feet. She is heavily into absurdist, post-modern cartoons. She can quote and act out all of Bill Cosby's recorded routines. She plays a very sexy air guitar. Inexplicably, she loves me.

After I discovered the supermarket sushi place we went out for sushi every Wednesday. We learned everyone's name—Anthony the chef, Yun the owner, and the wait staff. Anthony gave us his best cuts of fish. He taught us how to tell the different grades of fish: belly is #1, with the most fatty acids. It tastes almost like butter. Side is #2, and back is #3. People who order big, fancy rolls with all kinds of fish and fillings get #3 fish. Average nigiri Sushi customers get #2 fish. We got #1 fish. He told us that all Sushi chefs are Korean. He carved up oranges into cats and Mickey Mouses for dessert, and accompanied the performance with a running patter. He had been a fabric designer in Korea. He teased me about my weight mercilessly—and I was nowhere near my high point at the time. Yun, the owner and creator of the special sushi offerings and other delicacies the restaurant offers, started giving us Lagniappes—fancy, inventive extras at the end of each meal. We'd walk out groaning.

Anthony left to start his own place. Other chefs followed. None had his flair, but all were clearly instructed by Yun to give us #1 fish. And lagniappes.

Hilary went to Pasadena to get a degree in physical therapy a few years after she got married. She got the degree, returned from Pasadena, and moved in with me again, intending to stay until Mike's lease was up. When I asked why, she said, "He lives in a disgusting boy house. You don't even want your feet to touch the carpet." I was happy to have her back, but had a dim view of the effect on her marriage.

We started going out for Sushi again. Yun and the staff welcomed her, and showered attention on us. He sent us an exquisite lagniappe before we even finished the big platter of hamachi, maguro, salmon, hirame with vinegar and chili, and seared ahi tuna salad.

We ate a bite or two of the lagniappe. It was a salmon roll with a light touch of lemon and garlic and a spray of Japanese herbs. We couldn't finish it. We couldn't leave it ungratefully on the table. We hid it in our napkins and took it out to the car, where Magnus was waiting for us. Hilary said,

"This won't keep, and it's so good it's a shame to waste it. Do you think Magnus will like it?"

"Let's see."

We let Magnus out of the car and gave him a slice of the salmon roll. His eyes lit up like fireworks.

What was that? I've never tasted anything so exquisite.

We gave him another piece. And another. When it was all gone, he nosed around frantically looking for more.

Hilary was laughing and shouting, "Sushi dog! Sushi dog! Only in the Bay Area could this happen." She was doubled over, holding her belly, spinning around the parking lot.

She has referred to him as Sushi dog ever since. And every time we go out for Sushi and Yun gives us too much food, which is every time we go out for sushi, Magnus gets his share. Last week he got maguro nigiri sushi and hamachi nigiri sushi.

I didn't know then that raw salmon can kill a dog. We were lucky. Or maybe that's just a testament to the quality of Yun's fish.

CHAPTER 40   LIFE HAPPENS TO SUSAN S.

Susan S. decided over the summer that she needed a new career, and that it was going to be in social work. She scouted out schools around the country, chose one, applied, and was accepted with remarkable alacrity. The school was in St. Louis. She placed all but two of her dogs with families, packed the necessary items, and put the rest of her stuff in storage. She showed up at Mass in a rental truck, sideswiped a car turning into the parking lot, filed the accident report, and was gone in a blur. She'd already rented a small house outside St. Louis.

Her first few months were happy and busy. She joined in the flow of classes and study. She found a good choir to sing in. She reveled in the city's 19-century neo-Baroque and Renaissance architecture. She'd call me and say, "You won't believe this place I just found. It's amazingly beautiful." She'd try to describe it, but didn't have the architectural jargon for the job. It didn't matter. It only mattered that she was exploring and enjoying her new world.

A few months in, she got a phone call from a kuvasz rescue operation in L.A., letting her know that two of the dogs she'd placed had been abandoned on their ranch after their family imploded and decamped. She went to L.A., rescued the dogs, and brought them back to St. Louis. She then had four kuvaszok in a small rented house with inadequate fencing. She stripped a room, put a rubber mat on the floor, installed the dogs' crates in it, and had to leave them inside all day. Her evenings were spent in dog care again. School work slipped further and further behind.

Another year passed. She quit grad school and tried to piece together a new life. She looked into being a dog trainer. She worked for the Obama campaign. She got a temporary job doing telephone fundraising for the Symphony. She worked for the 2010 census.

She told me her life was in St. Louis now. Her money was gone, she couldn't dream of coming back to California, and she had to make the best of being where she was.

Her calls came in less often, and more and more often it was several days before she returned my calls. When we did manage to connect, she wistfully suggested that I put Magnus in the car and drive out to visit her for a week or two.

I hadn't had steady work since the banks failed in September 2008. The few jobs that were coming in had budgets that were 75% lower than the previous year. I didn't trust my car to hold up for a 1,500 mile trip, and couldn't afford to rent one.

The visit wasn't going to happen. The chances were very slim that Susan would ever see Magnus again. It made me cry, for all our sakes.

Over the following year Susan S. got back on her feet. She found a steady job. She placed Greta, the best dog from her last litter, with an old friend in Seattle. She rented a better house in a less isolated, more interesting neighborhood. She still didn't call, though, and I felt the thread between us stretching thinner and thinner.

Yesterday, after weeks of silence, she called to tell me she was moving to Seattle to live with Greta and her new owner, who has a nice house on five acres of land, and welcomes the other three kuvasok.

She wouldn't be alone any more. She'd be in her home town. There would be plenty of companies and organizations that needed someone with her now-updated skills, and she'd be back in an environment and a culture she was at home with.

"I can go home for Thanksgiving," she said. "I'll practically be your neighbor—it's only a day's drive. I'll be back on the coast."

"Susan, this is great. I'm so happy for you. It's just what you need."

"Yes. I feel more hopeful than I have for a long time."

We went on to talk about kuvaszok—I'd spent the afternoon looking up breeders and seeing what kinds of lines they develop. I like Magnus's sturdier looks. Some breeders prefer a more delicate, gracile type. "Vi and Luca are like that. You'll see what they're like when you meet them. You'll love them." When we exhausted that topic, she raised new ones. She was breathless. She didn't want to hang up.

Dog people are resilient. I can't wait to see her.

Chapter 41 — Autumn Routine

"What a beautiful dog."

I was starting to get tired of this. Though it gratified my vanity, I was thinking of printing up a card with kuvasz facts to hand out so we could get on with our walks. I started making up silent snappy retorts.

"Can I pet him?"

He's leaning against your legs and gazing right into your eyes. What do you think?

"What kind of dog is that?"

Wolf killer. Your dog is looking a lot like a snack right now.

"How do you keep his coat so white?"

I bring him to a salon every other week to have his roots done.

"He has blue eyes!"

Yeah, he's the dog from *Dune*.

"Can he see?"

He's looking right at you, pal, and he's got your number.

"Does he shed?"

No, those are snow drifts in my living room.

"Is he a Newfoundland?"

Well, I guess if his fur were *black* instead of *white* he might *look* like a Newfoundland.

"He looks like a Polar Bear."

That's what the 3-year-olds at the tot lot always say.

"Puppy!"

You've got to be kidding.

Why should you mind? This is the best part of my job.

I got over that phase.

Cooler weather arrived. Leaves crisped up and grasses turned to tawny dust, waiting for the rains. Nights drew in until we were walking in the dark all the time. Other dog people put lighted collars on their dogs, but even with no moon, Magnus's coat was bright enough to see. "That's a nice coat at night. I'd never be able to find Nate without his collar," NateMom said.

Nate the vizsla's collar puts out rippling waves of pink and purple, so recognizing Nate and Christopher and their Mom in the dark is easy. Christopher is elderly, and doesn't have any use for Magnus—he's the dog that snarked Magnus on our first vizsla walk. Nate is a little nervous in general, but tolerates Magnus well. Magnus simply makes sure we're all safe, and stays close to me. We tend to walk at the same time, but if they come out later, we do an extra loop with them. She's a tall, comfortable, slender middle-aged woman with intelligent features, clear eyes and short, no-nonsense hair. She was one of the first Silicon Valley programmers, back before there were any college courses in computer science. All training was done through corporate programs, and female mathematicians were considered the best talent.

We always talked easily of family and dogs and other simple matters. We met other dog people, and trailed around the park with our pack.

Making new friends was now routine. Off-leashing was routine. Being full partners in all we did was routine. Monitoring my old man's breathing and energy level to make sure he didn't get too tired was routine. Brushing and examining and massaging Magnus' old bones was routine. Dog food days were routine. I was happy spoiling and grooming and tending and watching my beloved. My health was stable. My mood was good. Magnus was clearly very happy, and getting stronger all the time. I was, too. By this time I could wear him out, instead of the other way around, which was the point of having a dog in the first place. I hadn't realized how much joy I'd get out of it.

Mornings, I put the teakettle on and open the patio slider just wide enough for the kids to go in and out. I read and sip tea for a while, then take Magnus out for his morning pee. He makes this last longer by dancing around me on the needle-strewn earth under the redwoods, leaning against me, giving me love-eyes and smiles, and diving into the dirt. When he's well drained, we go back inside for breakfast. He'd trots in briskly and stands before his bowl, head cocked. I combine a cup of stew, a cup of kibble, and a bunch of supplements with a cup of water in his bowl and stir it up. I put the bowl down, and he looks at me, waiting for permission. I say, "This is for you," and gesture at the bowl. He goes to the bowl politely and then spoils the effect by eating like a starving timber wolf. This process is not so indelicate that he can't spit out vitamins, so I cut them up. Sometimes he separates them anyway and spits them out.

When he's done eating, he trots on bouncy toes into the living room and dives on the indoor-outdoor rug I bought to make the floor less slippery for him, or goes to the ottoman and flips pillows off it with his nose, or dives into his big bed and tries to flip it over—or all three. Then he comes up to me, pushes my arm up with his head, and gazes at me gratefully. Sometime he kisses my hand with the élan of a baron.

When I'm downstairs, he lies across the front door, occasionally ambling into the living room for a bit of a stretch. When I go upstairs, he follows me. If the cats and I are in the office, he lies down across the office door, or just behind my chair. (One of the few things I didn't have to learn the hard way was checking for his big white feet or tail before wheeling the chair back.)

If I go downstairs, by the time I come back up his front paws are hanging over the top step and his great head is watching from above. For some reason this always touches me. It's the look of grave concern on his face that breaks my heart. In a good way.

In mid-afternoon, I walk him around the complex to limber him up. When the sun starts to go down, he comes to me at the computer, shoves his head under my elbow, and pushes my arm up to let me know it's time to go to the park. If I have to keep working, he understands, and lies down again until I'm finished. If I'm downstairs, he runs around the living room tossing pillows until I get the cats in, collect our gear, and open the door. He shoots out and trots to the car. I open the door and gently touch his butt to get him to climb in. He stands in the back seat and follows me with his eyes as I go around to get in the driver's seat. Then he snuggles down into his red brocade blanket while we drive to the park.

 He stands up as we approach, and licks my face and whimpers a bit. I park, let him out and snap the fanny pack around what used to be my waist. He trots ahead, giving me a grin over his shoulder, and beelines to a row of big oleanders with their long leaves, where he commences sniffing and peeing. I walk briskly past him under a brief stand of redwoods, and hear him cantering up behind to overtake me and launch out onto the field. I hang out with the dog people and exchange notes on the dogs. We watch the young dogs run around with nothing between their ears but air. Magnus plays a little, just to be social, but isn't much interested. After a while, he starts woofing the players. Kuvaszok like their flocks to be calm and quiet. Rowdy flocks mean only one thing: trouble. Maybe even wolves. When he gets to this stage, I walk on.

 I'm back to walking at a brisk pace, and don't wait for him when he hangs back to catch a scent. He trots to get level with me again. We go into our loop. After the first half mile, he slows down and we amble along.

 Occasionally he darts in front of me, blocks my way, and slows me down. I can take a hint. I slow down. If someone approaches, especially a man, he positions himself between us.

Let me handle this, dear.

 At first, he tried to block bikes in the same way, and nearly got his head smashed a few times. That's when I taught him to heel, patting my hip and holding a treat where I wanted his nose. He'd dog my footsteps staring at the hand until I released him with a circling gesture. This pleased me no end. Almost as much as it pleased the bicyclists.

If he senses potential danger, he heads straight for it, ears, head, and tail high. One night we approached a blind T in the path, with big, overgrown shrubs on both sides. Magnus burst ahead to make sure it was safe. Just that once. He sensed something, I suppose.

Every walk includes going down the wide stairway to the little creek. The little ravine is so deep that hundred-year oaks growing up from the bottom rest their branches on the park above. The far side of the ravine is lined with ivy and other plants that have spilled down from people's gardens. Most of the year, the water is only a few inches deep, and trickles faintly. Magnus hops from the bank to the streambed and drinks. When he's done, he patrols up and down the bank for a few minutes, then heaves himself over the roots of a great oak, runs up the stairs and crosses the lawn to check out the playground. As time has gone by and we've gotten stronger, I've found ways to extend the walk by crisscrossing trails. From half a mile to a mile to two to three and sometimes a little more. He now owns the park. It's his pasture, his beat.

We drive home. He gets his energy back by the time we get there, and dances from the car to the door. We have to turn a blind corner to get onto the front walk. I asked him once to wait for me there, because I don't want him to take someone by surprise. Just once. He now turns and waits for me at that corner, every night, and wheels around on his hind legs to move ahead when I catch up. When we come in the door, he greets the kids nose to nose, and heads for his bowl on food alert. I fix his meal, put out baby food for the cats, open the slider so they can come and go, and putter around for a while before going upstairs for Netflix hour. Magnus stays downstairs to guard the open slider unless I call him up. When the kids come back inside, we all go upstairs, I hoist him up on the bed, whistle them up as well, and we go to sleep.

I almost always wake up with at least one cat as well as Magnus. Or two cats and no dog, he presumably having been invited to leave.

I suspect a certain set of claws.

Sibling rivalry is routine.

Chapter 42　　　　　　　　　　Dumping People

I'd seen him around, riding his red bike in his white jacket, with his all his earthly goods hanging from the handlebars and bicycle frame in plastic bags. On an evening that was promising frost, with the moon full and riding high, we walked up the scrubby hill, and saw him sitting on the bench beside his bicycle, bundled up in sweaters and a hooded parka. I said hello. He said hello. I said, "Do you have everything you need?"

He said, "Yes," in a clear, cheerful voice. "Thank you for asking!"

"Oh, that's good then. Sleep well."

"You too."

I felt troubled, but he seemed okay. He had evidently been living in the little coppice of scrub oaks and small trees that had aroused Magnus' interest months ago.

A few weeks later, we were walking in another part of the park and passed a bench where he was sitting, with his bike leaning next to him. Magnus started to approach. I said, "Magnus, mind your business." Magnus started to turn away, but the little man said, "It's okay. I like dogs," and reached out his hands. Magnus shared the love for a few minutes. The man's eyes got dreamy, and he smiled.

He was a young Asian man, and he was keeping himself very clean and neat. He seemed almost proud of having figured out how to survive and maintain standards in his unhoused state.

I wondered at it when we walked on. You don't see a lot of homeless Asian people, and this man was clearly well brought up. He was polite, well-spoken, and wasn't nursing anything from a paper bag. How did he fall off the ladder? Where was his family?

I didn't see him after that for a long time. A year later I started seeing a scruffy, ragged-haired, fortyish-looking guy with several soiled shirts hanging off his body, unbuttoned. He had a black string around his neck. He rode a red bike with bags hanging off the handlebars and frame. He had the wolfish look of someone who didn't want to talk to anybody and knew what would happen if he tried. He wouldn't make eye contact when we passed him sitting on a bench. I figured the nice young man must have gotten on his feet and moved on, leaving his space vacant for new residents. Someone is leaving heaps of beer cans near his bench by the coppice. This new guy was an entirely different kind of creature.

But one who is little and Asian. This isn't a different man. It's the same nice boy, but a year further into his homeless career—a year that has hardened him. Some months later, I saw his red bike leaning against that bench, out in the open, and he was nowhere in sight. I worried that he'd lose his most valuable possession. For the next three evenings, that bike was still there, un-stolen. I went up to examine it, and saw that the front wheel had been stomped on or otherwise warped beyond use. We never saw the man again.

He was living in one of the richest towns in the country.

So we dump dogs. We dump people, too.

CHAPTER 43   SPOUSAL RELATIONS

When Susan S. gave us our first review, she said, "Oh, look, he's let you comb out the mats around his ears. You two are still in honeymoon mode." That was almost a year and a half ago. I can still brush his ears, or any other part of him that needs it. This is a honeymoon with staying power.

I freely admit that Magnus is a surrogate husband. I'm terrible with men, which is a terrible characteristic in someone who has a terrible need for emotional connection. It took a long time to figure out that being celibate was better than having unhappy relationships. That wouldn't work for a lot of people, but it works for me. I have men friends and I like them, but friendship is as far as it goes.

In Magnus I have a hunky, manly friend who takes me out of my own head. I have an extraordinarily fine and entertaining companion. I have a gentleman and scholar who escorts me to parties and events. I have someone who accepts my apologies and explanations gracefully. I have Magnus Biggus Gaius, Minister Plenipotentiary to Silicon Valley for the Kuvasz Nation.

If my attitude and behavior to God were as fine as my beloved's attitude and behavior to me, my place in heaven would be assured.

It makes me happy just to look at his head. As I walk around the house I come on him dozing and stop to gaze at him. He opens his eyes, smiles at me, rolls onto his side, and raises one paw. This means he wants a massage. He usually gets it. So what if he's spoiled? He's old and arthritic and retired and perfect.

In the morning, I pat the bed next to me and say his name. He gets up from the foot of the bed, stands over me, grins, and settles down gently with his back against my side. Sometimes he throws his head back over my chest and presses closer. This tends to push me off the bed. I push back. I wrap my arms around him. I bury my face in his fur. It smells good, slightly musky, with overtones of orange and coriander.

Sometimes I turn the tables, and kneel beside him, teasing him and pushing him around. He rolls on his back and waves his paws in the air and grins at me. Sometimes he gets so relaxed he lets go and pees. This doesn't irritate me. I cheerfully get up, strip the bed, and wash the bedclothes.

Once he got so relaxed he pooped. I haven't cuddled quite so close since then. Even love this true has limits.

He makes all kinds of disgusting respiratory noises, yeeEEEEchs and AAAAWWWWKs, hawkings and snortings and sneezings. In a man, I would consider this behavior deliberately designed to gross me out. In Magnus, I figure it's involuntary.

At least he doesn't snore and he doesn't fart.

On walks, when he's breathing too hard I roll the skin of his throat between my fingers until he steadies. I never tire of telling people he's a kuvasz, what a kuvasz is, how I keep his coat so white, and so on. I never get jealous or want the attention he gets for myself. I feed him cookies by putting them in my mouth and bending down to snout level. He takes them very gently, with hardly any lip contact.

You should have seen his face the first time I offered him a cookie that way. He was horrified. His eyes went big and round.

You think I would take your food out of your MOUTH? YOU may be that crazy, but I'M certainly not.

"It's okay. Go ahead."

I kept the cookie near his nose. After a while, he took it. I petted him. He gave me an odd look, sighed, went into the living room, turned around, and lay down on the floor. Watching me.

I'm not going to turn my back on her after a trick like that.

Chapter 44   Dan, Dan, Cookie Man

My neighbor Dan leaves cookies on his doorstep for Magnus. Every time we pass, Magnus swerves towards Dan's door. If he doesn't find a cookie, he stares at the door and cocks his head. I think Dan listens for us, because he often pops out just when we get there. He lets Magnus into his kitchen, and lets him drool on the tiles while he goes to the cookie jar and starts doling out treats. "You don't even have to sit for a cookie, do you?" he says. "You just get them for free." He stoops over Magnus and pets him roughly and baby-talks him. Magnus does the leaning-against-the-legs thing and gazing-into-the-eyes thing.

Dan is nearing sixty. He's tall and thin and rangy, and has a brief fringe of graying hair and big wire-rimmed glasses. He's a confirmed bachelor, shy, intelligent, with a gentle, thoughtful manner. He loves dogs and cats, but his allergies are so bad he can't keep them, so he has vicarious relationships with my critters.

He was especially fond of Rodney, my dear departed Norwegian forest cat (another gorgeous gift from someone who couldn't keep him anymore). You'd see them kissing when Roddie was on the fence, the gray head nuzzling the blond one. One night I was slow in coming to Rodney's rescue when he was being attacked by a particularly territorial neighborhood cat. By the time I got outside, Dan had driven off the aggressor, and was standing over Rodney, giving me a filthy look. I had this treasure, and was neglecting him. It's true, I was. Too busy with my job and committees and events.

One Friday after a week of after work meetings and late nights, Rodney left a little pile of poo for me in the dead center of the mat in front of the sink. Its meaning was clear. I dropped my things and collected him in my arms, and performed the homecoming rituals.

I'd sling him up on my shoulder and pace the living room while he told me all about his day. Rodney had a wide range of vocalizations, and used them all. I would comment and ask questions. I'd take him to the bathroom sink and run a trickle of water so he could sip from it. Open the cupboard under the stairs so he could check for mice or monsters. Sit on the stairs with him and give him safe love, protected on all sides. The stations of the cat.

In the evening, when he felt it was time for bed he'd seek me out, face me, say something to get my attention, then turn toward the stairs and look at me over his shoulder, saying "follow me." I always obeyed. Once upstairs, if the weather was hot, he'd fling himself on the bed, roll onto his back, and cry Get it Off Me. I could brush him every night, and never get to the bottom of his thick beautiful fur. Every morning, I'd wake up to his gentle kisses and his loving gaze.

Dan isn't crazy about Hammett, though he's nice to him anyway. He says, "Hammett's too macho." Dan says he never sees Margaret. He still misses Rodney. I understand. So do I. Rodney was to cat what Magnus is to dog.

The first time Magnus saw Dan, he charged, barking. I wasn't worried. I knew Dan. I dropped the leash. Dan squatted down, held his arms open, and said, "Come on, boy!" Magnus ran into his face and commenced kissing him.

Dan said, "If you need help walking Magnus, I'd be willing to take him." I said, "Sure, take him out any time." Soon after, Dan came over and asked if Magnus would like a walk. I got the leash, snapped it on the collar, and handed it to him. As they walked off, Magnus looked back at me with a frightened expression and pulled back. I said, "It's okay, Magnus. Good boy."

When Dan and Man returned, I asked how it went. He said, "Well, he hung back a bit on the way out, but perked up on the way back."

I was awfully worried about you, Nan. Are you okay?

We tried having Dan walk my old man a few more times, but then decided it wasn't working. Dan then said, "If you have to go away, I could help you take care of him."

"That would be great, thanks so much."

"Do you think he'll let me?"

"Why don't you take him for an hour or two now and then so he gets used to being in your house?"

You really do not understand me, do you?

"Okay."

We took Magnus inside, and walked him through Dan's townhouse. He sniffed round thoroughly. We stood on the patio for a while chatting. Magnus went in and out calmly. A week or so later I asked Dan if he wanted to take Magnus for the afternoon. He was agreeable, so I brought my man over. Dan rang my bell in an hour or so. "He's been a little anxious, so I thought this was long enough." We repeated this experiment a half dozen times. The last time was during a heat wave. When Dan brought Magnus home, he said, "He just lay in front of the fan looking bored. He was ready and eager to go when I asked."

Dan gets to be cookie uncle, but that's about it—although now that the cookies have turned into liver treats, Magnus is rethinking the issue. When I let him out, he runs to Dan's door and stands in front of it, trying to make Dan come to the door by staring at it as hard as he can.

Out of the blue one day, Dan asked, "When you're walking Magnus, do people ever come up to you and say how beautiful he is?

I laughed.

Chapter 45   Cyndi

Twenty-some years ago I was a freelance illustrator in Boston, Massachusetts. When I needed typesetting, I used Cyndi's firm, sending my orders in by courier and getting the galleys back by courier. I had never met her. I used her shop on the recommendation of a guy who sublet space from her, and who I happened to be dating. It was a complicated relationship. One day she insisted on making the delivery herself, which activated my uh-oh antennae. At the door I said, "You really didn't need to do this. It's out of your way, and I don't need those galleys tonight. Why did you really come?" I didn't move aside to let her in.

"I've heard so much about you that I wanted to meet you."

"From Gary?"

"Yes—I hear congratulations are in order," she said.

"Oh. Am I pregnant?"

Cyndi froze. Very carefully, she said, "Gary says that you two are getting married."

"So you just had to come check out the merchandise." He'd sucked her in to his high-pressure campaign to blackmail me into tying the knot. I tried to drive her off. She didn't drive off easy. She befriended me instead. She was very supportive when I broke off with Gary.

Years later, I asked her why she decided to be my friend. "It takes a certain quality of mind to come up with snappy comebacks like that on the spur of the moment. I thought you were seriously fucked up, but if nothing else, you weren't going to be *boring*." She'll forgive all kinds of faults if there's a chance of being entertained. Or challenged, it seems.

Cyndi comes to San Francisco for Mac World every year, and tacks on a few days to spend with me after the convention. It was time for my three days again, so I packed Magnus into the car, drove to The City, and picked her up at her hotel. She's a smallish woman a few years older than I, with a narrow face, a good figure, and permed black hair that she usually wears in an asymmetrical cut. Her manner of speech is emphatic, with strong stresses on selected syllables, clear and deliberate consonants, and rhetorical repetitions of phrase. She's very much a cat person, incidentally.

As I was lifting her bag into the trunk—I may have fibromyalgia, but she has arthritis and can't lift more than ten pounds—she opened the passenger door, and said, "So this is the *dawg*."

"That's my man Magnus."

"My *god*, he's huge."

"He's just a little guy."

"I don't think I could handle that. But I can *see* why you've grown so attached to him. He's *gorgeous*."

I went on for a bit about character, intelligence, probity, wit, and so on. She let me. We'd decided to go to Golden Gate Park and look at the fabulous new DeYoung Museum, so I drove across The City to Golden Gate Park, parked in some God-forsaken spot and proceeded to get us completely disoriented. I had no idea where we were or where the DeYoung was. It didn't matter. It was a lovely day. As it grew warmer, I took off the heavy wrap I'd brought, and Cyndi stood still, gaped at me, and said, "Oh—my—*gawd*. How much weight have you lost since last year? I couldn't see it under all those wraps. You're absolutely *gorgeous*. Your hair is gorgeous, your clothes are gorgeous, and you are stunning."

I wanted to melt into the path. I said, "Magnus walked it off me, and I had to buy new clothes, and I never wanted to be one of those old ladies orange hair, so I chopped it off."

"It's gorgeous, Nancy, *really*."

"It was supposed to be a kind of penitential renunciation. I had no idea it would be flattering."

We spotted some dogs running off leash in a little bowl-shaped lawn and brought Magnus over to meet them. He greeted a few of them, but wasn't particularly interested, so we put the leash back on and started wandering along the paths. People did the Magnus-reaction thing. Cyndi immediately saw how predictable it was, and got a half-smile on her face every time another dreamy-eyed man passed us. We sat on a bench in a rose garden so she could rest her arthritic back for a few minutes. The roses weren't in bloom, but the space was sunny and pleasant anyway, and a man with a little white dog was sitting a few benches away from us. She was off leash, and came over to check out The Man. I took his leash off and we entertained ourselves watching His Bigginess court her Princesshood. Both of them were very, very good and didn't stray off.

"See how good he is?"

"Yes, I see," indulging me.

We finally found the DeYoung, at which point I suddenly realized we couldn't go in with a dog, largely obviating the purpose of the outing. So we walked around the building, interpreting the architecture, which, for radical Modernist architecture, has a level of meaningful symbolism, an aesthetic relationship to its site, an organic integrity, and a pleasing ratio of proportions that Modernist design rarely manages to achieve. Cyndi went into an open courtyard while I waited outside with Magnus, and came out breathless, saying, "I'll hold the dog. You *have* to see this!"

She was right. There were wells of light and angles of sight and textures and materials and geometries arranged and combined to delight and soothe the senses. We continued around the building, finding varied combinations and proportions in every angle and wall that somehow created a harmonious whole.

Isn't it a pity that we don't enjoy our own places until we have an out-of-town guest? I hadn't been to Golden Gate Park for a decade.

We had a dinner date with a friend of Cyndi's after we left the park. My favorite self-deprecating joke at the time was, "Do you want to talk about my dog?" Cyndi had already heard it, and we'd only been together three hours. I used it on her friend. On the way home Cyndi said flatly, "You're in danger of becoming a one-joke person."

I didn't see the harm in that.

We followed all our traditions. I had bought good coffee for Cyndi (I gave it up years ago), and sausages and cheeses and eggs and bakery bread and herbs, and Cyndi made breakfast. We ate and yakked. We played with the cats. I told dog stories. We planned dinner at her two favorite restaurants, and we took Magnus to the park. Cyndi had recently taken up hiking, so she was more than game.

She met the dog people and the dogs. She was friendly and affable. She was clearly enjoying herself, and she spent some time walking behind us, watching Magnus. She said, "Nancy, he's limping on his left hind leg."

"Is he? Other people have said that, but I can't see it."

"You've never had an old dog before. Years ago I lived with two dogs, and one of them injured his knee. We had to be really, really careful with him, and I learned to judge his gait. Magnus has a problem."

I walked behind him and tried to see it. "I guess I'm just used to it. I'll take him to the Vet on Monday."

Lesson 6: Don't assume your kuvasz is okay because he acts like he's okay.

We had a nice visit over those two days. The year before hadn't gone so well. I had been cold and rejecting and Cyndi reacted by being clingy. Of course, that was when I was so sick. But I'd always had the idea that Cyndi treated me like a less-competent, inferior sister. A few months after that visit I had an insight. I realized that she was not the tower of power I thought she was:

she was protecting me from her troubles and insecurities because I had so many problems of my own. I called her and told her I'd had an insight. She said, with a voice that trembled, "What does that mean for our relationship?'

I said, "Good things. She sighed audibly and said, "You scared me. I don't think you know how much I love you." So I told her, and we talked for a long time, and we were all better when we signed off.

Then I realized I'd been doing the same exact thing to another friend that Cyndi'd been doing with me—and getting the same resentful reactions.

I called her. We're all better now, too.

CHAPTER 46   A LITTLE THING CALLED THE ACL

Dr. Paul folded his long body up like a carpenter's ruler to get at Magnus's leg, and moved the limb in all directions. Then he did the same with the other legs, and went back to the lame leg. He stood up, and said, "It's a little loose. He hasn't broken the ACL, which is a very good thing, but he probably stretched it."

"What's the ACL?"

"The anterior cruciate ligament. It's what makes the knee swing like a hinge. If it's stretched or broken, the ends of the bones slide over each other and wear down the cartilage. How far have you been walking him?"

"We've built up to about three miles, sometimes more."

"That's way too much for a dog his age and size," He said, very nearly glaring at me. "No more than two miles a day, total. And for the next six weeks, no more than to do what's absolutely necessary. If that ligament doesn't heal properly he won't be able to walk at all."

He gave the knee joint an injection of anti-inflammatory drugs, and sent us home with arthritis meds and instructions to REST!!!!

I didn't know that three or four miles were too many. Obviously strenuous, high-impact exercise was out, and it was clear that he didn't have much lateral strength. Walking at an easy pace seemed reasonable. And now my vainglorious plans for extending Magnus's life were hurting him. There's a sin for you.

I was thinking of my Mom, who has exercised religiously all her life and thinks nothing of going on a six-mile walk at the age of 80. But from what I gather, Magnus had been under-exercised for years, and in dog years, he's a few years older than she is, so a) he didn't have the foundation strength to begin with, and b) he was just too old.

My sister called, and asked after my man. When she heard about the ACL, she said, "Roscoe is only three years old, and he ripped his ACL right open. We have to get surgery for him, and it's going to cost $3,000."

"I can't do that for Magnus. It doesn't make sense at his age. But you have to do it for a three-year-old."

"I know. I try to keep him from screaming around full speed off leash, but he just won't stop. Well, now he's gonna stop for a long time. If he is going to tear himself apart, we'll just walk on leash from now on."

Roscoe is a chow chow mix, a brown behemoth who bullies Lisa. The other half of the mix must be Rottweiler or pit bull. He often bit her when he was a puppy. He barks and bosses her around the house. He drags her arm out of the socket on leash, which is why she tried off-leashing. He ran off so many times that they installed an electric fence. He won't do anything she asks. The man who wrote "Marley and Me" about the world's worst dog hasn't met Roscoe. The next year, he broke the other ACL, and had to have another surgery. Lisa was outraged, but it seems at least to have slowed him down a bit.

I started massaging Magnus's leg to keep the circulation up and the inflammation down. I thought of icing the knee, but couldn't think of a way to keep a gel pack on the joint without irritating him. I passively exercised the leg by gently moving it in imitation of walking. We stopped all walks except for duties for a month.

Then I started driving him half a mile to the playing fields and walking him, just a little, on leash, on the soft turf. This was painfully boring. I let him off leash once, and he immediately ran up to a fence with a barking dog behind it. Magnus started barking back and leapt up in an exuberant display of fence-fighting, all four feet hanging five feet in the air. I was on the cell phone with Susan S. at the time, and we both started laughing. "That's my boy," she said. I put the leash back on.

I slowly increased the distance, a block per week, and tried to keep my man from dancing and trotting in the morning. This was not easy, but I managed by replacing play with affection. We didn't go back to off-leashing in the park until after Easter Sunday.

Meanwhile, what did I do for exercise? Turned pages of books. Pounded keyboards with my fingertips. That sort of thing. Of course, I had an excellent reason. It would upset my darling to be left alone in the condo if I went walking by myself.

Chapter 47

The Kuvasz List

If I couldn't enjoy walking Magnus, I could enjoy learning more about kuvasz, training, and geriatric care. I found a chat list for California kuvasz and signed up for a daily digest.

A lot of the discussions were about upcoming shows—who was going to which ones, what dogs they were bringing, where they'd meet, and what they thought about the judges. I posted about Magnus right away to introduce myself to the group, and asked if anyone lived in Northern California. Only one person did, and he was over an hour north of me in the Central Valley. Almost everyone on the list lived in or around L.A.

I was surprised that so many people kept heavy-coated kuvasz in SoCal. I felt guilty keeping Magnus on the Peninsula, which is definitely cooler than L.A. because the temperature is moderated by the cold Pacific marine layer (a.k.a. fog).

Some of the discussions were about illnesses and deaths. I asked for advice on the knee injury, and people posted on successful, but expensive, ACL surgeries, arthritis medicines, and so on.

One woman posted the news that her seven-year-old prize bitch had died of laryngeal paralysis. Others posted their experiences with this disorder, citing heavy panting, difficulty breathing, inability to tolerate exercise or heat, and so on. They discussed which surgical options they preferred, and whether surgery caused as many problems as it solved.

I realized that from the very start, I always knew where Magnus was because I could hear his raspy breathing. I suddenly understood that this was not normal. I looked up Laryngeal paralysis.

The Larynx is designed to switch tracks between the airway and the alimentary canal: it covers the entry to the lung for eating and drinking, and covers the entry to the stomach at all other times. If it doesn't work properly, food can get into the lungs and cause pneumonia, or the airway can get blocked. Since panting is the only way dogs can cool down, it also shuts down their heat exchange system. It's commonly associated with hindquarter paralysis.

Magnus's medical chart displayed itself in my mind's eye. On the very first page, Dr. Paul had noted "chronic panting." Remember when he stroked his chin and said, "The hindquarter weakness could be neurological?" He knew. From the start. I wish now that he'd told me, and told me what to look for. But he may have felt that there was nothing we could do, and probably wanted to spare me the worry until the condition advanced.

Based on the kuvasz list stories about young dogs who couldn't walk across a room on a cool day, I figured we were okay, but I did start paying closer attention.

Chapter 48 — Does He Shed?

It's a known fact that in the kuvasz, the fur follicle and the root of the fur shaft both carry a positive electrical charge. Tiny ligaments at the base of the shaft hold the fur in place for approximately six months, at which time they weaken to the point that the forces of repulsion are stronger than the physical attachment, and the fur is ejected from the follicle. The collective strands of fur then expand to fill the available space, much as gas injected into a vacuum canister expands to fill it.

Interestingly, the vacuum created by housekeeping appliances is insufficient to collect kuvasz fur, which has enough of a kink to weave itself into all fibrous matter.

Magnus visited Amy's office with me one day for about an hour. Before we left, I saw a six-inch long strand of something white and kinky floating in the air above her desk.

The dust bunnies in my house grow legs within a week.

Kuvasz undergo a seasonal process known as "blowing the coat." I think you can guess what this means. Magnus blows his coat all year because he belongs on a Carpathian pasture, not in California. If I brush him properly, which I do about every two weeks, the fur I collect fills a small wastebasket, compacted. Uncompacted, it would fill a large trash bag. Brushing properly means starting from the tail, holding the fur back against the grain with one hand, and getting the grooming brush through the fur right down to the skin. I do surface brushing in between proper brushings. This provides my man and me with frequent opportunities for intimate bonding. Until I hit a snarl.

The kuvasz list started a thread on "weirdest places you've found kuvasz fur."

"In my baby's poopy diaper."

"In the butter dish in the refrigerator."

"I once went two years between dogs, and I still had dog hair in the house."

"In my keyboard at work."

But the winner was "In my appetizer at a cafe in Mykonos, Greece, during a two-week cruise in the Mediterranean."

The list reviews vacuum cleaners about once a year. Me, I just get on my hands and knees with a grooming brush to get the fur out of the carpet. On the hardwood floor downstairs, I reach down and grab handfuls when I notice them. As time goes on, I notice them less often. My once-meticulous housekeeping habits are in decline.

Chapter 49   Da Pacem

Being out of the park and staying close to home is boring. Apart from the prosy stuff—eat, sleep, work, love, and Magnus care—the most active thing I was doing was rehearsing for Easter.

We were working on some new pieces, and given that very few of us are strong sight readers, that's literally painful. Enough of us were off beat and off pitch that the result was cacophony. It's particularly hard to keep your pitch up when you're not sure what note you have to hit and you're not sure whether the beat is in triples or duples or whatever, and you're trying to keep track of accidentals, archaic key signatures, and special marks for temporary tempo changes—assuming one actually knows what all this stuff means. My music is marked up with little up and down arrows for sharps and flats, numbers for counting out rests, lines leading from a note in one part that will help me find the note in my part, and Nancy-language like "swing it," which is how I label triples. Bill shakes his head.

Some of our singers have formal training. Some of them can look at a score and read it like a comic strip. A few also have perfect pitch, which means that if you ask them for a middle c sharp, they can sing it for you. I'm not one of them. It took me eight years to figure out that the pitch I hear in my head is about a quarter step higher than what comes out of my mouth. One might reasonably ask how I got involved in this choir.

In 2000, a neighbor and I were trying to put together a caroling party. We couldn't agree on a date because she was singing so many Masses for a Bach festival. I asked if she was Catholic. She said no. She asked if I was Catholic. I said yes. She asked if I went to Mass. I said no. She asked why, and I said, in a spirit of sycophancy, "Because the music sucks." She said, "Oh, you have to meet Bill Mahrt. He directs a choir that sings the traditional music." She gave me the number. There was no try-out. Bill said, "Give it a few months. If you belong, you'll know it."

I didn't belong, but I didn't know it. I kept singing. Heaven knows why, since I often crept away to cry after I got snapped at for musical transgressions. "Heaven knows" is probably a literal, not a figurative, way of putting it. It's pretty clear by now that God wanted me in church. But there are other reasons, including the fact that singing in this choir is a rare opportunity.

We sing Gregorian chant and Early Music for church services—a liturgical setting, as opposed to the concert settings where most people hear Early Music. This kind of worship isn't for everyone. But the Latin Mass, with its regular prayers for the ordinary (prayers that happen at every Mass), and its carefully coordinated psalmody for the Propers (special material for each day) is a form of meditation that grows deeper with practice.

Except during the dry weeks, of course, when God is nowhere to be found. Most weeks are pretty dry for me. I'm the "Lord, I believe, help me in my unbelief" type of Christian.

Singing the Mass helps. You have to put so much effort into getting the meaning of the Latin and the sense of the music that each psalm, verse, and prayer you acquire has great value. The chant becomes more beautiful over time as you realize that it's not just an assortment of verses, but a grand cycle of rhythms and melodies, crescendos and diminuendos, across the liturgical year.

After eight years, I've learned the repertory and can finally feel the music and sing by ear instead of counting rests and grabbing for notes. There's a lot to learn. Our notebooks now hold over 270 songs and about 20 full Masses in addition to different chants for every Sunday and Holy Day of the year. The music fills my head. At odd moments I let the Da Pacem play itself out for me—a little prayer for peace with a little melody that walks up and down musical hills:

Da, pacem, domine
In diebus nostris.
Quia non est alius
Qui pugnet pro nobis
Nisi tu, Deus noster

Give us peace, O Lord,
In our day
For there is no one else
Who fights for us
But you, our God

Chapter 50 — Easter Week

Mom flew in on Tuesday of Easter week to hear the music. She sings in a choir in Rhode Island. Her choirmaster likes to stand in front of the singers with an electric guitar and drown them out. It hardly matters, because the music is about as interesting as milk toast. I knew she'd appreciate what we do, and had begged her to come.

The Easter music is the high point of the year. Christmas is nothing in comparison. It starts with a setting of the Lamentations of Jeremiah—Jerusalem! Jerusalem! Repent!—getting darker and darker as Good Friday draws near and the cantors chant the Passion, then Saturday, the Easter vigil with its hours of plain chant and psalms, and then exploding in paeans of joy on Easter Sunday with a double choir ringing out Alleluias in a church filled with lilies and hydrangeas.

By flying in on Tuesday Mom missed our best motet, *Sancte Deus* by Thomas Tallis, which we traditionally sing on Palm Sunday, at the start of Easter week. If you never listen to any other piece of polyphony, listen to this one. It's spooky and gorgeous and lush and has the best alto line of any piece of music I've ever sung. The climactic point is on the word *damnare*, the damned, appropriately enough.

It's a plea for redemption. Sends chills up the spine.

I asked Bill if please, please, we could sing it on Holy Thursday so Mom could hear it. He didn't answer, but on Thursday the music included *Sancte Deus*. I alerted Mom to watch out for it, and to forget about reading the Latin, which she had been following diligently. "Just listen to the music. All the meaning you need is there." After Mass, she said, "Wow. It's such a cry of longing."

She finished the week with us, attending all the services and celebrations, instinctively finding the best conversationalists and keeping herself entertained while I rehearsed and worked on client projects. Magnus didn't try to boss her during this visit. He quietly kept her company, and let us have our time together as a good husband should.

I know you're mine. I can share.

When she left, she said, "I'm so glad I got to experience this. It was wonderful. Can I bring some programs to show our choir director?"

"Think it'll inspire him to let you actually sing?"

She packed the chant programs in her little bag and flew out on Monday. I never did hear what her guitar-playing choir director thought of them.

Chapter 51 — Of Course It's My Fault

When Magnus was well healed and had built back up to two miles on leash, we went back to the park. He was ecstatic. I made a new set of rules. Instead of beginning and ending the walk on hard asphalt paths, I started at the other end, on the greensward, so he could start and end on soft ground. Instead of setting the pace and making him catch up with me when he stopped and sniffed, I let him set the pace, and stopped when he stopped. When we reached about halfway, I'd sit with him for a while and rest. I kept a watchful eye on that left leg, looking for signs of weakness.

The dog people welcomed us back, and were very solicitous. They asked how he was. "I see a serious decline since last year. He's not the same dog," I'd say. They'd say, "A year is a long time in the life of a dog. Especially a big breed like Magnus."

One evening, several women I'd never met joined us on top of the grassy hill. One of them went down on her knees in front of Magnus, and started examining his bad leg. One of her companions said, "She's studying to be a veterinary physical therapist, and noticed his injury." I started crying.

"I over-exercised him, and now he's suffering for it."

The future therapist, now massaging Magnus's limbs, said, "No, that's not how it works. They don't selectively fail on one leg from over-exercise. All the legs go. He probably had some kind of injury on this leg."

I didn't believe her. I knew it was my fault. I wept.

After about two weeks of this I noticed that the joy was leaking out of Magnus's face and leaving murky vaporous streaks behind him. His head was low, his eyes were serious. He was watching me all the time.

She is so sad. How can I help her?

I figured it out and lightened up. So did he. He gained strength.

Not long after, as we were pulling into the park, I saw a woman walking a big white dog with a black nose. I parked the car, let Magnus out, and walked back to meet her. Her dog was a German shepherd about Magnus's size. The men greeted each other with great civility, started walking together, and collaborated on scent investigations. It's not often that Magnus is interested in socializing with dogs, so this was lovely.

The other woman had never been to the park before, so I showed her all the high spots. We followed the paths to the greensward, where a big Malamute mix greeted our boys. The boys trotted around together, and Magnus was firm and sure on his legs. Three Alpha males, seeing qualities they admired in each other and being splendid. I was so pleased with my man, so happy to see him engaged in polite conversation—so different from last year.

Lesson 7—Don't imagine that the beginning of the end is the end. Enjoy your kuvasz, and let him enjoy himself.

Chapter 52 — Bones and Bifocals

I took the handrail off the stairwell when I first moved in because it was ugly. 13 years later, I got my first pair of bifocals. With bifocals, you can't see your feet. You're probably not even aware of being able to see your feet, but trust me, you can. You also see curbs and steps and changes in pavement surfaces a lot better than you think you do.

Losing your feet at the same time as your reflexes are getting slower and your sense of balance is going a bit off and your nerves aren't what they used to be and your consciousness of the long-term results of injuries has been sharpened by years of experience is just not fair. My Mom laughs, and says, "Ha! How do you like getting old?"

Cripes. I was only 53.

So I missed a step on the stairs, sat down hard, and cracked my tailbone. Having a cracked tailbone isn't much fun. To sit, you have to hang your tailbone off the edge of a pillow. Standing isn't so bad. Walking is a matter of waiting for the next breathtaking twinge.

So, naturally, I kept taking Magnus for his walks. After all, who matters more, him or me? He isn't getting much of in the way of walks this week, though. I can only hobble along for a mile or so.

Normally, he wanders off and casually expects me to keep track of him. Now he's staying right at my side, on alert. If I gasp, he stops and watches me closely. He licks my hands. He hovers and fusses.

I know you're in pain, love. You don't have to do this.

Turn about is fair play. Mutual service, graciously given and as graciously received.

Chapter 53   Dolly

Dolly might have weighed four pounds when we met her. We were halfway down the oak-and-redwood bordered green when she spotted us, and trotted toward Magnus, calmly, quietly, and confidently. She stopped a respectful distance away to ask permission to approach, got permission, dashed up to Magnus, raised her tiny head to his massive one, put her front paws up on his chest and said, "Hi! I'm Dolly." It never crossed her mind that he or any other being would offer her harm, and she was correct in that assumption. He smiled down at her and gazed into her eyes. There was no domination tension in his neck. He did not want to dominate Dolly.

Dolly was not instant flock, as the high-strung vizslas were. Dolly was not an instant subordinate, as bumptious puppies were. Dolly was not instant enemy, as the occasional stranger can be. Dolly was instant peer, as all intelligent, well-socialized, alpha breeds are. Dolly was in the class of Doberman, German shepherd, Rhodesian ridgeback, Rottweiler, and so on. But Dolly was a six-month-old Boston bull terrier.

The breed was originally a cross between an English bulldog and a white English terrier. It was bred to be a fighting dog. Unlike many other miniatures, this breed's build has not been distorted. It does have the flattish face of a bulldog, but its legs are the right length for its body, and its musculature is compact and balanced. Its disposition hasn't been distorted, either. It is a natural, dignified, forthright, amiable, courageous dog. I can't imagine an individual Boston terrier who more perfectly embodies this description than Dolly.

She's tiny, even by Boston standards. The largest Boston terriers weigh in at 25 pounds. Dolly will never weigh more than ten. She's the darling of the male dogs, with the heart of a lion, the spirit of a lark, and the unexpected grin of a 1930s cartoon dog. She doesn't rule. She reigns.

She is so fast that she can't be photographed—all you get is a blur. One of our greatest pleasures is to come on the green and find Dolly running joyfully with half a dozen big dogs chasing her and vying for her attention. She picks first one, then another, receiving the greeting each dog in turn. She takes it as a given that they all want to be with her, and that they all deserve to bask in her condescension, as a wise queen should.

One afternoon, they were the only two dogs on the green. As Dolly went to investigate an interesting scent, Magnus followed. When Magnus went to investigate another, Dolly followed. They led each other around the green for half an hour, the 9-pound, satiny girl and the 85-pound shaggy retiree going in and out of sunshine and shadow together.

When Dolly wanted to play, she ran circles around Magnus, charging in at him so he could lunge and bow and bark at each attack. There is only one other dog who figured out, first, that Magnus can't charge and wheel, and second, how to compensate for that to give him pleasure.

This idyllic scene was invaded by a bumptious puppy who stole Dolly out from under Magnus's nose. My poor old man watched his favorite girl run off to play with an ignoramus of a German pointer. He had the dignity to take it in silence.

We didn't see Dolly for a few weeks after that, and wondered where she was. At the end of one walk, as twilight was receding into night, we came upon her and DollyDad at the end of the green, near the street. She was on leash. We were happy to see them, and I asked why we hadn't seen her for so long.

"She surprised us by going into heat early. We'd meant to have her spayed, but wanted her to get her growth before we did it. We were afraid to take her out, so the poor thing has been cooped up all this time. It's making her crazy, so I finally had to take the risk. I'm still afraid to let her off leash, though."

"Oh, I don't think you need to worry any more. Look at Magnus. If she was still in heat, he'd be all over her."

"You think so?"

"I know so. We once met a Golden who was about to go into heat, though her owner didn't know it yet. Magnus was on her like white on rice. He bothered her so much she planted her butt on the ground every time he came near, and wouldn't budge until he let her be. The next time we saw her Mom, she said Bailey had gone into heat a day or two later."

"You're sure, then?"

"Absolutely."

The next day Dolly's reign resumed. We found her and her Mom at the top of the hill, where she greeted Magnus in the usual way, and ran circles around him. He loved it. Casey and CaseyDad joined us. Casey invited Dolly to play, and Dolly ran off with her. Casey was chasing balls. Dolly wasn't interested in balls, and returned to Magnus.

Come on, man! Join us.

I'd love to, Princess. But you know I can't run with you.

I'll help you.

You're very kind, dear. It's pleasure enough to simply be near you.

Oh, now you're just talking. But you're still a fine old gentleman.

I suppose dignity is something we can keep, even if the legs go.

You're always dignified, even when you play.

Ah, dear girl, if I were five years younger, I'd know how to make you happy.

Could you let me make you happy instead?

You do, Dolly, you do.

Well, good. I'm awfully fond of you, you know. Oh, excuse me, there's Casey again. I want to say hello to her.

I'll be here.

CHAPTER 54 OSTEOPATH

One of the dog people told me there was a terrific veterinary osteopath in the East Bay. I remembered his name, because it was the name of a boy I'd been in love with in second grade. Now wouldn't it be funny if...

Forget it. Life doesn't work that way.

Magnus seemed well enough. He wasn't getting as excited about walks as he used to, but the limping was way down. If he was less lively, he was also content. Still, I was in funds, and wanted to find out what the expert had to say. We made the hour-long drive, found the office, and registered.

The doctor was a jolly, chubby, cherry-cheeked gent with white hair. He put Magnus's legs through the motions, and said, "I'm not seeing much. Let's go outside to the parking lot and see his gaits."

This was one of the times I was glad Magnus is so good at off-leashing. He heels by second nature when I walk purposefully beside his head, so I didn't have to worry about him darting out in front of a car. We walked in a circle, following the doctor's instructions, and then trotted. He said, "I see nothing much wrong with him. Whatever injury he had has healed. I'll give you a cocktail of vitamins to keep up his health. Other that that, keep doing whatever it is you're doing."

Great news. I bought the fancy anti-arthritis vitamins, and got a list of others he should take: B3, E, and Omega 3 Fatty Acids. It cost almost $400, but it bought me the knowledge that I hadn't destroyed my darling.

Soon after that, I ran out of Missing Link. I didn't reorder, because it's for "skin, coat and more," and B, E and Omega 3 are all for skin, coat and more, too. So I reasoned.

Chapter 55 — Another California Kuvasz

The Kuvasz list was a big help. People were very ready to share information and advice, and some of the more gossipy bits on dog show politics—my, are there ever politics—are entertaining. I started an email conversation offline with a kuvasz guy in Sacramento.

Steve had bought a puppy from a large, well-regarded breeder in Missouri who consistently produces champion dogs. He named his boy Attila. He bought a panel van and customized it to transport Attila, and calls it the HunMobile. It has fans and insulation and other amenities to maintain a kuvasz-friendly temperature. It has enough space for Attila and Steve to sleep in on the road and during shows. That'll save him a lot of money, so it's probably a wise investment.

I told Steve how I met Magnus, not mentioning Susan S., but telling him my guy's name, age, what I knew about his history, and so on. We sent emails back and forth for a few weeks. I told Susan S. about "meeting" him, and said, "He just went to Doublering and bought himself a champion." I was being somewhat derisive.

She said, "You did the same thing, except you didn't pay for the dog."

That was unfair. I was paying, every day.

I said, "That's not what I meant. I meant that I think what you do is a lot cooler."

I could hear her smiling at me, and I couldn't figure out what she was on about.

I emailed asking Steve if he planned to breed Attila. He wrote, "Yes I am, but I'm not out to make money on him. He is definitely my companion. I'll breed him because there are so few good males out there, and I feel a responsibility to expand the breeding stock."

I wrote back saying, "I understand that breeders are very careful about what they pass on. The woman who gave me Magnus had to neuter an entire litter."

He replied, "I know who you are! You're Susan S.'s friend! I was going to meet Magnus one Sunday after she was done with Mass, but it didn't work out.

"You know, it broke her heart to give him away. But she thought it was the right thing for him and the right thing for you."

I was surprised he hadn't figured out who he was earlier. How many people adopted ten-year-old male kuvasz dogs named Magnus on the San Francisco peninsula during Easter a year ago?

I was more surprised that Susan hadn't told me she knew Steve. I called her.

"Why didn't you tell me you knew Steve?"

"I was going to let you figure it out on your own. Don't you remember me saying I was going to bring one of my dogs to meet a friend?"

"I wasn't that into the dogs then, Susan."

"I was having fun watching that interaction unroll on the list."

"You're on the list?"

"Yeah. I'm a lurker."

"You're a lurker? Why?"

"Oh, I just don't want to get into it with some people."

Politics, I suppose. "So, who is he, anyway?"

"He's been a kuvasz person way longer than I have. He's a trainer; he knows all the bloodlines; and he's an old friend of the Doublering people."

"I had no idea. I thought he just went out and bought a dog."

"So what does that tell you?"

"That I shouldn't make assumptions?"

"I guess."

Steve and I made plans to meet each other—he was bringing Attila to Palo Alto for a session with an obedience trainer who specializes in German shepherds and kuvaszok. He didn't want to meet off leash at our usual park, and insisted that we introduce them on leash with plenty of knowledgeable dog people around, because two male kuvasz would certainly challenge each other. I took his word for it.

On a hot Tuesday morning went to a small, pleasant bowl-shaped park surrounded by big firs and redwoods, tucked into a little corner off Sand Hill Road. The sky was a pale, steamy blue with little wisps of marine layer expiring in the heat as they reached over the coastal range. Four or five straight-backed, healthy shepherds, plus Attila, the trainer—a smallish middle-aged blond woman—and the dog people were standing in the faint shade of a young tree with a thin crown of leaves.

Steve saw us immediately and walked toward us with Attila off leash. I had Magnus on leash, and slipped the clip. You don't want a leashed kuvasz around an unleashed one, in my opinion. The trainer shouted to me, "Put that leash on! You don't know how the other dogs will react to a newcomer." I was on her turf. I obeyed.

Steve and I greeted each other. He was about my age, maybe a little younger, of average height, with a slight build, soft brown hair, and a gentle voice. Attila was fluffy, all combed out, with an enormous mane and wide cheekbones. We walked slowly towards the little tree. "I just bathed him last night," Steve said, "so he's extra-fluffy today."

"I decided to give Magnus the curly look this week, so I spritzed his coat."

"His coat is perfect. It's just curly on the back, and wavy on the sides, as it should be. I see that he has the traditional Hungarian head, long and squared. Attila's is more of a wedge shape, but both forms are acceptable." He continued to examine my sweetie. "He's a fine dog, just as Susan said."

"I'm very impressed with his intelligence and character. He learns fast, and seems to understand what I'm asking." Magnus made a slight move toward Attila—the move that starts to set the neck into an arch. Attila made a slight move in response. I wasn't concerned. I'd seen this resolve peacefully many times. Steven leapt in, got his hand on Attila's collar and told me to get hold of Magnus. I did, but said, "Magnus's behavior toward other dogs has been perfect for almost a year now."

"How many intact two-year-old kuvasz males have you met?"

"Ah. None."

The Shepherds were in various stages of repose beside their owners. They seemed ultra-mellow, moving as little as possible is the heat. They didn't look like vicious dogs to me, and largely ignored Magnus. Of course, their people were all at their sides, and since the men weren't worried, why should the dogs be?

The trainer was taking individual dogs and owners onto the lawn for focused sit-and-stay training. I asked Steve if he was planning to have Attila compete in obedience.

"Yes."

"Isn't that an unusual choice with a kuvasz?"

"That's why I want to do it. I want to demonstrate that kuvaszok are intelligent, and not the wild, uncontrollable dogs so many people think they are."

"That's great. If I had gotten Magnus when he was young, I might have tried freestyling with him."

"Why freestyling?"

"Because he's so graceful and attentive, and if I gesture to right or left, or circle, or whatever, he follows my lead, even without training." I told him about Caroline Scott and Rookie. He said he'd check them out.

At this point, Attila walked away from me, and I saw something large, black, and soft between his ankles. Between his ankles? The black object was swinging. Perhaps I should say "objects," since these things typically come in pairs. I was impressed.

"My turn is done, so we can go. Come see the HunMobile."

We wandered off with the boys to a stand of trees along the driveway, now off leash. Introductions established, the boys were content to coolly ignore each other. Steve's big white van was under the trees. He opened the doors and pointed out all the custom features with a combination of pride and self-deprecation. He had thought of everything, from safe surfaces to storage, refrigeration, and communications.

"I've got a lunch date with the people I used to work with today, so we've only got about fifteen minutes," he said.

"Why did you leave the job?"

"I was laid off."

"What were you doing there?"

"I'm a writer. Mostly technical, but I can do other stuff."

"I'm a writer too. Commercial hack."

He laughed. "I may try to get some hack work myself. I have to do something."

He didn't seem too anxious. Presumably he'd had good Silicon Valley jobs for years, and had some savings. Then again, he has a very expensive hobby. In addition to his kuvasz interests, he manages a German shepherd rescue operation. "I generally have four or five dogs in my care at any one time," he said.

"Sounds like a lot of work."

"It is, but it's worth it to see these wonderful animals get into good homes."

We talked of this and that. I don't remember much except that it was quiet and pleasant, and the dogs were placid and happy. After a bit, Steve got up, put Attila in the nice, cool van and said goodbye. Magnus and I went to the Nissan, opened the doors, windows, and sunroof to let the superheated air escape, got in, turned the AC on full blast, and went our own way.

I called Susan S. later to report on the meeting, "Attila's cheekbones are really wide. They make him look more Asiatic."

"Some people like that look."

"It looks strange to me, compared to Magnus."

"Magnus has a fine head."

"I couldn't believe the size of Attila's testicles. They were hanging down to his ankles."

"Was it hot out?"

"Yes."

"They have to keep the sperm cool, so they let the sac way down in hot weather."

"I'll say. He was practically stepping on those things."

I told her about Attila's brushed-out look, and about spritzing Magnus to get the curly look. She laughed. "You're trying out new hairstyles on my dog?" She laughed again. I like her laugh.

Chapter 56

Poor Old Guy

Magnus gradually stopped playing with me. He stopped standing up in the back seat and licking my face when we pulled up to the park. He stopped dancing onto the green. He walked with his head down, slowly. I got sadder and sadder watching him, thinking about how brilliant he'd been last year. He was still walking, but it wasn't that much fun anymore. I grieved. He panted. Poor boy.

I don't feel all that well for some reason.

I mourned.

I should have known better.

Chapter 57 — Hot Spots

A red, ring-shaped bald spot appeared on Magnus's shoulder. I took it to be mange or ringworm. I trimmed the fur away from it, scrubbed it with Betadine, and smeared it with antibacterial ointment. All the dog people said it was a hot spot, and that I was treating it correctly.

I was at the vet's for another reason, asked him to look at it, and asked him what he'd do about it. Dr. Paul said, "I'd trim the fur around the affected area, shave it, scrape the skin a little, and scrub it with an antibiotic."

I said, "That's what I'm doing."

He said, "What are you scrubbing it with?"

"Betadine." He was surprised I kept that in the house, since it's a surgical scrub, but I've done that for years. It comes in handy.

A week later, I found five or six small spots on his neck. At this point, I should have run to the vet, but I thought I had it under control. I shaved and scrubbed. A week after that, I found eight or nine spots on his rump. I ran to the vet.

"Is it allergies? Should I boil his bedding? Should I keep the floor dust-free? Is it his food? My laundry detergent?"

"Nancy, you can do all those things if you want, but this is coming from inside the dog. He has a systemic bacterial infection. Are you giving him anything in the way of immune system support?"

"..."

Missing Link. He'd been off it for a month. When we got home, I went online and ordered a large container.

Doctor Paul gave us antibiotics and a medicated shampoo that I was to bathe my man with weekly. I wasn't looking forward to that.

Within days Magnus was dancing in the morning again, standing up and licking my face as we drove up to the park, dancing onto the lawn, and so on.

I called Susan S. She said, "Why did you wait until the hot spots got so bad?"

"I couldn't see them through all that fur."

"Weren't you brushing him?"

"I brush him all the time."

"How do you brush him?"

"With a wire grooming brush. With rounded tips."

"From the top down?"

"No. I usually start at the back."

"That's not what I mean. You can't brush a kuvasz like you brush your own hair. You have to pull the fur back and get right down to the skin. If you were doing that, you'd have caught the hot spots early on."

"How was I supposed to know that?"

"I guess you wouldn't. I didn't think to tell you, since it's second nature to me."

"Live and learn."

At Magnus's expense, as usual.

Half the fur on his back was shaved off, and there were more bare patches on his neck, around his head, on his sides and a very big area on his rump. I decided to have his coat trimmed, because the contrast between the naked places and the five-inch-deep fur elsewhere was too stark.

Amy told me she got her dogs groomed for $35 each. I took my man to the groomer's and was quoted $90, minimum. I asked if she could recommend some electric clippers. She led me to the $175 set. I picked the $75 set, because I wasn't going to be using it all that much. I didn't go for the cheapest set, because I wanted the you-can't-cut-chunks-out-of-your-dog feature. Dr. Paul said the medicated shampoo was drying, so I also picked up some all natural, avocado-oil-based conditioner.

We went home and took our first post-house-of-poo bath.

I brought all the supplies into the bathroom and put them in handy places. I had to lug Magnus into the tub by main force—literally picking up his torso and hauling him in, then picking up his hind end and swinging that in too. He didn't actively fight the process, but he wasn't going willingly. I kept one hand on him, gentling him, while I got the water to the right temperature, and started soaking him down. That got him struggling to get out, so I held him gently, apologizing and trying to explain that I had to do this if he was going to get better.

I can't believe her. I'm perfectly clean. I mean, she loves me and she feeds me well, but this is just not necessary.

He stayed as far away from the faucet as he could. I started massaging the medicated stuff into his fur. It had to stay on for 20 minutes, so I kept massaging the whole time, praising him and cooing to him.

Hmmmm. I could get used to this.

Rinsed, freed from the tub (no hauling needed), and toweled off, lover boy ran into the bedroom, turned around, shook himself off, and grinned at me.

That actually feels better, sweetness.

"Not so bad, was it? Now you get the avocado oil massage."

Mmmmmmmmmm. Good hands.

Finally, I brushed the lotion through his coat and down to the skin. The lotion made the combing easy.

When he was dry, I clipped him, using the largest comb attachment to leave as much fur as possible—about an inch. Without his ruff and mane he looked pencil necked and geeky, his big rugged head stuck onto the wrong dog entirely. But people at the park still said he was beautiful.

The next bath was a lot easier. The getting wet part was still not great, but the rest of it was just dandy.

Susan S. and I had debated trimming a kuvasz for the hot summer weather. She said it was a bad idea, that if you cut the coat the guard hairs don't grow in properly, and that all I should do was thin the mane by cutting into it, at an angle perpendicular to the body. I'd done that already, and gone a bit further, figuring that if the coat didn't grow in completely, it hardly mattered in this climate.

But now he was shaved down, good idea or not. As the months went by, the coat grew in nicely, and by winter he had a full, thick mane again. With plenty of long, strong guard hairs.

Chapter 58   Dog People

Dog people have a special air about them. I'm not talking about your average pet owner, but the kind of people who know all the breeds, follow the shows, know about training and medical care and nutrition and which procedures are good and which are to be avoided. They have strong opinions on all of this. They are generally dedicated to one breed, and often keep at least two, one older and one younger, to make it easier when the older dog passes.

Don't even think about a young pup, ma'am. I'm all the man you need.

Dog people see PETA as a semi-terrorist organization that's dedicated to eliminating pet ownership on the grounds that all animals should live natural lives. Dog people circulate petitions on upcoming legislation that mandates neutering of all dogs or regulating breeders minutely. They hate puppy mills, but don't think existing legislation defines them clearly enough. They also don't think much of back-yard breeders—people who have a nice, intact dog, and know someone else who has another nice, intact dog of the same breed, and arrange play dates at critical times. Unlike serious breeders, they don't research bloodlines, choose pairings to improve breed-standard traits, or test for hereditary diseases. This tends to weaken the genetic stock.

When you talk dogs with dog people, they enter into a kind of trance, a special place in their heads where dogs, and only dogs, exist. Sometimes they look into space when you ask a question, and seem to consult their inner doggitude before answering. Then they answer with precise details and absolute assurance. They foster rescue dogs, train their dogs for agility or as therapy dogs, help other dog people socialize their pets, and have quick eyes for any kind of injury or discomfort.

Dog people are a breed apart.

CHAPTER 59   TOUGH GUY

Magnus started limping noticeably on his right foreleg, stopped horsing around with me, and was moving more cautiously in general. Back to the vet we go, hey-ho.

Dr. Paul moved the limb around, and said, "I can't tell what's going on from the outside. I have to take x-rays. Let me borrow the dog for a few minutes" He took the leash, and had to drag Magnus away from me, Magnus looking over his shoulder with wild eyes, gasping.

They're taking me away from you again. You couldn't possibly know what they do to me here. You'd never permit it.

When Dr. Paul had the films, he called me into the consulting room. "Look at this. See where the humerus meets the ulna?"

"Yes."

"There should be a black space there. There is no space. That means there is no cartilage, and the bones are rubbing directly on each other at every step. Are you giving him Glucosamine?"

"I started him on that the first week."

He knelt and checked the right leg, then the left. "He's clearly been favoring this leg for a while. I can feel that the shoulder muscle has begun to atrophy. I'll give you a prescription for anti-inflammatory and pain reliever for that elbow. Give it to him every day. That's all we can do."

Susan S. wasn't kidding when she told me that kuvaszok won't show pain until they're in agony. I ached to think of those bones grating against each other at every step, and it had probably been going on for a long time. He's a tough old coot. What's a little pain?

You'd think that they could slip a little silicon pad in there and glue it on. It'd hardly be internal surgery—those bones are almost fully exposed.

Hilary, complete with her new physical therapy degree, says it isn't that easy. Elbows are tricky.

The meds eased the pain, and Magnus perked up. We started playing under the redwoods outside the front door again.

Chapter 60 — Little White Dog

We'd just left the greensward and were walking along a sandy path that borders the ravine when a thin, whippet-like dog with a smooth, short coat dashed up to meet us. He was mostly white, with a few buff patches, and he was ready to play. This was the other dog who immediately understood that Magnus couldn't run and wheel and zig and zag, and invented another way to play. He circled Magnus, barking and darting in and out. Magnus pivoted and lunged at him when he came near, barking back. After a while, they decided to go exploring together. They trotted down the ravine, checked out the stream, climbed back up, and went along the trails together.

I didn't see a person. I didn't see a collar or leash. I worried about the little guy. He was healthy and well-fed, so he hadn't been out on his own for long. I thought it was irresponsible for an off-leasher to let their dog get so far away. When Magnus got tired and slowed down, the little snippet took off, looking for livelier companions.

I enjoyed that. What a fine little fellow. Now, what have we here?

And off he went on his rounds. It was another beautiful day. Birds singing, sky shining, temperature mild. We walked past wild lupines, spherical mounds of dark, delicate foliage crowned with tall spikes of clustered blue or mauve or white flowers. A stand of sage was undulating tall and silver along the path. There were larkspur, blue-eyed grass, and other wildflowers in the grasses along the verge. The dreaded foxtail grasses were still green, clutching their barbed seeds that slide through fur and skin and meander through flesh until they come out the other side. The oaks and chaparral plants gleamed in their tough olive drab.

The big playing field beneath the hill had been closed off with high, chain link fences. Architect's renderings were posted at the entrance to the schoolyard showing planned improvements to the baseball, softball, and soccer/lacrosse fields. The usual club of Lab ladies with their tennis-ball slingers was gone. The Bernese mountain dog people were gone. The vizslas were gone. All the dogs that usually peopled the place were gone.

Out of this desert came a pair of dog walkers. The women stopped to chat with us for a bit, and asked if I'd seen a little white dog. I said I had, and thought he was a very nice dog.

"He's out here with no collar and no leash and no owner."

"I know. He doesn't seem like a stray, though. He's well fed and clean and well socialized."

"He must be a yard dog that escaped."

"He'll find his way home when he gets hungry."

"I hope so. It would be too bad if he got picked up."

"Maybe he's been chipped."

"We can hope."

"If I see him again, I'll try to catch him."

We were headed in opposite directions, and walked on. I didn't see anyone else that evening. And I never saw the little white dog again. Presumably his people fixed the breach in their fence.

Chapter 61 — Dog Introductions

Watching dogs greet each other tells you a lot about their relative status and intelligence.

Magnus greets unknowns by standing still, holding his head high, and letting them sniff him. He only investigates them after they've gotten the information they need about him. This is Alpha dog stuff. The moment is always a bit iffy. I stay close and watch all meetings, helping him remember the rules by saying, "Be polite. Good job."

If the other dog is overly submissive, whether she rolls over on her back or cowers, Magnus is apt to over-dominate, and so I call him off. If the other dog gets right in his face before sniffing, it is a clear challenge that he stands up to.

Silly dogs dash up to him and sort of bounce around. This is bad manners, so he barks at them to make them stop. If it's a puppy and doesn't stop, he's liable to flip her over with his paw and loom over her. Dog people recognize this as teaching the puppy manners, but if I see it coming, I call him off. Pet owners thank me. Dog people say, "Let him teach her," and I release him. He puts the youngster in his place, and that's that.

Smart but playful dogs he immediately bows to, barks at nicely, and makes a few token lunges at, and then turns away.

If another Alpha dog approaches—you can always tell, because they approach calmly and slowly, giving my man a chance to see what they are—he will walk up slowly to meet him face to face. If they each see an equal, they will turn together to walk on and share the patrol. If they don't see an equal, the one who considers himself to be superior turns and walks away. We have met one such: a strong, young Doberman with an unusually deep chest. He wanted nothing to do with Magnus.

When Magnus shows fear, I know the other dog is crazy. A crazy dog does not understand the rules of engagement. We have met one such creature, a friend's Doberman bitch. They approached each other calmly, and seemed fine, but suddenly she bit him, red blood blossoming on his shoulder. Magnus ran away in terror. He didn't run away from the Great Dane: they were communicating, deciding who was top dog, and playing by the rules. But this crazy bitch he wanted nothing to do with.

We met her one day in the park. She and a golden retriever we love were running down the grassy hill in good order. She walked behind Magnus to sniff his butt, slid forward as he stood calmly, and casually planted her teeth in his flank, just for fun. He exploded, very naturally. The bitch's owner tried to dive in and grab her, shouting at me to do the same. I just stood there, because this was in earnest, I didn't want to get bitten, and Magnus had the right to defend himself until the Doberman was under control. Mircha finally did grab his bitch, and as soon as she was in restraint my man backed down.

"She started it, Mircha. She bit him for no reason whatever."

"No she didn't."

"You didn't see it because Magnus was between you and her."

"But she was doing just fine with Timmy. They've been playing together for half an hour."

"Timmy isn't Magnus."

I stalked off. Mircha called "I'm sorry, I'm sorry," but I wasn't having any. He has a big, strong, aggressive guard dog that needs a firm hand and isn't getting it. Meanwhile, my guy held his own in the engagement, protecting himself without hurting the bitch.

We haven't seen them since. Someone told me they'd gotten over $600 in tickets from animal control. You'd think that would be a clue that a little training was in order.

Chapter 62   Toby

It was yard sale season, and the complex was doing a big one. I went through all my stuff, selected less-than-special knick knacks and such, got out some big, hand-lettered signs I'd made years ago, freshened them up, and made sure I had plenty of ones, fives, tens, and quarters.

The next day was an average one for California—perfect. I got up on time for a change, put on a sundress and an apron with big front pockets, dragged my patio table and umbrella to the end of the driveway, and set up shop. Other residents were doing the same, so there was a lot of bustle and chatting and checking out of wares. When everything was ready, I brought Magnus out to sit in the shade with me. He was the only dog for a while. Our neighbors fussed over him. He started to draw in customers. One sweet young neighbor put reindeer antlers on him, which he tolerated surprisingly well. People ran to get their cameras.

While we were eating lunch, Magnus decided to void on the parking lot, in his inimitable style, waddling along and spraying pee from side to side in graceful arcs. "Look! He's making art!" someone laughed.

"It's finger painting for dogs"

General guffaws. I was embarrassed. Magnus didn't care.

It is what it is, hon.

Sheri, who had fallen in love with a blind cockapoo a few years earlier, decided to bring him out and let the boys socialize. We often walked together at the park, and the two got along fine.

Not at home, though. As soon as Toby smelled and heard Magnus, he went ballistic, launching off Sheri's lap and straining his leash. I was very glad he was on leash. Magnus backed up, bewildered, and looked around anxiously. I just led him away.

I had to answer the usual questions about a hundred times that day. It helped pass the time. One of the women I'd talked with the night before saw a small abstract painting I'd done years ago—a yellow-and-orange daub—and asked what I wanted for it. "You can have it," I said, thinking, "You actually want that piece of crap?"

"Really? You're just going to give it to me?" She was all excited.

"Sure."

"It's going to look great in my front hall. I'm going to hang it up right now."

She came back with a stack of DVDs. "Here, take this. It's three seasons of "Six Feet Under."

"Wow. Thanks"

She and I had been at odds some years before. Now we weren't.

Being blind doesn't bother Toby a bit. He tears around, instinctively stopping short of obstacles, and explores as avidly as any other dog. I noticed one day that he walks on the pace, with both right legs moving forward at the same time, then the left legs.

I know about pacing because that's the gait my stepfather's Standardbreds used in races, pulling little bicycle-wheeled carts called sulkies. Pacing is a good gait for sulkies because it's very smooth, with very little up-and-down motion. I have no idea what advantage it gives a dog who isn't pulling a cart.

"Sheri, look. Toby walks on the pace."

"What does that mean?"

I explained, and she said, "Oh. So he does. I never noticed that."

"I didn't know dogs used that gait at all. It seems unusual to me."

"Interesting."

Many months after that, I noticed that my beloved also walks on the pace. So do most other dogs. The things we fail to notice.

Sheri had helped me with training early on, making suggestions and pointing out when I was confusing His Bigginess. Now I helped her with Toby. When we ran into them around the complex, Toby continued to be aggressive with Magnus, who by this time had learned to hold back when little dogs over-reacted, and just held his head out of their way. Sheri would try to make Toby stop with verbal commands, but it didn't take. I got fed up the day Toby bit Magnus in front of our own door, and drew blood. I said, "Sheri, Magnus is pretty restrained, and won't hurt small dogs, but Toby's going to do that to the wrong dog one day and get seriously hurt."

She said, "You're right. I know. I have to make him stop."

The next time we saw them, Toby was a perfect gentleman. Sheri said, "I got a squirt bottle. He learned to behave in no time at all."

"A squirt bottle?"

"I think the idea is that it distracts them. Anyhow, it works."

Now Toby and Magnus hang out together, and walk around the complex, trying to see how many spots they can mark, and marking over each other's markings. Sheri says, "Men," and laughs. Dan Dan Cookie Man usually emerges with treats for the boys. We stand and chat for a while about them, and watch them, and feel kindly toward each other because of them.

Chapter 63 — Timmy and TimDad

TimDad walks with a wise, noble, golden retriever. He doesn't exercise Timmy by throwing balls around, as some retriever parents do, but takes him on a brisk two-mile walk every morning and evening. He also works from home, so Timmy gets to be with his pack all day. He's a calm, well-satisfied dog.

We were walking with them when a chow chow mix approached. Timmy, ever affable, greeted him with his best park manners. The chow chow snarked at him and circled him aggressively. Magnus puffed up, arched his neck, shot between the two dogs, and drove off the chow chow with a single fierce bark and lunge. The chow headed off in a huff.

TimDad regarded this with a vicarious grin. "I've never seen Magnus in action before," he said.

"That's what he does," I said. "He protects everyone he knows." TimDad beamed.

TimDad is a bit under average height, sixtyish, balding, sturdy, and carries an air of authoritative confidence. He has a mild Russian accent. He has a wide, Slavic face with a wide, curving smile and crinkly, blue, intelligent eyes. He quietly appraises people. He does not take you on trust, and is slow to warm up. He doesn't volunteer much information, but you can tell he has opinions. Put a white fur coat on him, and he'd make a pretty good kuvasz, actually.

"When did you emigrate?" I asked soon after we met.

"In the 'eighties."

"Before the wall came down."

"Yes." He was smiling broadly, with those crinkly eyes.

"How did you get out?"

"The U.S. had what the Soviets wanted."

"What do you mean?"

"The Soviet crop had failed, and there wasn't enough wheat. America had a surplus. In exchange for wheat, the Soviets had to agree to grant exit visas for a certain number of people. People with good educations and marketable skills. They lost some of their best and brightest in that deal."

"Did you come straight to Silicon Valley?"

"No. We had friends in New York, and stayed there for a while."

"What brought you out here?"

"A job."

That was all he was willing to give me. I let it go.

After some months of walking with Timmy and TimDad on a regular basis, they appeared in the company of a diminutive woman with a buxom figure and a pronounced limp. "Hello, Nancy. This is my wife." We exchanged pleasantries, and enjoyed the soft spring weather. TimDad had never once mentioned his wife. I knew he had a son, because I'd had to "borrow" a poop bag once, and he pointedly told me that it was biodegradable. I said, guiltily, "Oh, I use old grocery bags." He said, pointedly, "I noticed."

"I should be more eco-conscious."

"My son has had a great influence on us. He insists that we recycle, use fluorescent light bulbs, and so on. He has changed our way of living."

"It's wonderful that you are open to change."

"You have to be."

That was as much as I'd learned about his family, though I had made polite inquiries from time to time. He would smile and say nothing—he may have suspected me of flirting. When we parted that night, I said to TimMom, "Your husband has never said anything about you to me. He has kept all your secrets." She looked startled for an instant, then relaxed and said, "Good," with a smile that told me she got it—I was on her side.

A few weeks later, I met TimMom walking Timmy alone. As we went on, she apologized for her slow pace. I said, "That's fine. Actually it's perfect. Magnus needs to walk slowly, and most people go too fast for him." She was clearly pleased.

TimMom is far less guarded than TimDad, and we chatted easily. At the end of the walk, I said good night, using the Russian pronunciation of her name. She gave me a small, fierce look and corrected me with the American pronunciation.

She's an American now, and won't be taken for anything else. Presumably she has reasons for this. I'm sure I would if I'd grown up under Khrushchev and Brezhnev and the KGB.

TimDad started treating me differently. If I asked after Natalie, he'd tell me where she was and what she was doing, volunteering details. He told me more about his son, a concert pianist and graduate student in a technical field. As we reached the end of the green one night, I checked my car and said, "Oh, no, I've left my lights on."

"Let's see if you can start it."

He walked me to the door, all but holding my elbow to guide me, stood by until the engine cranked over, said, "That's good," patted the roof, smiled at me, and walked away.

Another time, he saw that my car was parked in the wrong direction. "You can get a ticket for that, you know."

"You can?"

"I can see the logic of it. If you pulled out you'd be heading against the traffic, and might cause an accident."

I never parked backward again. And I got biodegradable poop bags. When we meet up with them now, I give Timmy treats, and TimDad stops and gazes adoringly at Magnus, petting him, holding his face and talking to him softly in the darkening air.

CHAPTER 64 ASSUMPTION

Susan S. decided to fly out for the Assumption Mass. We were going to sing the Missa Ave Maris Stella—Hail, Star of the Sea, based on a hymn to the virgin—which we'd been working on all summer. We often prepare a new Mass during Ordinary Time, the months between Pentecost and Advent. Ordinary Time is so called because the Sundays are listed as First Sunday after Pentecost, Second, and so on—they're ordinal—but I think of it as vanilla season. Apart from the Assumption, which celebrates the Virgin's entry into heaven, there are no major feasts, no thematic music. It can get boring, so new challenges are welcome.

I sent Susan S. a copy of the Mass so she could study it, and she planned to stay with me for a few days. I was both looking forward to it and dreading it. Magnus looked awful, with his fur gone and a big ugly wart growing out of his right hip and the hot spots still showing on his skin. I feared her judgment.

She was going to rent a car at the airport and show up at my place under her own steam. She called ahead to see what was on for supper. I said, "Whatever you like."

She said, "I'd like a nice big spinach salad."

So I went to the market for greens and feta cheese and bacon and eggs and olives and a good crusty loaf of sourdough. It seemed fairly certain that she wouldn't have had much San Francisco style sourdough in St. Louis. I had everything ready to assemble when she got in.

Her face at the door was bright and cheerful, and her manner efficient and competent. There was no sign of sorrow on her, which made me glad. She greeted Magnus, kissing his big white snout.

Oh, what a fine surprise. I thought I'd never see you again, love.

Susan said, "Overall, he looks good. He has energy and seems strong, considering what he's been through. Who's you get to trim his coat?"

"I did it."

"You did?" She seemed surprised. "How did you do that?"

I told her about the fees for grooming, and deciding to buy the clippers instead.

"My, my. So now you're not only his personal trainer, nurse, and nutritionist, you're also his groomer?"

"Looks that way." I was fixing salad, tossing it first in olive oil, then adding lemon juice and salt.

"You've done a great job."

High praise from Her I'm-Not-Impressedness. I was smugly pleased. Margaret slithered through the living room on her way out the patio door. Susan said, "Ew, a cat."

Hammett ran in and got directly into Susan's face, demanding her attention. "You're a piece of work, Hammett." Then, looking abstracted, "I miss having kitties. They have such nice, soft, conformable bodies."

"They do. I like Magnus's big, strong body, but it's a different thing with cats. A different relationship, too."

"Radically different."

"You have to psych them out. Work with them cooperatively. They're much more like humans that way."

"They're not at all like humans. They're like cats."

"I mean that you can't boss them: they think for themselves."

"You think cats think?" She was teasing, but I didn't get it.

"Hammett thinks, absolutely. He's a plotter. When he wants to do something, he keeps trying different things until he succeeds. It may be more about sheer persistence than reasoning, but it gets results."

"Whatever you say. He's still a piece of work." She was looking at him with a glowing face, petting Magnus at the same time.

We talked choir and plans and critters while we ate. When we were done, Susan whisked the plates off the table, washed and rinsed and stacked the dishes deftly, and scrubbed down the counter with lots of soapy water. No discussion about it, just the easy cooperation of someone who carries her own weight.

We wandered upstairs to the guestroom/office, which I had cleaned and vacuumed and aired out for her. We sat on the bed and chatted idly. She was in a fey mood that I didn't understand. Margaret pussyfooted up the stairs and slinked in. She's very possessive about that room. I said, "You may have company tonight. Or you may find that someone has peed on your stuff."

"Does she do that?"

"She's been known to. It took eight months of keeping a plastic tarp on the bed sprinkled with Cayenne pepper to break that habit."

"Ew."

The next morning, Margaret slinked by while we were at breakfast. Susan said, "Ew, a cat," as if she'd never seen her before.

"Come on. You know Margaret."

"I've never seen that cat before."

"She was in your room last night."

"I never saw her."

This bewildered me until the penny dropped. Susan had figured out Margaret's modus operandi: she's the invisible kitty. In eleven years with my princess, I had never understood that. Margaret who peers around corners. Margaret who only comes within fingertip's reach. Margaret who rolls around on her back, inviting me to pet her, then runs away when I move to comply. Margaret the slink-around-the-walls girl. She'd been working me the whole time, playing cat and mouse. I was the mouse. Susan tumbled to that in an hour.

The Mass went well enough the next day. Susan knew it better than I did, which was good because all of a sudden it was as though I'd never seen the score before (it happens). I followed her lead. During the coffee hour after Mass Susan caught up with everyone, smiling and exuding competence and strength. You'd never know she'd been through a painful and disappointing year.

Back home, we sat on the floor with Magnus, and talked.

"I'm shocked at how far he's declined," I said.

"It's part of the package," she said.

"Isn't it my fault?"

"No, it's the dog. If I'd known he had so many problems, I wouldn't have given him to you."

"He had all these things in germ when he came to me."

"I didn't see it."

"You wouldn't have seen it. You weren't exercising him."

We were silent for a while. I didn't mean to accuse her, and she didn't think I did. She looked at his head silently for some time. "Who are you?" she queried. She was reviewing his ancestry, thinking about his relations. "I know who you are," she said. She didn't elucidate. Running her hands over his body, she said, "What's this?"

"It's a warty thing. I'm not worried about it. He's got a couple of fatty tumors on his butt, but they're actually shrinking, so I'm not worried about them either."

"Magnus, you're falling apart." She said this kindly and tenderly. "How old is he," she asked.

"He's a little over eleven now."

"No he's not. He's only seven or eight."

"You told me when I decided to keep him that his tenth birthday would be in July."

"Are you sure?"

"Yup."

"How rude. I gave you a ten-year-old dog."

"My sister would agree with that. But I don't care. I adore him, and he's been very good for me. Now it's my turn to be good for him."

"Magnus, your walking days are over."

"No they're not. We're still doing two miles a day."

"Okay then, his athletic days are over."

"That they are."

"You're not going to do anything heroic are you?"

"No. I can't stand watching people keep their animals alive past the point of joy. I'm going to keep him comfortable, keep him walking, and keep him happy as long as I can. When it's time, I'll let him go."

"Hear that Magnus? She's going to keep you comfortable and happy. You're a lucky guy."

"I'm a lucky girl."

I'll say you are.

We sang Vespers and went to Sunday dinner. It was so nice to have Susan S. around. I even stayed to sing Compline, which I'd been skipping because it's one thing too many for me, and leaves me useless on Mondays.

When Susan S. and I got back home after Compline and were getting ready for bed, I saw her nuzzling Magnus in her room. I quietly shut the door to let them have their moment. As I was shutting it, I saw her lifting Magnus onto the bed and lying down with her arms around him.

The door opened in less than a minute. Magnus came into my room, pacing nervously around the perimeter of the bed with his ears back and his eyes wide, putting his chin on the covers and giving me unhappy glances. I got up, and hoisted him onto the bed. He sighed, circled a few times, and lay down as tightly against me as he could get. He tossed his head across my body.

Nancy, that wasn't my idea. I would never cheat on you.

She'd been away too long.

Chapter 65 — Mrs. James

I was learning about elder care, and facing end of life care, and paying more attention to people around me who were doing the same. Susan A.'s tiny and shrinking mother has been in the extremes of old age as long as I've known her. She hobbles around with a rolling walker, sits in her room for hours reading and re-reading "The Cat Who" books, and comes to the table for meals at the appointed hour. Her stock of conversation is limited to grandchildren, "The Cat Who," the fact that her ex-husband was an Army dentist, and how remarkable it is that the foothills outside the windows change from hour to hour.

Susan A. has to keep after her to get her to eat. She lives on Progresso lentil soup. She drinks a mug of beer every evening from a glass shaped like a cowboy boot. She wears her antique Mexican jewelry with colorful housedresses from Sears. She sees and speaks to angels.

For years, Susan and John took her everywhere they went—the desert, the cabin, the Palisades. They never left her alone. Susan nursed her mother through fall after fall, surgery after surgery, and growing dementia. One night Mama fell out of bed, or fell getting out of bed, and broke her hip. Susan found her in the morning, naked, on the floor. She tried to get her up. She couldn't. John tried to get her up. He did, but he injured his back so badly that he had to have surgery—again. The doctors and nurses told them that Mama was a full-assist patient at that point, and would need a nurse on attendance 24 hours a day, plus orderlies to lift and bathe and move her. They told her she absolutely could not give this level of care on her own. She and John couldn't afford in-home health care. Susan had no choice but to place Mrs. James in a nursing home.

She agonized over this. We all told her that she couldn't keep on the way she had been, that her mother needed more care than she could give, that she had done a wonderful job keeping her mother alive and healthy for all these years, and that she was clearly physically unable to take care of her. She agonized anyway, and reviewed nursing homes, finally choosing the least objectionable one. She said, "All it has to recommend it is lots of fire exits and valet parking." She said, "Mama hates it. She wants to come home. No matter what I tell her, she just keeps asking to come home. She bites, kicks, and swears at the staff. I can't stand it." She was so drawn and drained and weary, it broke my heart.

She visited Mama every day. She brought pictures of the grandchildren and great grandchildren, and then brought the children themselves. She had other people visit. She did what she could to keep Mama happy, but nothing really helped. She was—and is—furious at the system. "It eats up people's every asset and delivers nothing for it but a death stripped of all dignity," she says. "A nursing home is a whitewashed descent into Hell."

Mrs. James was released from that Hell in a matter of months. She was, I think, 98.

The entire choir came to sing the Requiem Mass for her, a solemn chant and plainsong service. People showed up who hadn't been to Mass or dinner regularly for years. After the service we went in a caravan to the cemetery. Jean and Magnus rode with me. It was insufferably hot, a steamy August day, and I worried about leaving my guy in the car, even in the shade. I walked down the row of cars till I found John and Susan in his aged Porsche.

"Do you think Mrs. James would like Magnus to be at her funeral?"

"YES!" they said in stereo.

I went into the chapel, and asked if my dog could attend the burial. "Yes, as long as he's on a leash." I went back to the car, got out the leash, and walked with Magnus and Jean behind the procession of cars, down a hill, and into a bowl-shaped lawn with shade trees and flowering trees, a chapel, and a trellised shade structure. We gathered around the gravesite and the handsome walnut coffin, and sang another psalm. Magnus pulled on the leash, wanting to investigate what everyone was so interested in. I asked him to sit. He doesn't like to sit in public, so he refused to stay down. He tried to get between people's legs to reach the grave. He wanted to know what was going on. He knew it was important. I held him back while the priest read the burial service and Mrs. James's remains were lowered gently to their final resting place.

The air was soft with exhalations of the earth, the sky was hazy, the birds were singing freely in the trees. Mary of the X-rays and Tibetan mastiffs walked by and said, "It's too hot for him out here." I took him to a shade tree, and sat with him on the grass. People came over and spoke quietly with us. Others strolled around the grounds, trying to see what kinds of birds were in the trees. Magnus regained his calm, looking smart in his new blue halter.

We all went back to the house for a buffet lunch. Susan's middle daughter, Allison, had collected pictures of her grandmother at every age, from infancy to octogenarian, along with some intricate carvings Mrs. James had made, and set up a kind of shrine to her on an antique chest. We piled our plates with ham, smoked salmon, salads, and bread and settled down to listen to stories about her.

When she was in her eighties, Mrs. James went to a David Bowie concert with a Mary, Susan A., and one of the granddaughters. Susan and her daughter went into the mosh pit. Mrs. James and Mary went to nice seats in the mezzanine with their picnic basket and a bottle of champagne. Mrs. James decided that their seats weren't nearly as nice as the press box, and said, "Let's go sit with them." Mary said, "We can't go in there. We're not press." Mrs. James said, "Oh, we're just two old ladies, they'll figure we have a right to be there."

Mrs. James was right. She very much enjoyed the concert, the wine, the food, and the company.

When they went out to the parking lot after the concert, they found a group of young men clustered around Mrs. James's car, a vintage Mustang with a four-on-the-floor standard transmission. They asked her how much she wanted for it. She said, serenely, "I would never sell my Mustang," got into it and drove off. She could shift it without spilling her coffee.

I've never been to a funeral that was more of a celebration of a life. Good night and God bless, Ms. James. I wish I'd known you when you were still yourself. Take care of my love for me when he gets there, okay? I'll be along if I can make it.

Chapter 66 — Stumbling

Magnus's hind end tottered and wavered and collapsed a mile into our usual walk, his breathing grating and labored even at the slow pace we were taking. I sat down on the grass, pulled him onto my lap, held him in my arms, and massaged his throat gently as he rested his full weight against me. He likes that. Kathy, who was walking with us that day, said, "He needs to turn back."

"I know."

"Do you know what's wrong with him?"

"He's developing something called laryngeal paralysis. It's neurological. Hind end paralysis tends to go with it."

Kathy looked at me with kindness and pity. She lost her last cat a few years ago, and decided not to get another one because Mike is allergic. She knows what watching a loved one go down is like. She knows what Magnus means to me.

"He seemed so healthy last year. The vet said he was in excellent shape for a dog of his age and size. I didn't know he would decline so far, so fast," I said. "I'm afraid it's my fault."

"He's lucky to have you."

"I hope so."

He was in a bit of a daze. Suddenly, he stood up, pulled away from me sharply, and started walking away.

For heaven's sake, lady, I merely stumbled. Come along.

We finished our walk without further incident.

Naturally, I cried all evening.

The weather cooled down over the next few days, and Magnus improved, as usual. It was just the heat.

Two tiny dogs we know—their combined weight is about one-eighth of Magnus's—ran past playing catch-us-if-you-can. Magnus was off like a shot. I let him go about 75 yards, and called him back. He wheeled round and cantered up to us in perfect form, grinning. Jean said nothing, raised her eyebrows, shook her head, and made the O shape with her mouth.

We stood still so he could rest, but he decided to walk on. A young black Labrador trotted into Magnus's face to challenge him, snout to snout. Magnus arched his neck and faced him squarely.

I'm younger and stronger and faster than you.
But I am more noble and wise.
You're a PATHETIC WRECK.
You are callow and unlearned.
I RULE!

Magnus was about to retort when I called him off. The Lab stalked stiffly off to his people. He was not exactly a typical Lab. Magnus returned to my side, grinning.

Jean said, "It's all about quality of life."

We were at the top of the hill, and started heading back, into the gathering dark beneath the spruces and oaks. Magnus took the lead, glowing whitely in the dusk and looking over his shoulder every now and then to make sure we were in train. We passed the donkey paddock. We crossed the big bridge over the creek, which was just a thin trickle at summer's end, went up a short rise, and down again onto the green with its shadowy old oaks and redwoods standing sentinel. The peepers were peeping, the birds were sleeping. I got out the little wind-up flashlight, wound it up, and played it on the grass so we wouldn't trip on the rodent and vermin burrows.

Young men and women were playing soccer in the dark at the far end of the green, working out their social ranks with loud, sarcastic commentary on each other's skills (or lack thereof). Their bags and shoes and drinks were scattered in heaps that Magnus had to investigate.

Some of these kids have snacks, I believe.

I called him off. He then stopped to assess the state of the boys and girls, who really were loud and rowdy, and concluded that they were just playing, not fighting, so he didn't have to intervene. He walked on. As we approached the car, Magnus saw a dog he wanted to socialize with, and trotted briskly toward it. I called him again, and he trotted briskly and crisply back to me, tail high and ears on alert, full of life. I unlocked the car, flipped the passenger seat forward, and watched him climb into, and fill, the back seat.

Mom called. She asked how my man was doing. I told her. She said, "When will you know that it's time to make a decision?"
 "When there's no joy."
 "That sounds about right."
 "But, you know, there will be food for a long time."
 She laughed. She knows how he feels about food.

CHAPTER 67   TUMOR

When I got home one afternoon, the ugly wart on Magnus's hip had burst, and blood was running down his thigh. This didn't bother him. He jumped up when I opened the door, wagging and grinning and wriggling with anxiety and joy. I'd been gone a little over an hour, on errands. I'd left him home because it was way too hot to leave him in the car, even in the shade.

You worried me terribly, you know, taking off like that. What if something had happened? Who would have taken care of you?

I got out a washcloth, bathed the open wound gently, poured peroxide over it, and called Dr. Paul. He told us to come right in. I had to leave the poor boy overnight, and when I returned the next day to pick him up, Dr. Paul said, "We had to do much more extensive work than we expected. I found a large tumor under the skin, and had to remove quite a bit of tissue. See? That scar is about 4 inches long."

I can't believe what that man put me through. Why do you let him do these things to me? It's incomprehensible.

We went to the front desk. I paid up. The orderly who took my card grinned and said, "Why don't you just leave this here?"

Dr. Paul stopped on his way out of the lobby, and said, "Do you want a biopsy?"

I said, "What does it cost?"

"Eighty Dollars."

"What will we do if it's cancerous?"

"Exactly."

"What do you think?"

"I'm pretty sure it's benign."

"That's good enough for me."

We went home, with a shaved right hip, big blue stitches, and a thin red wound. It healed. The fur grew in again. The tumor didn't.

Chapter 68 — Medical Assistance

The dog people are very sympathetic. Magnus has become a kind of mascot in the park, being the only one of his kind and being so nice and having so many troubles. Everyone who meets him remembers him, and remembers his name, no matter how long it's been since they've seen us. Everyone stops and looks him over.

"Magnus seems much better."

"Yes, he does, doesn't he? I thought I was losing him a while ago."

"You've been given a reprieve."

"Has he lost weight?"

"No, he's lost hair. I trimmed the coat to make the shaved parts less obvious."

"He had a little surgery?"

"Yes. We had to remove a growth."

"The fur is growing in nicely over those hot spots."

"Yes. I give him regular baths now, and the skin is healed"

"How far are you walking him?"

"We still do about two miles a day. Slowly, but we do it."

"We don't mind slowing down for him."

"Thank you."

We'd been to the vet's 14 times by this point. I wondered what his original owners would think if they were to read this—or, rather, how they'd feel. My sister said yesterday that it was hugely unfair to give someone a dog for the saddest and most expensive part of his or her life. She has a point. Still, watching Magnus, even in decline, shows me what my man is made of. Better late than never, when it comes to love like this.

Chapter 69 — A Pointer Gets It

The first time we met Maple—a gangly, adolescent, black-and-white German shorthaired pointer—Magnus hadn't been out for several days because of the heat, and he was snickety. This long-legged pup was engaged in rapid evasive maneuvers against an invisible pursuer. His people were also invisible. When he saw my old man, he started galloping towards him, then stopped in his tracks about 20 feet away, sat down, and hung his head between his shoulders. Magnus was doing distance domination. He did the same thing to two females we met that day. I rather enjoyed his lordly presumption.

The second time we met Maple, he cut in on Magnus's time with Dolly. I believe this fact was noted and filed for future reference.

Two or three weeks went by before we saw him again. Maple ran rudely up into Magnus's face. Magnus barked a stern command. The pup dropped to his hindquarters and bowed his head. I saw Magnus's neck arch, his jaws open, and his head descend to lock on the pup's head. Maple screamed. I screamed "MAGNUS!" He came off immediately. The pup ran past, terrified, his head completely slimed. I didn't see any blood. His Mom ran past after him. "Is he hurt?" "I don't think so." "I'm so sorry!" She didn't reply. I already had the leash on Magnus's harness.

We had a very stern walk for about 10 minutes. Short lead, no sniffing, stay to my left. He resisted strongly, trying to pull away and finally refused to walk on.

For goodness' sake, I was just doing my job, and I stopped the instant you asked. Get over yourself, missy.

Dragging Magnus wasn't working, and was making us both unhappy, so I stopped, and snapped the leash off.

Another dog person came along and asked after Magnus. I told him what my bad boy had just done. He laughed. He told me mouthing another dog's head is a standard ultra-dominance behavior, intended to humiliate but not to harm.

"But the puppy had already submitted. He was sitting down and hanging his head."

The guy grinned. "Probably brought it on himself by doing that."

I was dubious.

As the weeks passed, I kept hoping I'd meet MapleMom again so I could apologize. Our paths didn't cross until mid-October. Maple crept toward Magnus slowly and respectfully, and lay down on his belly when he reached us.

Oh. You again.

Magnus stood over him with the arched neck of dominance, but otherwise kept still. This lasted for a breathless moment, until he released the pup by moving along.

"I am so sorry for what Magnus did to your dog the last time we met. I was horrified. "

"Really?" MapleMom said.

"Oh, yes."

"Why? Older dogs always correct Maple. He's two years old, but he can't seem to grow up."

"Well, he certainly approached Magnus politely today. Maybe he's learning."

"It's about time."

We al walked on together, Magnus serenely ignoring Maple, and Maple hovering in his wake, trying to look cool. Magnus wasn't buying it. But he let Maple stay with us for the rest of the walk.

Chapter 70 — Leash Training

Susan S. asked, when I related the mouthing-the-puppy story, what leashing and being hard on my man had communicated.

"That I did not appreciate him taking the puppy's entire head into his mouth?"

"But he stopped when you called him off."

"Ah. So as far as he knows, I punished him for obeying me."

"You confused the dog."

This would have consequences.

Jean and I took him to the beach the following Saturday. We were there to escape from a severe September heat wave, as were hundreds of other people. I had to keep Magnus leashed in the crowd.

He didn't want to be leashed. He wanted to go meet all the people and see if they had any food and make sure they were safe and check out their dogs. He wanted to do his usual job—inspect and assess the environs.

Now what have I done? I don't understand you.

Lesson 8: Don't ever, ever use the leash as a punishment.

He pulled away from me to check out some folks. "Mind your business, Magnus." He dragged his feet. "Come on, Magnus." He simply stopped. By this time I realized what I'd done, so I stooped down, hugged him, ruffled his ears and neck, and told him he was a good boy.

So, are you angry with me, or are you just losing your mind?

We finally got to a section where other people had their dogs off leash and the crowd was thinner, so I snapped off the lead. Immediate dancing in the sand, a little trot with leaps thrown in, head down and swingin', eager and grinnin', right at my side, elated.

Ah! You're back. You had me going there for a bit.

The beach was deeply shelved in three levels, with swells at least ten feet high, and tingling foam surging far up the steep beach. There had been some heavy weather at work creating overnight geological change. You can go to a sandy beach on the California coast one week and see two shelves with gradual slopes, and the next week see one shelf pushed high against the coastal cliff with a steep drop to the waterline. It's impressive.

Warning
Rogue Waves Frequent
Wading And Swimming Dangerous

Rogue waves tend to attract a certain kind of surfer, and there are usually quite a few out there looking for them. That day, only a few people were out. They weren't surfing, but sitting or paddling around—the waves may have been breaking too close to shore because of the beach's steep slope. But plenty of other people were wading and swimming, and parents were letting small children play in the waves. Jean and I rolled up our slacks and waded into the icy water. The weather was so hot that people were wearing light clothes and bathing suits. Usually you need at least a windbreaker, even in high summer. On this Saturday, the temperature, the wind and the sun were all in perfect proportion.

Magnus came to the water's edge to try to lead us back to a safe distance, but we did not comply. He then went about 15 feet off and took up the watching stance: neck out, head low, eyes focused on his charges. You see pictures of working kuvasz doing this all the time. Staring at sheep to the south. Staring at sheep to the west. Staring at sheep to the north. We were the sheep. People were walking between my kuvasz and his two-sheep flock, blocking his view of us. As they passed he loosed a wavery, muted howl I'd never heard before.

This is intolerable. Why don't you get out of that water?

A slim young woman in a white shirt stopped to pet and praise him. She was on her way off the beach. He followed.

If you're going to act like this, I'm leaving. I can't trust you anyway.

He did not come when I called him. He didn't even look at me.

It worked. Jean and I left the waterline, collected and reassured my old man, walked on a bit, and sat one level above the breaking waves. He lay down beside us, happy—or at least happier.

I hope you got my point, young lady. Don't ever pull a stunt like that on me again.

Said with a smile while squinting into the westering sun.

I didn't know dogs could squint.

Lesson 9: Sometimes it's best to just do what your kuvasz says.

Walking back through the crowd on our way in (off leash this time), a man sitting on a blanket with his lady lying beside him gave Magnus a soft-eyed smile that invited introductions. Magnus accepted, gently approached the couple, and then stood directly over the woman, who first shrieked and then wrapped her arms around him as he bent to kiss her, the man looking on admiringly.

Jean said, "You shouldn't let him just walk in on people like that."

"The man wanted to meet him."

"He did? How do you know?"

"He gave me the look."

"Oh. I didn't notice."

"I did. You know how closely I watch him in crowds. And you know how people are with him."

This couple was fond. And fondling.

We'd left our shoes at the foot of a long flight of stairs that led up from the beach, so we collected them and started climbing up the headland, slow but steady. At the top, people wanted to pet him, so we stopped. I, of course, kept my eyes on Magnus—you never know—so I didn't notice that everyone else was staring out to sea. A tiny girl in a dark pink dress was petting Magnus. A tinier terrier behind me was growling at him. A pleasant-looking young man turned to me and said, "There are at least three whales out there," pointing west.

I took my eyes off Magnus, turned, and saw a whale surface and blow. Another whale blew to the north. They were both about 100 yards off shore. A third whale surfaced and blew near the first, its huge, long, dark body arching above the surface of the waves and then rolling down, rolling and rolling and rolling until its dorsal fin rolled up and disappeared under the waves. More blowing. Another large dark body with a dorsal fin rolled in the swell. Hordes of sea birds—it was hard to tell what type against the afternoon sun—were diving in the same area. Dolphins or porpoises were leaping and diving to add to the melée—or carnage. A shoal was under attack. Another shoal was under attack to the north, with two whales feeding on it. The frenzy went on until the pair nearest us rose vertically out of the water, belly-to-belly, nose-to-nose, with a third of the length of their bodies out of the water. We could see their striated white bellies. Cetaceous victory dance.

"You can't get better than that."

"That is more whales than I have seen in my entire lifetime."

They were probably Finbacks or Bryde's whales. Bryde's whales are slightly more common and are known to be coastal, but Finbacks are known to circle schools of fish at high speed in order to roll the school into a tight ball, then surface and roll back under on their right sides to scoop the fish into their maws. That matches the behavior we saw, so our whales were probably finbacks. They are the second-largest whales on the planet. They can eat as much as two tons of fish per day. Between 1935 and 1965, commercial "fisheries" killed about 30,000 of these intelligent, social mammals every year. About 60,000 Finbacks remain to swim the seas today. So few, and so magnificent. We were very lucky to see them. They will be lucky to survive.

(Data from the American Cetacean Society.)

Chapter 71 Goats and Donkeys

There are two goats in a paddock just off the park. They are not guarded by a kuvasz. Their owner takes them for walks using long, heavy leashes. One day last year the goats were grazing near the bridge by the green when my kuvasz and I walked by. Magnus was curious. Magnus approached the goats. One of the goats turned to face Magnus and lowered its head. Magnus moved closer. The goat moved forward until its hard, bony forehead was pressed against Magnus' hard, bony forehead. The goat pushed a little. Magnus got the message. That goat didn't need a guard, thank you.

There are also two donkeys in a paddock just off the park. (There are two more donkeys in the playground, but they are wooden and painted and have little seats on them and are mounted on big springs.) Not long after we met the goats, we met the donkeys. They were out in the greensward, grazing on fresh, well-irrigated grass and the little white clover blossoms stitched into it. Magnus was curious. He approached the smaller of the donkeys. He circled it. The donkey tried circling away. He kept on the donkey and tried to sniff its butt, which is perfectly good manners among dogs, but not considered quite the thing among donkeys. The donkey's right rear hoof shot out and caught Magnus on the head. It must have been a light warning kick, because he didn't so much as yelp.

Magnus developed the irritating habit of going down to the donkey paddock to eat donkey dung. One evening, I heard the larger donkey heeing and hawing and braying and screeching like a brace of devils was after him. I turned back, and saw Magnus's head retreating from the donkey's hooves. The donkey then thundered down along the fence toward me in a hard canter, then thundered back up, then down again, then threw himself on the ground for a quick roll in the dust before pulling himself up in a tight spiral and galloping away, kicking his hind feet in the air and braying raucously.

I have never seen that animal behave other than placidly, unless someone was bringing him carrots.

Magnus trotted up to me smugly. "What was that about?" I asked.

I haven't the faintest idea.

"Did you nip his heels?"

You know I would never do such a thing.

"You did something, I'm sure of it."

Really, Nancy, it's just a ditzy donkey. I don't care to discuss the matter any further.

Chapter 72 — Dinner with Dutchmen

Just as we were wrapping up rehearsal for Vespers, two men came into the chapel. Bill greeted them warmly, hurriedly explained how we do the service, and introduced them as visitors from the Netherlands who sing chant and polyphony. We were a bit apprehensive, because part of the beauty of Vespers is the unity we've learned to create over the years. New singers, however accomplished, tend to disturb that.

The Dutchmen didn't. They didn't have to learn to blend with us. They led us. They read beautifully, created a new unity, and actually kept the pitch up. (We sag badly, especially on the Psalm 113, which has 29 verses.) They are both strong tenors. One of them was in his fifties. The other was in his eighties, which is astonishing. The male voice doesn't usually last that long.

It was a splendid service. For once, we women could sing the harmonic antiphons and the polyphonic hymns full-throated. Indeed, we had to. Those Dutchmen's' voices filled the chapel.

They came up the hill to John and Susan's for supper, where we gave them places of honor and made sure they had people to talk to. I did the salad. John did the potatoes. Susan A. did the vegetables. Magnus and Blue did staying underfoot in the kitchen, waiting in joyful hope.

After dinner, we went into the living room to sing Compline. Magnus was coming up to me and rubbing against me and trying to scratch his belly in a most undignified manner and causing himself to fall down, so we shut both dogs in the kitchen.

After we sang the final *Salve Regina*, I freed Magnus and Blue and we chatted for a while. Magnus worked the room as usual, except that his legs collapsed every few minutes. Susan said, "He's in trouble."

I said, "I've never seen him so weak." This was new.

Susan said nothing.

She had lost Bosco to cancer two months before. He'd been ill in various ways for several years, and she was expecting it, but his loss grieved her terribly. She watched my man solemnly, and sighed.

When Magnus rejoined us, I started stroking his back, so he laid down and stretched out full length, pulling up his foreleg so I could get to the good places. Massage seems to revive him a bit—if nothing else, he enjoys it, and it's a nice distraction. A couple of the men watched this. I think they were jealous.

Susan A. said, "Not many old men get such good love."

"He deserves it," I said.

"You two have a fine relationship," said one of the men.

The next day, we went to the park for our usual walk. Magnus was a bit wobbly, but basically okay. We ran into some fans of his, who asked after his health. I told them we were still having fun.

I'm giving him his head more often so he can take more pleasure in his walks. He led me to a steep ravine down to the stream—not at the place with the nice big steps, but a bit farther on, at a 60° slope reinforced here and there with cemented sandbags. I checked to see if there was a shallower slope for him to climb up, saw that there was, and let him go down. He drank for a long time, and even waded around the stream, which I'd never seen him do. When he'd had enough, he faced the steep slope. Worried about it a bit. Looked off to his left and noticed a shallower slope, considered it, then climbed the steeper bank out of the ravine. Good days and bad days, but still more good than bad.

Chapter 73　　　　　　　　　　　　　　Bad Days

Last week, we were doing our slow two miles pretty well. Last night we did the same, but with much stumbling and collapsing. Dolly and her Mom met up with us on the green. Dolly greeted Magnus, asked him to play, ran around him and tried to get his interest, but he seemed almost afraid of her, backing away and whimpering. Dolly gave up and ran around by herself in the dark. Every once in a while, she'd come back and try again, but Magnus just stood there, and it was humiliating. DollyMom said, "Dolly, leave him be. He's not up to it tonight."

When he recovered a bit, we walked on, and he decided to go to the ravine for a sip of creek water. DollyMom and I were doubtful. Magnus looked back over his shoulder to smile at me, to see if I was coming. I moved up even with him, to show that the next step was his choice. He went down the stairs to the creek. Dolly ran after him, and ran round the stony creek bed, and ran up the stairs, and ran around in the bush beneath the enormous twisting oaks. Magnus finished drinking, and strode up the slope without a hitch. DollyMom said, "It was like this with Dolly's predecessor. It would seem like she was full of life, and then in a month she went straight down. Just enjoy him while you have him. He's a very special dog."

The next day, as I walked him around the complex for his morning and afternoon stretches, his hindquarters collapsed repeatedly.

Of course, belly-scratching while walking doesn't help—he pretty much throws himself to the ground. But still, his butt sank, and he got a bewildered expression, and turned his face to mine.

What's happening to me?

I'm considering vitamin B12 shots and acupuncture. Susan S. has suggested I try howling at the moon on alternate Wednesdays.

After choir rehearsal, Susan A. asked how Magnus was. I said, "He's not good. If he continues to decline like this, he probably won't make it to Christmas."

"Don't give up. Ask the vet. There must be something."

John interjected. "Try vitamin B12 shots. They're working just fine for me." He cackled.

"I'll ask the vet. But his problem isn't structural."

"The body needs B12 to regenerate nerve tissue. Don't forget folic acid: you can't absorb B12 without it." More cackling. John has a trick of leaning forward and tilting his head to one side when he cackles. It's part of his charm.

"Just don't give up," Susan said. "Try anything."

John called out, "Folic acid!" as I was walking away.

I took Magnus to Dr. Paul, and told him about the collapsing.

"I'm certain he has neuropathy," he said.

"What can we do? Anything?"

"There is no surgical solution. We can try one of two things: inject an anti-inflammatory, or try the B12 shots."

"Why an anti-inflammatory? This is neurological."

"I know," Dr. Paul said, "but for some reason it seems to work."

"Well, he's already on anti-inflammatories, so let's try the B12."

"Okay. He's on a low dose of Rimadyl so you can add a half-tablet at night." Rimadyl is the arthritis medicine.

About six hours after the B12 shot, we met Dolly as we were walking onto the greensward. She ran to Magnus and stood up and put her paws on his chest, and he cantered off with her. They didn't play long, but they played, and did so joyfully.

The B12 is not a panacea—he still has trouble breathing from time to time—but it is slowing the decline and giving him better quality of life. Blood tests also showed that Magnus was hypothyroidic, which contributes to laryngeal paralysis and neuropathy generally, so Dr. Paul added thyroid hormones to the daily mix.

I went back over Magnus's old bloodwork, and saw that the thyroid had been steadily getting lower at each test. I should have intervened earlier. I should have tracked his bloodwork more carefully. No one tells you these things.

CHAPTER 74 — BICYCLE MAN

The combination of B12, folic acid, and thyroid medication had astounding results. Not only did Magnus improve right away, he continues to improve. I haven't seen this much dancing and grinning and cantering since last year. Yee-hah!

We were walking back toward the car, mosquitoes drilling my shoulders in the unseasonable autumn heat, tree peepers chorusing in praise. A bicyclist approached us on the bridge near the green, pedaling slowly. I herded my honey to the edge of the path to let the man pass. He continued straight on at us, staring at Magnus. A lot of riders are hostile to dogs, so I touched Magnus's neck to keep him still. The cyclist veered off at the last minute, saying softly, "Where'd you get the polar bear?"

Chapter 75 — Someone's Out There

In late October, we had just gotten onto the green and were chatting with another dog person when Magnus went on full alert: head up, tail raised, ears forward, stance wide. He gave a deep, loud woof. He stood there staring for several minutes, completely focused, repeating that single woof every few moments.

"Something's there," I said.

"There are goats across the way."

"No, he's used to the goats."

Neither one of us could see a thing.

I know she's out there. Not too close, but close enough.

The next evening, we were crossing the first bridge when Magnus whirled around and ran in the opposite direction. He'd never done that before. I followed. He tried to get under the bridge but was blocked by a fence. He ran around the corner where he knows there is a break in the fence, ran into the ravine, and started searching up and down the creek bank, plunging into the brush, on full alert. He didn't find whatever or whoever he was looking for. All that evening, he repeated this behavior—dashing off, sniffing the ground, raising his head to sniff the air, ears forward, tail up.

When we were on our way back, crossing the bridge at the far end of the path near the holding pond, he sniffed the boards insistently, back and forth and back and forth. He decided to go under the bridge, and there was no fence to block him. I was concerned that he'd slide down and be unable to get up, but reasoned that he could go downhill to the shoreline and climb up elsewhere. He went under the bridge, sniffing, and turned to me with something black and stiff in his mouth.

Squirrel in an advanced state of rigor mortis.

"Drop it!"

He dropped it and scrambled out.

The next night was a milder replay. Whatever scent he had picked up was getting cold.

Last night, we were coming up under tall trees to the same bridge on the return lap of our walk. Magnus was sniffing the shrubbery, and I was on please-don't-eat-any-nasty-stuff watch. I turned away from him and saw what I thought was the silhouette of a small dog at the other end of the bridge, with ears, up on alert, half-crouching and backlit by a streetlamp. There was no dogwalker in sight. I thought, "Someone's let his dog get awfully far away from him." Magnus emerged from the shadows and the dog fled, flashing a thick, bushy tail. All of this happened in a single instant.

I thought of the wolf that terrorized the townspeople of Gubbio in the middle ages. They pleaded for help from Saint Francis, who tamed the wolf by making the sign of the cross and blessing it. I didn't have time to bless the coyote.

Magnus didn't see the coyote—his night vision is getting dim—but he smelled him. On the side of the bridge where the coyote had paused there's a concrete wall built to prevent accidental falls down the steep bank of the marsh. Magnus had been interested in this wall for several weeks. After the coyote fled he paced back and forth along it, straining to see over it. At its lowest point, it came up to his chin. He couldn't get over it. He stared down the slope on the other side of the bridge. After about five minutes, he started pacing the bridge again. This proved futile.

We continued on our way under a moon that was a silver sliver shy of being full. A soft breeze teased us. Something flew over our heads, invisible, calling queeeeeeeee-quee-quee-quee-quee-quee in a treble voice over a deserted park.

Chapter 76 — Onward

Magnus continues to improve. True, if the temperature is over 70° F, he is slower and weaker, but that's always the case.

On cooler nights he canters for joy, trots the first half-mile, continues to break into trotting from time to time, holds his head up, and expresses joy in every lineament of his figure. His trot has regained the old, crisp, bounce. His canter is a little crabwise, but it's firm and well-arched. He slows down a bit as the walk goes on, of course, but finishes in good form. He's dancing from the car to the front door again, and getting air as he wheels around the corner. He's teasing Hammett again—snouting him, faking lunges, getting boisterous when Hammett tries to spend quality time with me. His after-dinner dance is raucous again.

He hasn't been this good since last December.

My happiness is indescribable.

He may make it to fifteen, after all. Knock wood. He'll definitely reach twelve unless he develops another disease—such as cancer, to be realistic. In any event, he's having a grand time, and I'm having a grand time watching him.

Chapter 77 — Cookies and Corpses

I'm drawing the line on eating random rancid delicacies he finds under the bushes—several times lately he has vomited up frothy bile and oak leaves, and you never know if the dead animal has been poisoned or carries germs and parasites. A couple of nights ago, he stayed under the oak trees long enough that I knew he had discovered death's bounty. I called him angrily, went under the leafy umbrella, shouted "Knock it off!" took hold of his halter, and pulled him away. He was startled, betrayed, and ran away from me with a confused look in his eyes.

What? All I was doing was eating something that smelled good. Now you don't want me to eat? What next, hon?

He was wary of me for the rest of the walk. The next day, I worried that he might be ill, sinking. He moped. He walked around with his head down. When I held my arms out to him, he looked at me suspiciously instead of coming into my embrace.

We went out for morning duties. Dan-Dan Cookie Man's doorstep had a cookie offering on it. Magnus approached within three feet of it, looked at the cookie, looked at me, looked at the cookie, looked at me, and didn't take a step. I realized that I'd taught him not to eat stuff on the ground. I guess the distinction between rotten squirrel corpses and bacon-flavored biscuits was not one he could make. I said, "It's okay, go ahead and eat it."

He looked at me, looked at the cookie. Looked at me. I made an inviting gesture towards the cookie. Slowly, he moved toward it, lowered his head, and cautiously ate it, keeping an eye on me. I told him he was a good boy and that I loved him.

We did the necessary business, and went inside for breakfast. I fixed his meal, added the supplements and medications, and set it down on his little feeding rack. He looked at me, looked at the bowl, and so on just as he'd done with the cookie. I encouraged him again, and at length he settled into eating, looking at me from time to time to see if it was still okay to eat stuff on the ground.

I spent the rest of the day hugging and petting him every hour or so, telling him I loved him, and by evening he was himself again. As dusk approached, he asked for his walk in the usual way, slipping his head under my arm to gaze imploringly at me, then going into the living room to toss pillows around with his nose.

We went to the park. Magnus cantered onto the greensward—and did not go under the oaks to sniff out random rancidness. I praised him and gave him a cookie. He danced along lightly, avoiding the bushes, cocking his head at me with his usual smiles.

He'd figured out what I wanted in one try again.

They say dogs have the intelligence of four-year-olds. There is no way a four-year-old would have been able to make that kind of deduction without the benefit of language.

CHAPTER 78   MAGNUS'S BLOODLINE

Magnus was one of Susan's last two champions. When I met her, she wasn't showing any more—it's a rich man's hobby, and she didn't have the funds to keep it up—but she was still breeding. When she neutered her last litter because of the bone disease, she ended her kuvasz bloodline. It was the right decision: in the years since, almost every dog from that litter has died of bone cancer. The only one who survives is the one whose bad genes were expressed in the developmental disorder.

During the ten years she was still showing she produced an astonishingly high number of champions for a small-scale breeder. She had at least one winner every year she entered the Kuvasz Club of America (KCA) and American Kennel Club (AKC) shows, and she often had more than one. She even bred a national champion, Gywndura's Sovereign Quest. My guy is Sovereign Quest's nephew, and his full name is Gwyndura's Quest's Charlemagne. His original family shortened that to Magnus.

In 1996, Susan had an eye on Ederra's Canis Major Arrakis, with a mind to breeding him to Gwyndura's Quest's Bravissima, Sovereign's sister. She got in touch with Major's owner, and they agreed to meet during a show in Albuquerque. Magnus was conceived in a few furtive meetings behind the hotel, and was born on July 12, 1997.

On Major's death in 2003, the Kuvasz Club of America's quarterly magazine carried 12 pages of memorial ads taken out by grateful people who owned his pups. He was one of the outstanding kuvasz sires of all time, and left a long line of successors.

And here when I met Magnus I thought he was a pretty, fluffy dog, and that Susan was an average kind of gal (although certainly not ordinary). She doesn't blow her own horn unless you ask her to, and even then you have to push.

CHAPTER 79   HAMMETT FIGHTS BACK

For ten years had Hammett enjoyed Magnus's current status as king of the hill. Every morning, I woke with him in my arms. When he saw my eyes open, he would stretch his paw slowly toward my cheek and play Claw Mommy's Face. I thought it was cute. I'd grab the paw. He'd reach out again. I'd grab the paw. He'd give me the demure look.

When he played I Can't Get Down off The Roof (yes you can, kiddo), I humored him and brought out the ladder.

When he figured out how to escape through the kitchen window by hooking a claw into the rubber strip on the screen and folding back the wire cloth, I told everyone how clever he was. When I got a movable wood-framed screen to keep his clever claw away from the rubber strip and wedged the screen into the window frame by locking the sliding window hard against it, he immediately learned how to pull the wood frame out. When I positioned the wood frame between the sliding window and the screen and locked the slider down, he rotated it inside the frame to effect his escape the first day. I told everyone he was a genius.

When he played "Sit on Mommy's Book" I put up with it affectionately. For some inexplicable reason these adorable traits lost their appeal in the face of Magnus's policy of appreciation, service, humor, and devotion. This has not escaped the little genius's notice.

Something has to give here. If slobbering all over her works, maybe I should try it.

The other day he did the oddest thing—snuggled against my chest in the morning, purred loudly, and licked my arm. His normal purr is only audible if you press your ear against his chest.

What is this new act?

What is this sitting on the fence outside the kitchen window, when the patio door is open in the back, mewling piteously for me to come and rescue him? (I do, of course.)

What are these new, loud, affectionate greetings, and subsequent hangings around and rubbings against me? His greetings have always been "Oh. You're home. Let me out."

What is this sitting next to my book, or cuddling against my chest while I read, instead of sitting on the book?

What is this not-bothering-me when I'm at the computer?

He hardly ever jumps on the desk to bother me any more. Just sits on the bed beside the computer and dozes politely until I go over to kiss and stroke him.

My neighbor said, "Hammett has been a lot friendlier to me lately." I said, "He wasn't friendly to you before?" She said, "No. He ran away whenever he saw me. Now he lets me pet him."

It's been a year and a half, and I still haven't gotten rid of the competition.

I was wondering when this would crop up. Wouldn't have credited Hammett with the patience to hold out so long. Then again, a big chunk of his intelligence is his persistence.

Meanwhile, if he's willing to be a lot nicer to me, I'm willing to be a lot nicer to him. That's a major concession for a cat to make—especially a piece of work like Hammett.

Chapter 80   Anxiety

Magnus hopped out of the backseat and started trotting to the front door, smiling over his shoulder at me. He suddenly stopped short and hung his head. Then, as if he'd been hit in the head with a mallet, he went down and all four legs splayed out from under him. He tried to pull himself up, straining his neck and forelegs and failing. His hind legs were completely inert. His eyes were huge. His ears were pressed way back. His breathing was rapid and ragged.

    I dropped my things, sank to the ground, began massaging his neck and throat to keep his larynx from tightening up and spoke to him calmly, in a low voice. He looked into my eyes and relaxed. A hot stream of urine flowed out from under his body, soaking the fur. He held my gaze with a look so trusting and calm it broke my heart. A tear slipped out, but I reminded myself that this was not about me. It was about my old man, and I was not to upset him. I just kept telling him I loved him, kissing his snout, and holding him.

    What was I going to do? I couldn't leave him in the parking lot to go get help. I couldn't lift him. I hated the idea of dragging him inside. I thought it was the end. I blessed him with all my heart. He wagged his tail gently and smiled at me. The light slowly came back in his eyes. We loved each other silently for a while.

    I stood up and collected my things. I said, "Come on, Magnus."

    He got up, and walked slowly to the front door. We went in. He lay down on his rug. I got a bucket of warm water and some facecloths and bathed his belly and legs. That felt good. The rear leg got going in sympathy with the scrubbing. I dried him off.

    All afternoon, I checked in on him from time to time to see if he was still breathing. He was. As he lay napping, his legs twitched, playing with Dolly in his dreams. As dusk drew on, he got up and asked for his walk. He teased Hammett and tossed pillows around with his snout. I was afraid to take him out, so we went to the yard under the redwoods for duties. He did the rocking-horse canter, the trot, the diving and pawing at the ground, the head-butting and leg-leaning—all his little games. I looked at him in wonder. Why was I surprised? He'd always bounced back before.

I had a piece of cold steak for dinner. I cut off the gristly bits, went to the door my man was guarding, and gave him each bit in turn. He followed me back to the table and watched me expectantly. I cut and chewed. I took the last bite between my teeth, and bent down to give it to him with a cookie-kiss. He took it with is teeth, very gently.

I like to think that it was my love for him, and his love for me, that revived him.

Lesson 10: Never give up on your man.

These episodes will recur. I'm going to carry a tarp and the cell phone in the fanny pack when we go walking. If he goes down mid-walk and can't get back up, I will roll him onto the tarp, and call Jean to send a couple of the girls to help me carry him back to the car and get him in it. When we get home I'll find Dan or Jesus or someone to help me carry him in—if he hasn't recovered by then. We'll manage.

CHAPTER 81   THANKSGIVING

I overslept, probably because I stayed up late making stuffing and bread dough for sticky buns. Then again, I wasn't exactly eager to drive the 70 miles to Manteca, do a Nan-Can-Cook exhibition, and drive the 70 miles home in Thanksgiving traffic. Besides, I hate being a portable relative—the one who never hosts, but always visits. The one who always has to pack up the car with gifts and food to make the holiday circuit. I put up with this for a couple of decades, and then solved the problem once and for all by moving 3,000 miles away.

But Amy lobbied me hard to go to Diane's for the holiday. "Biggie can come," she said. "We're bringing the boys, and Diane has a border collie that is trained to assist her. It'll be a very dog-friendly day."

"What are you planning to have for dinner?"

"Well, turkey, of course. We found a new recipe in *Cook's Illustrated* that we want to try. Stuffing. Mashed potatoes."

"I can make southern-style green beans, with bacon."

"Yum."

"And cinnamon buns. It's not a holiday for me without those."

"That will make Skip very, very, happy."

"Do you want me to make the stuffing?"

"How do you make it?"

"Oh, I just do a traditional bread-and-celery type thing. Fresh rosemary. Water chestnuts for crunch."

"Sounds perfect."

"When do you want me to be there?"

"Any time."

"Come on, Amy."

"Okay, come about noon. We'll be eating at four. Do you remember how to get there?"

"Not really. Give me the address and I'll Google it."

She gave the address as Espana Street. Google Maps didn't find it. Skip said to call when I got to Manteca and he'd guide me from there.

The holiday traffic was vicious. The last fifty miles were stop and go, up to seventy mph, slam on the brakes, sit a while, creep a while. I succeeded in picking the wrong lane every time I had a choice.

No radio, no company. Magnus was sleeping, and besides, we know he's a man of few words. I got to Manteca. Skip gave me directions: look for Best Fit, and take the next left. After several miles I started passing endless orchards and reasoned that I'd missed Espana. Amy called. "Where are you? You should have been here fifteen minutes ago."

"I decided to go to Yosemite. It was Magnus's idea." She laughed. I said, "I turned around a few minutes ago."

"Go back until you see Best Fit. It's right before the entrance to the 90. Diane's street is the one just before it on the right."

"Okay."

I did as I was told. I saw Best Fit, but no Espana. I turned around and saw that the street beside Best Fit was labeled Pestana.

Close enough.

Skip was standing outside when I drove up, and helped me carry things in. He pointed out that my tires were under-inflated. Magnus trotted to the door expectantly, and was greeted by a surly Border collie and the two yipping Maltese. Diane tried to greet me and chat, but all the dogs were in an uproar—except Magnus, who, of course, was perfect. The Border collie, Cindy, kept her head next to my man's and growled at him continuously. She wouldn't leave him be.

It's her house. I don't really blame her. Whose idea was it to include the yappy ones?

I went into the kitchen, gave Amy a big hug, and started forming the sticky buns as fast as I could go—I was so late that the bird was already done. Diane came back in to the kitchen in her wheelchair—she has MS—and tried to talk to me again. The dogs were still riled up so it took me a while to understand that Magnus had already marked one of the bedroom floors. I grabbed paper towels and went off to clean up his super-sized trail of pee. He watched me while Cindy stood next to him with her head low and her neck stretched out, still growling.

I went back into the kitchen, cut up the bacon, started slow-cooking it, and returned to forming sticky buns. Roll out the dough as thinly as possible, spread it with melted butter, sprinkle cinnamon sugar on it generously, roll it up tightly from one end to the other, pinch the seam shut, cut it into one-inch slices and put them into a pan lined with brown sugar and butter. I only know how to make big batches, so we made three pans of buns. Meanwhile, we'd scooped the stuffing into loaf pans to warm it up and dry it out—it seemed a bit wet to me.

Diane's brother showed up with a Queensland heeler and a mutt who looked like a Queensland heeler. Six dogs now. New cases of nerves all around. Jasper renewed his barking fit. Cindy was still growling at Magnus. Magnus escaped to the patio, left another very large watermark, and topped it off with a super-sized poop. He came back in, holding himself in check against the general canine clamor. Cindy kept growling at him. The Queenslands were submissive and kowtowed to him, shuddering. Jasper ran back and forth, and barked and barked and barked and barked. Cupcake found a safe place on the back of the sofa and sat there solemnly, above the fray. Skip said the bacon was done. I poured off the fat, and got the package of fresh Vericots Verts out of the refrigerator. Green beans started falling on the floor.

"Oh. The bag is already open," Amy said.

"I see."

The beans on the floor disappeared in a whipping of tails.

I washed the remaining beans, laid them on top of the bacon, added a cup of chicken broth, and left them simmering.

Diane's brother was holding forth at length on the fish he'd caught and the crabs he'd caught and the feasts he'd held in Half Moon Bay. Amy and Diane humored him with polite questions and comments. He then held forth at length about carving a turkey with an electric knife. Skip said, "I've never used an electric knife. It's a good thing you're here," with a straight face. The patriarch was in.

Cindy went on growling at Magnus. Magnus was going into mental conflict mode. His ears were back, and his head was up, and his neck was tense, and I could almost see him vibrate. He wanted to correct Cindy's bad manners, but knew it wasn't his turf. I tried gently scruffing Cindy behind Diane's back and telling her to settle, but she was in command of her domain, and ignored me. As, of course, she should have.

Skip was plating potatoes, bread, and turkey, and pouring gravy into the gravy boat. Amy was making the salad. Diane's brother was asking everyone what he or she wanted to drink—grape juice or wine. I said, "Scotch." Amy and Skip laughed.

Mormons don't run to Scotch.

Diane said, "Magnus stays right with you, doesn't he?"

Cindy stayed right with Magnus.

I checked the stuffing. It was a boiling fluid. Skip passed by carrying dinner rolls and looked over my shoulder.

"We don't have to serve it," he said.

"We'd better not."

The beans were done, so we all sat down and started passing dishes. Skip said a meandering, improvised, Mormon patriarch's grace. The dogs settled on the floor around the table. We ate, ignoring them. The food was good. Diane's brother continued to hold forth over dinner on various topics. Amy said, "Nancy, Diane is trying to talk to you." I couldn't hear her, of course. Her voice is not as big as her brother's. I turned to her and tried to converse, but my mind is strictly monaural, and I just couldn't follow. She understood.

Before we even pushed back our chairs after dinner, Diane's brother said, "Well, I'm off. Thanks for all the great food." As he and his dogs went out the door, Diane gave me a sideways look and murmured, "Off to the office."

"The bar," Amy said.

"He calls the bar his office?" I asked.

That explained a lot.

We put the sticky buns in the oven, and started cleaning up and packing food away. Amy found a grasshopper pie and cut tiny slices for herself and Diane. Diane's home health care worker came back from her own holiday party, and slouched around with a loud, anxious Chihuahua in her arms, which didn't help the dog situation any. I started doing dishes. Skip passed by and said, *sotto voce*, "There's someone here who is paid for doing that," nodding his head in the Chihuahua woman's direction. I finished cleaning my own pans and bowls and left the kitchen.

"Are the sticky buns done yet?"

"I'll check them," I said. They were sitting in the oven, doing nothing. Skip walked past and looked over my shoulder. "The oven isn't on, " he said. "*Someone* must have turned it off after she did the dishes." He turned it back on. I gathered there were issues with the home health care lady.

Twenty minutes later we were eating hot, steamy, caramel-covered buns. We divvied up the leftovers. And then Amy, Skip, and I left to caravan back to the Peninsula. Just before the highway there was a cheap gas station we'd agreed to stop at. Skip slotted the nozzle into his car, then came over and said, "I want to fill up your tires properly, Nancy. I know you can do it, but I want to."

I used to bristle at this stuff. I didn't understand that men like to be helpful, to feel useful, until long past the time it might have done me any good in a relationship. I don't bristle anymore. I said, "Thank you, Skipper. That's so sweet."

Once out on the highway, the Skipper lost me in no time. He had radar detectors. I didn't.

Magnus flopped onto the back seat and fell asleep immediately. He snored and snuffled and took Cindy down properly in his dreams all the way home.

Chapter 82 — Risky Business

The next day, Magnus was exhausted from the strain, and his legs were wobbly. I was fairly beat myself. We went to the park, but turned back a little more than halfway, and went home to rest.

As a result, my beloved was very perky on Saturday. The coyote had clearly been through the park again, because Magnus kept veering off on new scents, backtracking, going over the same ground. He was calm when we passed Coyote Bridge, which surprised me. When we came back to it on the return leg, I thought he looked tired, sat down under the streetlight, and held out my arms. "Com'ere, Magnus."

Me, pass up a love moment? Not likely.

I folded him in my arms for a bit, then started to massage his neck, trying to quiet his breathing.

You're treating me like an invalid again. I won't tolerate this.

He pulled away from me irritably and eyed the old oak tree that stands among its stripling children on the north side of the bridge where the marshy creek flows into the pond.

There's definitely something interesting in there.

I watched him push through the young scrub. I thought that he might slide down the steep bank to the water. I knew the water there wasn't deep. I figured if he slipped down, I'd go to the waterline and call to give him direction.

I can't reach it. I'll have to try from the other side.

Magnus came out of the brush, and then went around it and down the bank.

I still can't reach it. It smells good and strong. I'll try again from above.

He drove up the steep clay bank and went into the coppice from a different angle. I heard rustling leaves and sliding noises. I heard scrabbling. I heard silence.

Dread gripped my heart.

I went down to the waterline as fast as I could without slipping on the slick clay.

Shit. I'm in the water. Can I pull myself out? No, it's too sheer. Shit, shit, shit. Now what shall I do?

In normal circumstances Magnus wouldn't use such language, but you know how he feels about water. Down by the shore, I heard him whimper, once, softly. I heard him breathing. He was very, very close. I went along the bank as far as I could, shined my little windup flashlight around, saw nothing, and called his name.

I hear her, but I can't tell where she is. There is too much echo here. I can't see. I can't smell in this water.

Suddenly there was no sound. No breathing. No splashing. I went back up the bank, forced myself through the scrub brush, scratching my arms—and very nearly fell off a precipice. Hidden behind what turned out to be a mini-islet, the creek bank had been sliced off vertically and reinforced by a concrete retaining wall. Teetering back and forth, windmilling my arms, I managed not to fall into the muck. I leaned over it and played the flashlight as far as it would go. Nothing. No sound. I ran up to the bridge, and played the flashlight around the water line of the marsh. Nothing. "Irresponsible! Irresponsible! You idiot. You've lost the dog. You've lost the dog. How are you going to explain that to Susan?" I went to the south side of the bridge and turned the flash on the waterline there. Nothing.

Silence.

Did he have a seizure and drown?

I refused to believe this. I knew that motivation, such as the desire to counter a threat or tease a cat, extracted extraordinary powers from mysterious reserves. I began to pray.

I went across from the pond to the marsh, which goes in a great curve away from the bridge. I went as close to the edge as I dared, and wound up the flashlight as fast as I could to get the most light. I saw what looked like a white tree trunk on the far side of the bend in the creek. I thought I saw it move. I had no idea if I could get over there—all I could see where I stood was the bank and the old oaks growing on it. It was too steep for me to climb down in my clogs.

Where is she? Can she see me? Can she smell me? What is going to happen to me? My heart feels like it's going to burst. I can't seem to get enough air. I can't move.

I went to the protective wall and peered over. The bank was topped by a level path about five feet wide. I went along it easily, searching the bank for whiteness, and finally saw him, in an oddly erect sitting posture about fifty yards from the bridge. He whimpered softly, once. He was at the foot of a good-sized oak. I slid down to the tree. The clay was like cold grease, and the angle of the bank was at least 45°. It felt like 60°. My clogs wouldn't grip it. Holding onto the trunk and some exposed roots, I lowered myself to the water's edge, and was very happy to find a tiny patch of wet grass that offered enough traction to give me some footing. Magnus's back was to me. I put my arms around him. He was rigid and soaked and gritty with mud and breathing extremely harshly.

She's here. She's here. She's here. Oh, she's here.

He sank back against my chest, and laid his head against my neck. I held him tightly, massaging his throat, telling him "I love you, it's okay" as I assessed the situation.

I knew you'd come. You'd never let me down.

I already had let him down, of course.

His hind legs were tangled in thick, exposed roots. The right leg was stretched out straight between two of them. He had his front paws on higher roots, and had been straining to haul himself upward, but his position was too vertical and his hind legs were too tangled up to stand and push. I couldn't stand to help him out either, because the bank was so slick. I had to turn him around from the half-reclining position I was in. His breathing was calm by this time, so I palpated that right hind leg. No reaction. It was either paralyzed or okay. I chose okay, and gently worked it out from between the roots. As soon as it was free, he took weight on both hind legs, straining upward. I gently eased his shoulders to the right, trying to turn his body towards me.

She wants me to turn around.

He turned around, and started trying to haul himself out of his hole under the roots. He hadn't the strength.

I was glad I'd put the halter on him. I'd actually considered doing without it, because I knew no one would be in the park the Saturday night after Thanksgiving, but for once discretion got the better part of vanity. I took hold of the harness with one hand, bracing myself against the roots with the other, and with every ounce of strength I had—he was a bit above me, and I had to lift him up over my head—I hauled him free. He scrambled onto the clay bank, and scooted up away from the water so fast it would have been funny if I hadn't been so horrified by what had almost happened. Once on the level path, he turned to examine my position.

Now, what's my Nan going to do? She doesn't have claws to dig in the clay. I do love her to pieces, but there's no way I'm going back down there.

I managed to turn myself around and shove myself far enough up to find a small crevice in the trunk. First handhold. I saw a smallish root, and tugged on it to see whether it would bear. It didn't. There followed some hands-and-knees scrabbling, but I did manage to get to the far side of the trunk, pushed off from there to reach the top, and then collapsed on all fours, panting from exertion and weeping in relief. Magnus came over and kissed me on the cheek.

That was a bit close, wasn't it?

We headed back to the bike path. Under the streetlight, I watched his gait. A little wobbly, but not bad considering the exertion and the panic he'd just been through. Within a few yards, he settled into a steady rhythm and a steady gait. He smelled coyote again, and started trotting back and forth over the ground. He kept this up all the way to the car, which was about a mile off.

Huh.

Mysterious reserves of strength.

We were both sore the next day, so we rested. We did go to Vespers and Sunday dinner, though, and told the company about our adventure. I expected some censure for taking such a risk with a dog who had been collapsing and having seizures, but no one said anything except "He's lucky to have you."

The next time we passed Coyote Bridge, I went to the bank of the pond, where Magnus often takes a mid-walk drink, and invited him to go down to the water. He stood in the path, on alert, head cocked, watching me. I asked again if he'd like to get a drink.

You're out of your mind. Get away from there. It's dangerous.

Good thing one of us has sense.

Chapter 83 — La Luna

Everyone back in New England says that California has no seasons. It's not true, of course. It's just that the seasons are a lot subtler here. They don't slam you with ice storms or months of sloppy mud or sleepless Augusts of suffocating heat and towering thunderstorms or the heartbreakingly brief glory that is July.

Because of all that weather, I was largely unaware of the phases of the moon in New England. On the rare nights when the moon was up and the cloud cover was off, it was glorious. But I didn't develop an intimate daily relationship with her until Magnus started getting me outside every evening, and I saw her almost every night she was out. Where she was, how she moved, how she lit the landscape, how she bleached the night sky and blinded the stars.

I've drawn close to La Luna. I love the delicate slim sliver of the new moon with the faint image of the rest of her illumined by soft reflections from places on earth where the sun is still shining. I love the fact that when that new moon is near to the horizon, it looks almost horizontal, like a soup bowl. When it's nearer to the zenith, it stands more upright, and looks like an archer's bow.

I watch that strip of light advance by degrees across the moon, night by night. It grows amazingly fast, stunningly fast, and suddenly the full moon gives so much light that you can see the green of the grass and the trees and the shadows become impossibly black, an utter negation of light, and Magnus's coat catches scattered photons and glows as he moves under the trees.

If you check the moon's position against the backdrop of the stars at the same time every night, you'll see that it moves slightly to the west from night to night. That shows its movement through its orbit.

As for why the moon rises at different times on different days, and why it rises 39 minutes later on Tuesday than it did on Monday, and 29 minutes later on Thursday than Wednesday, NASA says its orbit is eccentric—it varies tremendously in altitude. And since orbiters orbit faster when they're closer to us, and slower when they're farther away, its speed is erratic, too.

But too much data kills the romance. Tonight the moon will be a perfect half-circle, and I'm looking forward to greeting her, and basking in reflected glory as she tugs on the tides of my heart.

Chapter 84 Lights and Music

Kathy and Mike asked us to meet them and a bunch of FOMFOK people at Sunnyvale depot to see the Christmas train. FOMFOK stands for Friends of Mike, Friends of Kathy—their hiking club.

Yes, Michael knows what that sounds like. He did it on purpose.

"What's the Christmas Train?"

"It's an old Pullman sleeper that the Salvation Army takes from San Francisco to Yosemite every year. They cover it with lights and decorations, and stop at every town on the line to play Christmas songs on a stage in the middle of the train."

"Sounds cute."

"It's very cute. After the train, we're going to walk around the neighborhood and look at the lights."

This is a big draw—people in their neighborhood have a very competitive spirit when it comes to holiday decoration. Two next-door neighbors have been collaborating for years on a display with figures that move and lights that flash in time to music. It's so well done that people take buses from The City thirty miles away to see and hear it.

It being a Saturday night, Jean and I were going to have dinner together, so I called and suggested that we eat first, then go to the train and look at the lights. She was game, and her 17-year-old daughter Laura asked if she could come too.

"You'll have to sit in the back seat with Magnus. Is that okay?"

"I don't mind."

Laura is a little blond elf who wears quietly creative clothes and long knitted scarves. She climbed into the back seat, gently moved Mr. Biggie to make room, had him sit up next to her, and put her arm around his shoulders. He looked bigger than she did. He started giving her a facial with his tongue, which she apparently enjoyed.

In Sunnyvale, we followed the trail of families streaming to the depot. I hadn't had Magnus in a big crowd for a long time, and hadn't really thought about it, but did get a little apprehensive when I realized we had to walk among people packed shoulder to shoulder with children riding piggyback on their parents. Magnus immediately whipped out his and cravat and his cummerbund, put them on, and went into Ambassador mode. Men took out their cameras and slyly took my-camera's-at-my-waist-I'm-not-really-photographing-your-dog shots. Parents called out to their children, "Polar bear! Come see the polar bear."

"Can I take a picture of my son with your dog?"

"What a beautiful animal. Can she pet him?"

"He's so sweet!"

"Polar bear!"

Magnus licked their faces, stood patiently for pictures, and went on to meet child after child. People lined up to get pictures with him. After about twenty minutes of this, Jean said, not entirely sarcastically, "I think I know how you could make some holiday cash."

This reminds me of my youth. The crowds, the shouting, the overlapping scents, the applause.

We worked our way up and down the platform, threading through families, looking for Kathy and Mike, who should have been easy to find with all those FOMFOKers. They weren't. We should have been easy to find too, with the stir we were creating, but they didn't see us either.

The train pulled in with a whistle and a hoot, recorded music filled the air, lights flashed and blinked in festoons and big red-and-white-striped plastic candy canes and trees and snowflakes and other pagan iconography all along the train. People in reindeer, elf, bear, and Santa costumes with oversized heads waddled down the steps to the platform and merged into the crowd for photo ops, handing out red-and-white striped candy canes made of sugar instead of lights. The Salvation Army band assembled on a stand built on a flatcar in the middle of the train and began their polka-style renditions of holiday classics.

On our second loop I saw Mike, rosy and wreathed in fogs of cheery chatter, round face shining, bearish body wrapped up in high-tech cold-weather gear. He held out his arms, and we bumped bellies and squeezed each other. Mike is the only man I allow to give me full frontal hugs. Everyone said hello to Magnus. A few people even said hello to me. Strangers kept stopping to meet Magnus, asking the usual questions, and taking pictures of him with their kids, so we were constantly interrupted, but no one seemed to mind. The FOMFOK folk were mellow. Jean and Laura stood by, smiling peaceably.

We milled around together, listening to the band. We wished some Silicon Valley entrepreneur had thought to set up a hot chocolate stand. It felt festive to be outside, warmly dressed, on a cold night. When the music was over, Kathy and Mike and company started walking back to their neighborhood. Jean was tired—as who wouldn't be after spending the week chasing six-year-old monsters around and trying to get them to absorb at least the basics of readin' writin' and 'rithmetic—and Magnus couldn't walk that far anyway, so we drove to the competitive Christmas displays district.

You couldn't see the stars for the ground constellations. Some displays were restrained, traditional, tasteful. Most were gleefully garish, with figures and lights gleaned from the couturiers of Walmart, Costco, and other purveyors of Chinese crafts.

The set piece, the adjoining houses of engineers who didn't waste their spare time, was a tour de force. These guys actually invented icicle lights years ago by stapling loops of white lights to strips of wood and attaching them to the eaves of their houses. That was just the beginning. Now they have broad bands of colored lights in alternating colors spiraling up the telephone poles and around the trunks of trees. They've strung globes and stars from boughs. They've woven varicolored lights into their matching hedges in diagonal patterns. They've draped casual skeins of colored lights along their foundation plantings, built an arbor surrounded by illuminated candy canes and lollipops, and peopled the lawns with robotic white-light deer. They put a really big reindeer on the peak of one of the houses. They've programmed every bulb and figure to flash and move in time to music. That evening it was 'fifties swing music and swing-inspired carols and songs playing over a local-area radio station they set up.

A small bus pulled up, radio tuned to the homegrown station. Cars prowled slowly by. People lined the sidewalks. Magnus was in the car—I didn't think he'd like standing around, and I didn't like to think what the stroboscopic lights might do to his central nervous system. We parked on a side street and got out.

The musicological elements of Jean's central nervous system lit up like the displays. I could practically see sparks coming out of her head. Her eyes grew wide. Her mouth went into O mode. She ecstatically pointed out the way different lights expressed different instruments.

"See the reindeer on the roof? He's the vocals. The lights on the hedges are the brass. Those candy canes are the drums, see?" We stood there until the repertory started to repeat—about forty-five minutes. "I can't believe how well they've coordinated the music and lights. Imagine the hours they must have spent programming this!" Her cheeks were flushed, her eyes were gleaming, and she was practically dancing as she pointed out smart details.

I'm usually only good for about fifteen minutes of this stuff, but that night I liked the music—fifties dance-hall swing is my favorite form of pop—and belatedly realized I'd never understood what the engineers were doing. That's why we need friends who are smarter than we are. Or at least know different things.

I got revved up, and started studying the patterns. I particularly liked the effects for the brass sections—great blares of white and gold in timed waves across the hedges—and the bass line striding up and down the telephone poles. The strobe lights in the trees were too much for me, but then I'm easily over-stimulated.

After we toured the neighborhood and revisited the uber swing display, Jean allowed me to drag her back to the car and bring the evening to an end. We had to sing in the morning.

Chapter 85 Night Herons

I'd always assumed that the large, squawking birds that swoop out of the trees around the greensward at night were crows. On a clear, cold night with a full moon, as we were coming back into the park at the end of our walk, one of the big birds settled on a bare branch just above us, and La Luna illuminated its long yellow legs and white belly. "Snowy egret!" I thought. "I didn't know they roosted in trees." I looked into the branches of all the deciduous trees, and saw a number of hunched avian silhouettes roosting in the bare branches. As we passed, I shined the flashlight on them to see what they were, and they fled with great beatings of their two-foot long wings to keep their identities to themselves.

On following nights, as the moon waned, I watched the birds' silhouettes against the sky. They certainly weren't snowy egrets, because their necks were short and thick. Their numbers steadily increased. So many eventually gathered in the greensward that they roosted in redwoods and live oaks, not just the bare-branched ash trees, and flew and swooped over our heads noisily, sweeping their wings forward and together, almost as though they were clapping hands as they took off.

A few nights later, I saw several birds sitting on the grass. They flurried and floated up to the trees when they saw us, which was immediately, but I thought I saw a pinkish grey color on their backs. For some reason, I thought of night herons. I had never seen one and didn't know what they looked like, but these birds had heron legs and beaks, and were obviously nocturnal. The next Saturday Jean came out with us, and I asked her what she thought they were. She said, "Night herons." We stood for a while watching them against the pale, overcast sky.

It's actually lighter in the park when the sky is overcast, because the city lights reflect back to the ground from the clouds.

I went online and searched for night herons. The photos matched the silhouettes I'd seen, and the maps showed that they live along the central California coast year-round. I learned that they prefer habitats on the verge of water, hunting fish and amphibians among the reeds and weeds at night, and sometimes settle in fields (or city parks). I couldn't imagine what they found to eat in the park, especially at the opposite end from the pond, but there must have been enough grubs or tree frogs or other damp creatures to feed them all.

As the days passed we started to see them sitting on the ground under the streetlights as we pulled in. Definitely night herons. Crowds of them, black-crested ones at that, staring into our headlights stolidly. I paused awhile, studying them, then parked and got out of the car, at which they all took off with a booming rush of laboring wings. Cars are not as scary as Magnus and I are.

The trees were full of them, and the air was full of them, and dozens were standing around the greensward, taking off in small groups as we walked on, before we could reach them.

And then one night they were gone. Maybe the grubs ran out. Maybe it was a marshalling place for an extended flock that had plans for a group migration. Maybe they just got bored.

We'll never know.

Chapter 86 — Sorry Season

A few days before Christmas, my old man's legs were so shaky again that he could barely stand. He seemed better by evening, so I took him to the park, where he fell again and again and again. We made it back to the car, but he didn't ask to go down the steps for a drink in the creek, and I had to help him into the car. I cried all the way home. I cried all evening, gazing at him.

I'm worried about her. I'd best stay as near as I can, poor thing.

I woke up with my eyes swollen half shut, looked in the mirror, and said, "Don't cry about it. It's bad for the dog. Do something about it instead." I decided to double his dose of thyroid meds and get him another shot of B12.

We ran out of Magnus Mealz, and I couldn't bring myself to make more. I didn't want to have to face a freezer full of unused packages. I went to the pet store, selected a high-grade canned food, and bought six cans. He liked it. He even schlooped while I dished it out. The kids loved it, and demanded their share.

I cried when I saw the big bag of Missing Link in the refrigerator, anticipating having to look at it after he was gone. I cried when I saw the poop bags in the closet, because they would remind me of my love after he was gone. I cried when I saw fluffy drifts of white fur floating in corners. I decided that when he was gone I'd use the grief energy to clean the house thoroughly. (I shouldn't have waited another day on that one. The place was a shambles.)

I cut down the length of the walks. I watched his hindquarters to see if he was tired, and encouraged him to sit with me and let me hold him if he looked shaky. He stopped going down to the creek.

She really isn't well. She's moving more and more slowly, and she needs to sit down and rest more often.

I started an intense campaign of spoiling my baby-love. He got rawhide chews—and was very jealous and possessive of them. My nobleman, walking around with a chew in his powerful jaws, trying to hide it from the cats, disappearing upstairs to devour it in peace. He got cookies for no reason. He got lots of lovin'. I spent more time playing with him on the commons, doing lots of bad lambie and making him laugh and nuzzle me and lean on me and trot around after me.

He started doing a pretend canter. His forelegs and back were into it, but his hind legs weren't. He rocked his body, and believed he was cantering because he was sending the messages to his legs and couldn't feel the lack of response. I didn't tell him otherwise because it was good to see the joy.

He developed new idiosyncrasies, such as having to walk all around the carport until he found an empty spot to walk through instead of just coming up from behind the car and hopping in. I found him in the bathtub one morning, staring at the faucet. That's not his favorite place—although those avocado oil massages may have changed his mind. Once I was hanging my head over the edge of the tub, washing my hair, and he tried to climb in with me.

He began to have occasional terrors. One night his legs got caught in the seatbelt as he climbed out of the car, and he stopped and trembled violently, and I had to hold him for several minutes until he calmed down. I finally realized he was completely night blind, and started using the flashlight to show him the way.

His terror when the complex's fire alarm went off just as we passed it one morning was more understandable. I knew how to disarm it, and did, but he vibrated with fear and shock for at least ten more minutes. I did make a round of the buildings to see if there was any smoke, even though that thing goes off if someone takes a shower with the bathroom door ajar or burns toast. It's so sensitive that none of us believe there's a real fire when it goes off, which is probably not a prime safety feature.

He started sleeping in. I would get up, leave him sprawled across the bed, leave the shades down, dress quietly and go downstairs. He would follow in half an hour or so.

He started to eat around the kibbles, and to leave half the food in his dish. This was serious. Magnus not eating?

Chapter 87 — Cyndi's 2nd Visit

Cyndi paid us her annual visit at the beginning of January, forewarned of Magnus's state. "I can see the old man in him more strongly than I did *last* year," she said. "But he's *not* as badly off as you've been making out." He was walking slowly along, head low.

I said, "You're probably right. He's walking. He's happy. That's all that matters."

Right. Liar.

She was getting over the flu, had been having health and heavy family responsibilities for months, and was in a low state herself, so we planned to do as little as possible. Just hang and talk and pet the critters. We did go for sushi, of course, but had plain nigiri sushi, not too much of it, and only a little saké, and went to bed fairly early.

When I woke up, I smelled coffee, and knew Cyndi was downstairs. I went down—in my red flannel doggie pajamas, of course—and we made breakfast and chatted and lazed around, until we noticed that it was a splendid day and unseasonably warm, and I said, "Let's go to the beach!"

"Oh, yes, let's!" Being a typical female, it took Cyndi about 45 minutes to get ready. I am not a typical female. I get out the door in fifteen minutes. I don't do makeup or style my hair, of course, and don't fuss over what to wear. I pulled on jeans and layered on a couple of jerseys, got Magnus into his harness, and sat in the patio in the sun, waiting impatiently for Cyndi.

At length we got into the car. Magnus settled into his red brocade blanket, and Cyndi asked how long it had been since I'd vacuumed the upholstery. Hey, I scraped off the top layer of dirt and dust the day before, what did she want? "My standards have dropped, I'm afraid."

"Yes, I can see that," she said dryly.

"It's a dog car now. It's impossible to keep it clean or even get it truly clean. So there you go."

I took the scenic route over the hill again, winding through the intricately rounded and canyoned coastal range, through stands of fantastically twisted live oaks and red-skinned madrone and sky-reaching, long-leafed, spicy-smelling bay laurel trees, and then breaking out into meadows at a summit cloaked in green from winter rains, each curve presenting a new vista. "I see the ocean!" Cyndi said, and there it glittered.

"I've never actually seen the water from here," I said. "It's not usually so clear." It really was a fine day.

We curved and hairpinned downward, through deep-shaded stands of Douglas fir and Sequoia Semper Virens with ferny fens where little streams flow after the rain, and the fog feeds the Spanish moss in the branches and the lichens on the rocks, and you expect to see long-haired men in beards and broad hats, suspenders and boots step out holding little hashish pipes or sacks of fresh-picked marijuana in their resinous hands. But somehow that never happens. At least, not when I go there.

Down and down we went until we began to see the horse and flower and vegetable farms that line the coast, and a long straight road led us toward the pale winter sun and then into a little village, Pescadero, founded by Portuguese fishermen and frequented by day trippers. Its shops offer a curious mixture of yuppie gourmet goods for us and Kraft mac and cheese and Cheerios for the real people. We got water and ginger ale for Cyndi, sugar-free iced tea and an incredible flaky, buttery cinnamon pastry for me (I'm all for daytripper gourmet goods). We let Magnus get out and stretch and pee. Cyndi and I sat in little wrought iron chairs between a couple of big, old-timey barrels. I said, "This is probably his last trip to the beach," and started to cry again.

Cyndi put her arm around my shoulders. "It doesn't happen overnight, Nancy. He has plenty of life left in him."

"But it's neurological. He's not going to get better."

"He's not that bad. Enjoy him while you have him."

"I'm trying. But at this rate, I think it's a matter of days or weeks before he crosses some threshold of function, and can't walk at all."

"That's not how it works. He'll go up and down for a while. Just because it's been coming at a certain rate, doesn't mean it will continue at the same rate."

"That hadn't occurred to me." I felt slightly comforted, but didn't really believe her. I did manage to shut off the tears, though.

We got to Montero beach just as the sun touched the sea. We stayed on top of the cliff to watch. I'd never seen a Pacific sunset through an absolutely clear sky—there's almost always some fog—so this was special. The sun was a deep golden red. As it sank beneath the horizon, the ocean acted as a lens, and magnified the light into a lozenge of gold that was refracted through the crests of the waves. The sun sank lower; the glow grew deeper; and for a long moment after the sun was down that red-gold bar glowed through the water.

We went down the long, steep, irregular stairs to the beach. The stairs were littered with tasty horse buns. Magnus snapped one up. (It came out two days later in almost exactly the same condition as it went in.) There weren't too many dogs or people, so I let Magnus off leash. We walked to the water's edge. Cyndi took pictures of the satiny patterns of tender violet and coral light on the wet, rippled sand. Magnus was not happy so close to the water, so he took off up the beach to the clay cliffs, and since it wasn't wading weather I followed through the soft, heavy sand. Cyndi stayed on the shore with her camera for a while, taking stealth pictures of Magnus and me hugging and walking and kissing in the rosy dusk. She rejoined us, and we all started looking for fossil rocks and sea glass, which Cyndi likes to collect.

When people began lighting fires we decided to head back to the car, with Magnus taking a decisive lead.

Good idea, ladies. Let's go.

We came to the foot of the stairs. Cyndi and I looked at each other.

"I didn't think about that," I said.

"I wonder if he can manage it," said Cyndi.

"If he has trouble, I'll stop and rest him. If he needs help, well, that's what the harness is for."

He looked at the steps, looked at me, and then launched himself up one step after another, stumbling a bit, but moving along just fine.

Chapter 88 High Technology

My windup flashlight wound down and died. I put it in the recycling bowl, and wended my way back to Walgreen's for a replacement. They had battery-powered LED flashlights. They had windup LED flashlights with built-in radios. All I wanted was a windup flashlight.

I left without purchases and went to Radio Shack. They had battery-powered LED flashlights. They had wind-up LED flashlights with built-in radios. Not being a patient shopper, and needing a flashlight that night, I asked to see one. A plump, pretty young lady with long dark hair led me to a display and handed me one. It not only had AM and FM radio, it also had a siren function that included two tiny red flashing lights; a USB cable with a plug for recharging your cell phone; terminals for a nine-volt battery; and on the wind up handle, a tiny compass.

I figured this was going to cost $45. It cost $9.95. I was defeated in my search for simplicity. I bought the over-engineered toy.

The alarm, I found, could actually be heard from as far away as ten yards. It didn't startle Magnus, not even the first time he heard it. He sort of noticed it. I liked the little red flashing lights. They are probably visible for more than ten yards. Say fifteen. I haven't figured out how I can use the compass, since it's on the side away from the LEDs, and of course once I take my trusty windup flashlight out, it's too dark to read the tiny letters or see the skinny compass needle.

In any case, if I want to get a good upper body workout, I can wind up my new multi-function tool as we walk, listen to the faint buzz of talk radio, try to scare off bats with the alarm, charge my cell phone, and stop under the park lights to read the compass and see which way is north. I suppose it would be easier to look at the

Big Bear and find the North Star by following the line of his front legs to the last star in the tail of the Little Bear, but when you have technology, it must be used.

Some days later, we were walking out of the park and passed an elderly homeless man sitting on a park bench, smoking. This homeless man had a white bike almost entirely festooned with possessions in useful plastic bags. I didn't greet or look at him, not wanting to intrude on his privacy, but just went to the car, got in, started it, rolled along for a few yards, and came to a decision. I stopped the car, asked Magnus to stand guard, and took the flashlight out of the pack. I walked back down the path, stopped at the man's bench, and said, "Hello."

"Hello," he said in a grave voice.

"I thought you might have some use for this," handing out the flashlight. "It's a windup flashlight. It has a little radio you can play. No batteries, and it's really light." I held it out to him. He wouldn't take it.

"That must have cost a pretty penny," he said.

"Ten bucks."

"I don't think I'm smart enough to figure out how to use it," he said, with slow, formal diction.

"Are you sure? I thought it might be useful."

"I don't think I can learn how to use it," he said, and reached for one of the cans of beer on the bench beside him. He took a polite sip.

"It's pretty easy. I can show you."

"No, I'm not smart enough for that."

"Well, alright then. Do you have everything you need?" I asked.

"Yes, thank you. It's kind of you to ask."

"Well, okay then. Have a good night."

"Thank you, I will. You have a good night yourself."

I gave up and went back to the car. You can't give away over-engineered technology even to homeless guys, not even for free.

Chapter 89 — The Girls

Any time you go into Jean's house you find females clustered together. The house is big enough for them to spread out, but they prefer to be close. The four girls are all big fans of Japanese animé, and spend hours writing and drawing their own stories. They all play orchestral instruments and know the Western classical repertory. They've memorized most of Gilbert and Sullivan. They compete with each other at computer games, goofy ones like "Dance Dance Revolution" rather than shoot-em-ups. Each girl has her own sense of style. And they love each other so tenderly and sincerely it brings tears to my eyes.

After Laura's spring violin recital, Madeleine said, "Why am I in such a good mood?" Irene said, "Because you're happy for your sister's success today." Madeleine said, "That must be it." The three girls cruised the refreshment table together with their shoulders touching, making private jokes. They have a lot of private jokes.

They adore my old man. From the moment they met him, they played with him and fawned over him, and made much of him. I used to worry that their own dogs, Ida and Joe, would get their feelings hurt, but they didn't seem to mind.

One Saturday night Jean and I were chatting in the car in her driveway after dinner. Another car pulled up behind us, buzzing with excited young voices. Jean and I got out of the car. Magnus stuck his head out the door to see what was up. While Madeleine was introducing her friends to her Mom, she saw Magnus and said, "This is Magnus. You have to meet him." Young people surrounded the car with chirping voices. "He's so beautiful!" Hands reached into the car. "Look at those blue eyes." Magnus leaned out to pull in the love. "His fur is so white!" All the usual exclamations and fuss.

When they'd had enough of my man, Madeleine waved her arm in my direction and said, "Oh, yeah. I almost forgot. This is Magnus's friend, Nancy."

Chapter 90 — Back to The Ravine

At the end of January Magnus decided he wanted to go down the stairs to the creek again. The first time he did it at the beginning of the walk. After that, he did it at the end. I started cautiously extending the walk until we were back up to two miles. I went slowly, and tried to rest him from time to time, but he wasn't having any. I'd sit down, and try to pull him into my lap when he looked tired, but he'd only stay a few seconds before getting up and sniffing around.

I guessed that he'd had some small strokes or seizures before Christmas, and lost some function—temporarily. He was getting those functions back now. This understanding lifted my spirits enough to be able to get back to writing and doing client work. And singing as I moved around the house, and kissing the kitties, and actually cleaning the house and cooking for myself.

I bought chickens, some liver and tripe and so on, and made an enormous batch of stew. Magnus hovered around the kitchen waiting for fresh treats. He got his appetite back. I went back to basic discipline—no free treats—and Magnus stopped hanging around with his tail between his legs.

I called Susan S., and wondered at all of this. She said, "That's life. He's living."

Yesterday morning he cantered towards me when I was bad-lambie-ing. It was just three or four steps, but it was a real canter with air under all four legs.

CHAPTER 91 — HACHI

Hachi is a magnificent dog by anyone's standards. He's very tall and wolf-like, with malamute facial markings, a dark overcoat and creamy undercoat, a brisk, efficient gait, and a gentle, intelligent manner. He's half malamute, half German shepherd, and all splendid. Magnus loves him. We don't see him often, but when we do Hachi is all attention.

This obviously has nothing to do with the fact that I'm a known high-octane-treats carrier and Hachi is a known snack fanatic.

We were passing near the park on the way home from a client meeting late one afternoon and decided to go for our walk early. We had just started walking down the green when Hachi spotted us and I spotted him and called him, and he came runnin'. HachiMom joined us and asked after Magnus, who immediately joined Hachi in side-by-side exploration.

HachiMom is a small, vaguely Asian-looking woman with a patient nature and intelligent eyes. She had wanted a malamute since she was a girl, for reasons she can't explain. Years later she heard about a family that had intended to breed Malamutes, but had a little accident and wound up with a mixed litter. She drove north to get hold of one as fast as she could.

She's the only dog person who always sets her pace by Magnus's pace. She watches him sharply for any sign of weakness, and turns back with us when she sees it. She watched in amazement that afternoon when he cantered up to us—a real, sustained canter, which I thought I'd never see again. When he and Hachi weren't grazing and sniffing, he was trotting back and forth between us. Full of frisk.

He did wear himself out, though, and we had to turn back early, but he sure had a good time. HachiMom watched when his butt hit the ground on the way back. She said, "You're going to have to start watching how far you go."

I said, "Yes."

She said, "I have to start thinking about what to do when it's Hachi's turn, now that he's seven."

I said, "He's just a pup." She smiled.

What she did, incidentally, was start exercising Hachi by letting him run beside her while she biked in the hills. The last time we saw him, he was more magnificent than ever.

When we got back to the car that night, Hachi tried to get in with us. She was clearly annoyed and called him sharply.

The next day, Magnus showed signs of old man's regret on our walk. We went slowly and gently, and didn't go too far. Two days later, he started looking weak about half way along the path, so I turned back. We had about a quarter mile to go when something snapped, his right hind leg turned into a rag, and he fell. I got down on the ground with him, and held him. He pulled away from me and tried to get up. He got up. I made him sit down and put my arms around him. A gaggle of teenagers came along at this point, and said, "Is he okay? Do you need help?" I said I didn't know. They asked again, and I said I didn't know again. They passed. I wished they hadn't. Why didn't I say yes? Stupid.

Magnus pulled away from me again, and stood up. He tried to walk. The best he could do was throw his whole right side forward and lurch through one or two steps. I called Jean on the cell, and left a message telling her where we were. I did not cry. I stood and thought. I remembered that when he's motivated, his nerves and muscles work better. I got out a meaty treat and put a piece in front of his nose.

He took a few steps and got the treat. I got out another one. He started to walk. I got out another chunk. He started to walk almost normally. We made it to the car, and he climbed into the back seat on his own as if nothing had happened.

Over the next few days he improved. He'd start to sag, and then haul himself up. I'd play with him outside, and he'd perform the ghost of a trot with the wagging tail and the big smile. As the day went on, the sagging would go away. Another day went by. He performed a true trot when I danced the bad lambie. He started getting edgy, woofing at strangers, needing a real walk.

So we went out, and as we pulled in to the park Magnus stood up in the back seat and licked my face and whimpered with excitement after two whole days of being cooped up indoors. He was great for about 100 yards, and then got very shaky. We went extra slow, with lots of stops, and I decided enough was enough. We turned back, and just as we got to the car we saw Hachi, who pranced up to meet Ms. Treats as fast as he could go, which is fast. HachiMom said, "How's Magnus doing?" I said, "Not so well. Something's up with the right hind leg—he collapsed a couple of days ago."

"I actually think he's doing very well for a dog his age."

We walked back into the park with them, just to hang out a while. Hachi was wandering off, so she called him. I asked, "How do you spell his name?"

"H-a-c-h-i. It's the Japanese word for August. I picked him up in August, so it seemed appropriate. It's also the name of a famous Japanese dog. My Mom is Japanese, and she told me the story. This Hachi was so loyal to his master that he went to the train station with him every day and saw him off, then came back to the station every evening to greet him when he returned. Eventually the man died, but the dog refused to believe it, and continued to go to the train station morning and evening. The people who worked at the station adopted him, and when he died they had a big statue made of him and put it up in the station. When people want to meet there, they meet at the statue. They ask 'Do you want to meet at the head or the tail?' When I went to Japan, my cousins asked me what I wanted to see. I said I wanted to see

Hachi. They said, 'Is that all?' and I said, 'Yup. That's all I really need to see.'

Magnus had rested a bit by this time, and Hachi decided to rejoin us, so the four of us set off down the park. Hachi ran around, but Magnus followed us slowly, cocking his head and looking at me inquiringly. I'd call him, and he'd trot briskly up to me—no stumbling or poor coordination. HachiMom said, "He keeps stopping. Is he okay?"

I said, "He can't figure out what the heck I'm doing. We never turn around and go back up the park. But look, he's trotting just fine. I wonder if that episode the other night was neurological, or just a regular injury?"

"It's worth checking, isn't it?"

When we got home, I put warm, soapy water in a bucket and then put the bad foot in it to clean off all the mud for a visual inspection. Magnus put up with that remarkably well. Then I made him lie down, and checked the pads, the spaces between the toes, and the top of the foot, palpating gently and looking for cuts, rusty 10-penny nails, coke bottle chunks, prickly sweetgum seedpods, and so on. Nothing. I started working up the leg, feeling around the metatarsals. Magnus jumped and jerked his head towards me. I apologized for hurting him, kissed his nose, rubbed the sore spot gently, and went to the cupboard to get him a nice big tasty chew. It seemed he'd sprained his ankle showing off for Hachi.

We went to the vet, just to check.

I can't believe she's dragging me here again. What are they going to do to me this time? More cutting and stabbing and being caged and having tubes inserted in places that are NOBODY'S BUSINESS?

He wouldn't let me calm him. Naturally, the next dog who came in the waiting room was a one-year-old, intact, male Doberman who wanted Magnus's blood. His owner handled him very well, and Magnus behaved, but it didn't do anything for his mood. After about 15 minutes, we weighed in and went to the exam room. After another fifteen minutes of waiting in the exam room, with Magnus snouting the door and the waste basket, whingeing, looking at me pathetically, and panting so hard I thought the poor guy was going to have a heart attack, Dr. Paul came in. He manipulated the leg, tested the joints, palpated the bones and flesh and so on, but didn't find a sore spot. "It's probably already getting better. We can give him an anti-inflammatory shot if you want." He continued to manipulate the legs as Magnus stood, bending the toes backward, setting the foot on the floor and watching to see if Magnus corrected the position so he could stand properly. "I'm not seeing much in the way of injury, but look how he lets his leg hang there when I pronate the foot. That's the neuropathy. But we knew about that already."

"Yes, we did."

So Dr. Paul went out and came back with a syringe for the shot, and took my panting, eye-rolling, resisting darling to the back room for some claw-trimming. (Long claws cause more foot injuries than anything else.)

By the time they released him, Magnus was in such a state of anxiety that the injured leg was flopping helplessly, the other hind leg was almost as bad, and he had to drag himself to the car with his front legs. Except for the anti-inflammatory shot, this exam clearly did more harm than good.

No shit, Sherlock. Excuse my language, but get me home, now. And don't ever do that to me again or I'm moving in with Dan. Remember, he gave me chicken liver this morning and all you gave me was rawhide.

I gave him another chew when we got home, and a good rub. Then I had to run the tap for Hammett, and rub him, and then I had to follow Margaret upstairs to shake, shake her bowly and rub her, too. "At least you guys still feel good and can do everything you want to do," I said. "Count your blessings."

I brushed Magnus up thoroughly and trimmed his edges. It shows off the lean lines and clean angles (even now) of his physique. He seemed to enjoy being fussed with.

One must keep up appearances as best one can, mustn't one?

I tied his big, red, Appalachian Trail kerchief around his neck to complete the effect. By evening, he was walking normally, nerve-wise, but trying to keep his weight off the right hind leg, pain-wise. I saw that the exam had set him back. No walkies for at least two weeks—two weeks of boredom and pent-up energy.

Why aren't we going out? It's evening already.

Poor boy. I've stopped playing with him, to keep him from dancing. Hugs and kisses aren't as good. He seems glum, and is getting off the bed before our morning cuddle, sighing when he lies on the floor.

Two weeks pass. Jean and I go out for dinner as usual on Saturday, leaving Magnus on guard duty in the back of the car. We have a leisurely meal, and I drive her back to my place so she can pick up her car. When we get there, he jumps out of the car, trots for the door, pirouettes on his hind legs at the blind corner, trots back to me, wheels around again and trots forward. We take him under the redwoods for duties and stand chatting for a bit. Magnus starts to trot to the front door (I was talking to Jean and ignoring him). I say, "Hey, Magnus, stick with me," and he wheels around again and canters up to me, full speed. Jean and I shake our heads.

"My dying dog."

"Yup."

Chapter 92 — Dog Intelligence

According to Stanley Coren, author of "The Intelligence of Dogs," there are three types of dog intelligence:
1. Adaptive intelligence (learning and problem-solving ability), which is specific to the individual animal.
2. Instinctive intelligence, which is also specific to the individual animal.
3. Working or Obedience Intelligence is specific to the breed.

Dogs who learn new commands in less than 5 repetitions and obey first commands 95% of the time or better define his top ten breeds:

1	Border Collie
2	Poodle
3	German Shepherd
4	Golden Retriever
5	Doberman Pinscher
6	Shetland Sheepdog
7	Labrador Retriever
8	Papillion
9	Rottweiler
10	Australian Cattle Dog

Here are the breeds Coren grades as understanding new commands in 25 to 40 repetitions and obeying first commands 50% of the time or better, which he considers to be merely average performance.

40	Soft-Coated Wheaten Terrier

	Bedlington Terrier
	Smooth Fox Terrier
41	Curly-Coated Retriever
	Irish Wolfhound
42	Kuvasz
	Australian Shepherd
54	Boston Terrier
	Akita

Ranking at 42 out of 79 breeds gives my beloved an F. Petrix.com ranks the Kuvasz at 65 out of 97. At least that's a D+.

What is going on here? Magnus is the smartest dog I've ever known. Granted, he's a very experienced guy who has clearly been well trained. But he is not into sitting and shaking hands or doing other useless, purposeless things on command. He is extremely reluctant to lie down on command at any time unless a massage is in it—what if a wolf showed up? Nor will he obey anyone but me.

His intelligence is all about assessing situations and making his own decisions—the adaptive and intuitive stuff. The same would be true of the Aussie. Both breeds as a whole are known for this, not just certain individuals of those breeds.

Testing intelligence out of context, using artificial situations, is the lazy way to go. I defy Coren to take a bunch of dogs into the woods, leave them there, and see which ones were still alive in a month. They would be the smartest dogs in the pack, trust me. And they'd include kuvaszok.

There was a listing on a kuvasz rescue site for a dog who'd been discovered living in the wild. Based on his appearance, the rescuers estimated that he'd survived on his own for months. Not only that, he'd found three goats to guard, and kept them safe.

D grades indeed. Frankly, I'm offended on Magnus's behalf.

Don't trouble yourself, my love. It's not worth the effort.

Chapter 93 Waterworks of a Different Kind

The condo was built in 1961. It was built in a hurry. The plumbing serves all seven townhouses in our row, and the water heater is in a closet outside my end unit. Hot water dissolves things, such as copper pipes, more quickly than cold water. The pipes burst at the water heater and blew a hole through my living room wall.

This was a special plumbing failure. Three previous breaks had happened under the slab in my kitchen, rotting the floor and a cabinet. This one steamed the furniture, flooded the living room, and boiled the hardwood floor. The plasterboard was swollen, blistered, and dripping. I tried putting a bucket over the spray jetting out of the wall, which was brilliant, since the bucket was horizontal and all the water bounced out. I tried putting towels around to soak up the water, but the output was too prodigious. I decided to shut off the water to the building, and went outside to warn the other residents. Lucky me. They were all out. This reminded me that, unlike me, they all had steady work, which I immediately thrust out of my mind as being too painful to ponder. I went to the water-heater closet and shut down the main supply and the water heater.

I called the management company, who started sending plumbers and restoration consultants over to get three bids for each stage of repair. The first was a plumber who'd been tasked to clamp off the leak. He asked where the leak was, and I took him to the water heater closet outside. Magnus was suspicious, but the man was around such a short time he just kept an eye on him.

A bit later two guys came in with huge fans and dehumidifiers, which they proceeded to deploy around the living area. Magnus stayed at their heels, strongly registering disapproval. I went to the tub of liver treats, got some out, and handed them to the men.

They made friendly noises and offered him the treats, but he lowered his head, put his ears back, and refused the little nuggets, giving the men a slitty-eyed stare.

I'm not falling for that, you two. Back off

They stayed for almost an hour, fidgeting with equipment and aiming the blowers at the wettest spots. Magnus stood in the patio door with his neck stretched out and his head low, ears forward, staring at them and drooling. Kind of like he did at the beach. Occasionally he'd look at me searchingly. I told him everything was fine, but he wasn't convinced. The men left, leaving the blowers on high. The kids ran in through the living room, hugging the opposite wall, and dashed upstairs to escape the fans. Magnus retreated to his guard post by the front door.

A couple more plumbers came to assess the damage. Magnus tried to block them at the door. I slipped past him, and went out to show the men the water heater. He followed close at my heels.

You have no sense of security, do you?

The next day another man came to assess the damage to the wall, see how much wallboard would have to be replaced, how much wood was soaked, and so on. I thought it might be easier for Magnus to take a walk around the complex than to stay inside with a suspicious stranger.

This was after living with a kuvasz for two years.

I wondered why he pulled back on the leash, looked over his shoulder, why he was walking so slowly, why he kept trying to go back to the house. I naturally assumed he was sick and about to die. As we sagged around the last corner, I got it. I'd left our home unguarded with a strange man in it.

When we went back in, he was on high alert. I fixed his breakfast and set it down. The man was working in the living room—or area, rather, since the floor plan is open—while I washed dishes. Magnus stayed between us. He looked at the man. He took a bite of breakfast. He looked at me. He took a bite. He checked back on the man, and then on me. That was the slowest breakfast in dog history.

When my bodyguard was done eating, he positioned himself across the backs of my legs and kept his eyes on the man until I finished the dishes. When I turned around, he tried to block me in.

If I can't protect the house, I assuredly can and will protect you.

After the man left, my guy went out to the patio to lie down on a big pile of plant trimmings I was going to put in the bag lying next to them someday, and eyed me watchfully. He didn't come in until late afternoon. He only came then because I called him in to give him treats and praise for doing such a good job of keeping me safe. Then he followed me upstairs to the computer and laid himself down directly behind my chair.

He kept me under heavy guard all evening, during our walk, through the night, and into the morning, when I did some fake whimpering because Hammett and Magnus had me pinned down under the blankets. Magnus bolted up off the foot of the bed, and stood over me, licking my face until I made him stop.

He did play with me later on, though, prancing like the mountains and leaping like the hills in the 113th psalm.

For the next few days, he wouldn't let me out of his sight. He barely let me get out of touching range. I had shown such poor judgment the past few days that he couldn't trust me to be safe and sensible, could he?

I can't wait till the men come to do the actual repairs.

Chapter 94 — Visible Kitty

All of a sudden, Invisible Margaret is in my face. She's hanging out with me, chatting me up, following me around. She let me pick her up and hold her for the first time in a long time. She was all bones. I could feel every prong of every vertebra. Her skin was loose on her frame. I hadn't seen the change through her long coat, and was shocked at how skinny she was. She'd seemed fine to me—active, alert, lithe—but that kind of weight loss is not normal. Remember, she's in charge of the dry food bowl, which is always full. She can eat as much as she likes, whenever she wants.

I decided she was in my face because she was deathly ill and needed comforting. I called Dr. Paul and made an immediate appointment. At the weigh-in, we found she was down two pounds, which was about 20% of her normal weight. Dr. Paul did blood tests, urine tests, and x-rays. He didn't tell me what he was looking for, and I didn't need to be told: it was either cancer or kidney disease.

It cost over two hundred dollars to find out that she was in perfect health. Relief then gave way to guilt. I decided to feed her up, and went to the pet store. After examining the labels of every brand of canned food I chose the one with the most protein and least ash content. I got several different flavors to see what she'd like. She liked them all.

She started to come around when I was preparing Magnus's food, and asking for her own. I fed her first. She started to gain weight, and continued to be companionable. I started picking her up as often as she'd let me, and she let me do so much more often that before.

Mom says she was lovesick for her Mommy. So it seems Margaret is fighting back now, too.

Good on you, girl.

Chapter 95 Veterinary Decision

Magnus's terror at the vet's office the last time we were there convinced me that it wasn't worth it to keep taking him in. His blood work shows that he's healthy on all counts except for the thyroid. I will pick up his meds and his B12 shots, and give them to him at home. Obviously, if he is wounded or breaks a bone, I'll get treatment for him. But I'm not going to put him through more tests or invasive procedures. If he can't be helped with meds and home care, I'll let him go.

My best hope for Magnus is a sudden ending, preferably during a walk. I know a dog who did that. Enjoying the company of other dogs and people, this sweet-tempered Doberman lay down at his man's feet, curled up, and simply died. That's what I want for my love.

Dr. Paul understands. When my guy got another case of hot spots, he didn't ask to see him, but just told me to come over and get the meds. He's giving me four syringes of B1-12 at a time. He's not suggesting further exams.

I'm more determined than ever to enjoy my love and to give him joy. I had some leftover salmon the other day—I'd bought more than I could eat—and realized that I'd forgotten to thaw his stew, so salmon is what my guy got for supper (cooked). He ate it up, working his way around the kibbles to get to the fish. I went upstairs while he was eating, and as soon as he was done he pounded up the stairs to the computer room to give my hand continental-style kisses and wag his tail for me and give me the happy eye.

You know I love salmon, girl.

Chapter 96 — My Hero

We're taking walks again. Short, slow walks—it's taking Magnus a while to regain strength after being off for four weeks with the sprained ankle. And who did we see last night but Hachi himself?

I was watching my old man graze in the deep grass—all the dogs love the tender new growth—and was startled to see Hachi appear under my nose. I didn't even hear him come up, though he was running full speed. HachiMom followed. Hachi eyed my fanny pack lasciviously and sat down in front of me.

HachiMom said, "He knows who carries the good stuff."

"Can I give him one?"

"It's up to you."

I gave him one. Magnus came over to get his share. We all started walking down the greensward. Hachi was at me, trying to get more treats. HachiMom said, "Hachi, don't beg." I've noticed that the person holding the goods has to give the order, so I said, "No more, Hachi."

HachiMom said, "You have to hold your hands out like this to show him there aren't any more treats."

"But he knows perfectly well there are. Maybe I should carry them in something more airtight."

"He'd still smell them. HACHI. Don't beg."

I held out my hands. "No more, Hachi."

"Hachi, don't beg."

Repeat twenty times.

I was secretly laughing, so Hachi knew I wasn't serious.

HachiMom said, "If you're going to be like that, you're going on a short leash." When Hachi pulled to get at my pack, she gave him a quick sideways yank. Then she pulled ten feet or so in front of us, to remove the temptation. After a while, Magnus wanted to graze, and I could see he was already tired, so I said, "You may as well go along. I don't know how much farther we're going."

"Okay. It's good to see you out and about again."

Seven-year-old Hachi and slim, straight HachiMom went along briskly. I hung out with my almost-twelve-year-old darling and watched him going slowly through a patch of new grass. His dental anatomy does not serve him very well as grazing equipment. Those long teeth only manage to snip off the occasional shred of sweet greens. We turned back when he got tired, and walked very slowly back towards the car, with stops to let him catch his breath.

Back on the green, I wanted to stay for a while because we'd only been in the park for half an hour, so I sat down, let Magnus lick my face before asking him to sit, and then encouraged him to lie down. This time he acquiesced easily.

So there we were, lovin' each other up in the dark on the soft grass, doing mutual eye-gazing and admiration, when something brushed my shoulder softly.

It was Hachi on his return run. Again, I didn't hear him. Stealth mode malamute.

Hachi dove for the fanny pack.

Magnus surged on Hachi. He moved so fast he blurred, dove across my legs and clashed with Hachi by my side, both dogs snarling and snapping. He drove Hachi away from and behind me.

Insufferable creature! Prepare to die.
Hey, lay off. I was just going to help myself to a treat.
Not while there's breath in my body.

Did I mention that dog people once told me that being on the ground with angry dogs is a good way to get bit?

I got bit. By Hachi. I finally managed to throw my body out of the fray, and watched it. I shouted at Magnus, but he was in high gear. I decided to trust his sense of proportion. He wasn't going for the throat; he was forcing Hachi down.

By the time HachiMom ran up shouting "Enough!" Magnus had Hachi on his back on the ground and was standing over him in the arched-necked posture, one paw on his throat. Hachi hadn't fully submitted. His lips were drawn back over clenched teeth in a frozen snarl. But both dogs were still. HachiMom grabbed Hachi's collar and hauled him off. She's a little thing, and he's a big dog, but she was in dominance mode herself. This was a good opportunity for Hachi to save face.

I'd have whooped you, old man, but my woman won't let me.
I doubt it. I seriously doubt it. I had you down, punk.

I was still on the ground, somewhat in shock, holding my arm where Hachi had bitten me. HachiMom said, "Are you all right?"

"I got bit."

"Did it break the skin?"

"I don't think so. It didn't break the cloth of my jacket."

I pulled up my sleeve. She examined the arm. "It's okay. There will be a big bruise, though. I'm so sorry! Hachi ran up to you too fast, and right into you. He shouldn't have done that."

"It's all right. I've been giving him treats, and he couldn't resist."

She was quiet for a minute. "You know, when I saw you sitting here, I was afraid that Magnus...I came to see if you needed help."

"No, we were just hanging out. He did a little better tonight than last night, but he's still weak. I didn't want to go in yet, and thought it would be nice to stay and watch the night come on."

"I really am sorry."

"I guess I'd better not give Hachi any more treats, eh?"

"Guess not. It really is good to see you two out here again. I was afraid after the last time I saw you..."

"Me too. But this time it was a soft tissue injury, not the neuropathy. Remember a month of so ago when the boys were playing? He probably sprained his foot then. We'll be coming out for a while."

"Good. See you soon, then."

"See you soon."

She put Hachi on a short leash, and walked off, still angry with him. If he was a kuvasz, I'd have advised against that.

Ah, Magnus. My old invalid can still put up a fight—and win. Without bloodshed.

CHAPTER 97   LEG HYDRAULICS

Magnus started knuckling in April—walking on the top of his right hind foot. My guess was that he'd probably been doing that for a while, and that was probably how he'd injured himself. I watched this, trying to think how I could help him hold the foot up properly. I thought of a light brace, L-shaped, that could be strapped on his leg somehow. I couldn't think what to make it with. I thought of a making him a leather boot with a restraint running from the top to the toe to hold the foot up. I thought of a leg brace with a hydraulic system that would pull the foot up for him, like the anti-slamming tubes on screen doors. I thought of getting baby-boots for him, went shopping, and couldn't find anything that would work.

I bought an ace bandage and strapped his foot into place with that. He gave me a very hard time about it.

Enough with the feet, dear girl. You know I hate that.

"You want to go walkies?"

Very much. You know that, too.

"Then settle down and let me get this thing on."

Our walk went wonderfully with the ace bandage. He went farther, more comfortably, than he had for a long time. But the ace bandage shredded about a half mile into our walk. So I got a Bag O' Baby socks and put that on over the ace bandage. It lasted for about one and a half walks before he shredded it. But who cares? We were walking, he was getting stronger, and very soon, when I called him to his big bed for bandaging, he came promptly, laid down, and grinned. Bandage meant walk time. Joy.

We went through two Bag O' Babies in about a month. At Sunday supper, Susan A. said, "They make boots for dogs, Nancy."

"They do?"

"I'm sure of it. Go Google dog boots."

I went to her computer, Googled dog boots, and sure enough, all kinds of companies make all kinds of boots. The number-one brand had just what I wanted: a boot in a lightweight mesh fabric with a semi-rigid sole, specifically designed to hold the foot at the correct angle. Doggie Orthopedics. On sale, even. I duly measured my sweetie's foot, and ordered a pair. They were bright blue with green trim. Very sporty.

Chapter 98 — Traffic Management

Magnus stops traffic. Literally. When we walk around the neighborhood in the morning, people driving past slow down to look at him, even in his age and decrepitude. If we're at a crosswalk, they stop to let us pass, and watch us cross the street.

Today, I was wearing white to match Magnus, and since it was hot we were resting in the shade of a tree on a patch of juicy new lawn. A white-haired couple walked past on the opposite side of the street, stopped, and stood smiling at us for a minute or so. We said a few polite words to each other, and they walked on with dreams on their lips. A woman driving past slowed to a crawl, with dreams in her eyes, which were on us. Another woman stopped her car and watched anxiously when Magnus stumbled (he was trying to scratch his belly, and sat right down in the middle of the street.) I think she was going to hop out of the car to rescue him if he couldn't get up. I'd have appreciated that enormously.

This happens every day.

Men give Magnus a look that says, "Now that's what I call a dog." They smile unconsciously. They turn their heads to keep their eyes on him as they pass. I love this, particularly when the man in question is burly and tattooed and has his head shaved. They almost never look at me, which is just fine. Next to Magnus, I'm invisible. But when they do look at me, they all but give me a thumbs-up sign.

CHAPTER 99   GREAT BLUE

One spring evening, as we were coming off the field and walking down the hill, we saw an enormously tall bird with a long head on a longer neck looking abstractedly up to the clouds. Long, thin, black crest feathers swept down from its crown. Its slate blue wings were folded into a neat oval across its back. We couldn't see its legs in the tall grass, but its head was nearly level with my shoulders, and I am not a short person. It had to be a Great Blue Heron.

I couldn't see what a shore bird was doing in a dry field some miles from the Bay.

Said bird moved restlessly as we approached, and finally took off, his great wide wings working strongly as his long legs swept the tops of the grass. I saw him on several more walks last spring, and again this spring, always on a windy day, sometimes in sweeping flight, sometimes standing stock still in the grass with his head pointed straight down, sometimes moving slowly through the grass looking at the ground.

I'm fascinated with him. Why is he there? If standing in a field is such a good idea, why is he there so rarely, and why is he there alone? Why is he so still?

When we got to the top of the hill last evening we spied Dolly and DollyDad. We hadn't seen them since September. We'd missed them. I shouted, "Dolly!" She stopped running and stared at me blankly. It had been so long she wasn't sure who we were. I called her again, and after a moment's thought she came running up to me at top speed (as if she knows any other pace).

She'd grown a lot—she was almost double the size she was when we last saw her. She jumped up to place her paws on my legs, and circled me half a dozen times and then found Magnus and circled him. His tail was going, and he was wreathed in joy.

Dolly, Dolly, Dolly. Aren't you looking well!
You're looking great, too, man. Where have you been?
I've been here almost every night, little one. Where have you been?
We come every day. I guess we come at different times.
Well, we're together now.
Yes we are. I'm so glad!

She started running circles around him—or spirals, rather, since we were walking forward. DollyDad said, "Hello. We haven't seen you in months."

"I generally come out after sunset, looking for the coolest possible temperatures."

"I'm sure he appreciates that. Even Dolly gets too hot in direct sunlight. He's looking great, by the way. You're doing a terrific job with him."

The last time they saw Magnus, we had just discovered B12 and hadn't started the thyroid meds yet. DollyDad was clearly surprised that my man was still with me, and as clearly pleased. Dolly was still running circles around us, and occasionally charging Magnus, who'd feint back at her with his old spirit. He loves me, but I'm the wrong species, and even old men have needs.

"I've been giving him B12 shots, and it's made all the difference."

"Really? It's like a miracle. He's doing fine."

"And next week his new orthopedic boots are coming."

"All the best-dressed dogs in the park will have them. Does that have anything to do with the bandage on his foot?"

"Yes. He's got neuropathy, and winds up walking on the tops of his feet and bruising them, or twisting his ankle. If I can keep his feet in the right position, he won't keep injuring himself."

We were heading down the hill when DollyDad swept his arm out in a wide circle, and said, "Have you been here recently?"

"Yes."

"Have you seen the Heron?"

"Yes, I did. Twice. It's a magnificent creature. I always see it in spring, and always when it's windy."

"I've noticed the same thing. Have you ever watched it catch a ground squirrel?"

"They eat rodents?"

"Absolutely. They stand perfectly still, and all of a sudden they stab their beaks into a burrow and come up with a squirrel."

"Fur and all?"

"Fur and all."

I got an immediate image of a long bushy tail hanging out of a long yellow beak.

"I thought they ate fish. I can see how scales could slide down its throat, but fur?"

"Yes, fur. We figure that this bird was blown here on a spring gale, and found the field by accident. When a big wind comes up, he takes advantage of it to get a free ride to a good meal. The bird is always here at dusk on a windy day."

"That explains why he stands so still, and why he's usually looking down."

"Yes. He's staking out a burrow."

"The other day, we walked all around this hill, and watched him the whole time. I never saw him strike."

"Keep watching."

At the Cornell Lab of Ornithology website, I learned that the Great Blue is the "largest and most widespread heron in North America." Their preferred habitat is a calm shoreline with fresh or salt water. In cold climates, they migrate as far as South America, but here on the left coast they're year-round residents. That doesn't explain why we only see our bird in the spring, but maybe, like the Night Herons, Great Blues have their seasonal rounds.

They are solitary feeders. They eat small mammals as well as fish, reptiles, and amphibians. It seems that they can get greedy, since they sometimes try to swallow prey that is big enough to choke them. We'll have to keep watch in case our bird needs us to do the Heimlich maneuver on him.

With the lengthening days, the park was full of people again. Jack, a dog who had been rescued from a medical lab, ran up to us. Two years ago he was a frightened, anxious little thing who didn't know how to be a dog. He would cower and tremble, never played with other dogs, shied away from people. Magnus and I used to work with him, helping him build confidence by being quiet and gentle and giving him treats. Today he's a real dog, at last.

"Look at Jack! He's so happy!" I said, giving him a treat. He wriggled and wagged.

"Isn't he great? I'm so proud of him." She had that distant look in her eyes that dog people get.

Three middle-aged women stopped to meet my man, exclaimed over his loveliness, expressed sympathy for his lameness, and praised my clever solution. One woman said, "He's the kind of dog who should be in a fairy tale. He'd live in an old castle in Hungary, protecting the young fatherless princess from the cruel intrigues of the court, and giving her sage advice."

I said, "He could be a kind of Aslan, protecting and guiding the people of his kingdom."

She said, "Exactly."

I said, "You get the prize for creativity. Everyone else says, 'Oh, his eyes are blue! How do you keep him so clean? How old is he?' No one has ever suggested he be in a fairy tale. I like it. Let's get hold of Pixar."

"Right!" She laughed. The women walked on beyond us. Jack and JackMom and Magnus and I walked slowly along until we came upon an elderly couple who were watering native plants they'd sown along the verge. Magnus laid himself down for a rest as we talked about native plants and the neighborhood, where JackMom had grown up, then moved a way and was now back.

Her parents had been friends with them in the old days, and they remembered her and the house she'd inherited, and promised to visit. I promised to strip the seed heads off some invasive grasses every time I came out.

A big man with a small cream-colored Chihuahua came by, and blond Jack and white Magnus convened with them briefly. The three women passed us on their return loop, and stood to watch the pale-dog conclave for a while, smiling. I said, "Pixar." They laughed quietly and walked on.

Jack decided he'd gone far enough and insisted on turning back. Magnus and I went onto the greensward and sat down, where Lucky and LuckyMom found us. "Is he okay?" she asked.

"Sure. We're just taking it slow."

"Good. I got worried when I saw you on the ground. "A couple of weeks before, she'd insisted that I take her cell number in case we needed help.

Lucky is a big, lusty, gangly young Lab with a waddling gait. When he was a puppy his Mom would drop the leash to let him run, and he learned to run with his hind legs apart so they wouldn't get tangled in the leash. Like the German pointer, he was taking a long time to grow up, but unlike the pointer his manners were good enough that Magnus never felt the need to correct him.

She stood and talked with us while Lucky sniffed about under the oaks. The little Chihuahua reappeared, and Lucky dashed out to greet him and maybe have a nice chase. The Chihuahua started screaming in fear, running away, Lucky chased him, LuckyMom chased Lucky, Lucky evaded her neatly, and the little dog's Dad chased and captured him and swung him up on his shoulder to safety.

As Lucky dashed towards us and away from his Mom, I called him. He came promptly to the liver treat source, so I got hold of his leash, and handed it to his Mom as she trotted up. Magnus refused to stay down in front of Lucky, so the four of us wandered off in the dusk, and another walk came to a close.

Days passed, many of them cool and breezy, and we saw the Great Blue almost every night for a few weeks. We never saw him strike. We saw him standing in the mown-down grass, holding his head up at a 45° angle. We saw him staking out burrows, hunched over, eyes on the prize. We saw him make his royal progressions, stalking gravely and slowly across the hill. Once we saw him fly away, his wide wings threading between the trees along the path. I wondered how he could navigate such narrow spaces. He didn't startle and fly away anymore when people passed. He has come to trust the park and its people. As have we.

Chapter 100

The boots came. They were an unqualified failure. They added half an inch to the bottom of Magnus's feet, and he couldn't figure out how far to raise his paws to clear the ground with them on. They didn't hold up his paw, either. He dragged his leg behind him, especially the weaker right leg, on any but the most level surfaces. On the greensward, he was no good at all—his foot got tangled in the grass. I went back to ace bandages and baby socks.

As the weather grew warmer, my love grew weaker again. Spring allergies were straining his heat exchanger, as usual. People started giving me hard looks at the park for over-exercising my poor old panting dog. I understand, but I want to tell them that when the sun starts to go down, he still barges around the condo poking things and jogging my elbow, begging to go to the park. Going for walks is his idea. Not that I mind.

He sets the pace. When I try slowing down, he looks back at me.

What's with you? Can't keep up?

Often he's weak for the first hundred yards or so, and then his nerves wake up and he gets stronger. Hilary the physical therapist says this is normal. When I couldn't stand the sight of his flanks heaving with every breath, I sat down and tried to get him to lie down, and stayed beside him, massaging his head and neck. He'd sit, but in a moment he'd get up impatiently and start walking. I'd follow, as slowly as possible.

After a while, particularly if I chose a soft patch of green grass to sit on, he got to liking it the massage sessions. He got to expecting it, lying down and stretching out, glancing up at me out of the corners of his eyes, smiling.

He rests his head in the crook of my arm. He lies there, gazing up at me. I try to kiss his nose without getting kissed back. We can play that game for quite a while, until he rolls over, and waves his forelegs around and tries to catch my arms. I start massaging his chest and back and legs and neck, running my hands through his fur, letting the loose stuff fly.

A woman with a little black dog saw this one evening, and stopped to ask, "What are you doing?"

"Magnus needs to rest in this heat, and the only way I can get him to stay down is to make it worth his while."

She watched me finger-comb his fur, and smiled as fluffy tufts went wafting away. "I've been wondering what that white stuff was," she said.

"Whenever you see white fur in the grass, you'll know we've been here."

"I like that. You look so sweet together. Our dogs do us a lot of good, don't they?"

Last night, I was thumping him gently with open palms, which he likes inordinately. I noticed that thumping different parts of his chest and belly made different sounds. I started playing rhythms on his body, laughing to myself. Bongo Dog.

I stopped drumming, thinking this was disrespectful, maybe even irritating, but Magnus lifted his head and gave me a quick glance.

Why stop? I was enjoying that.

So I bongoed on for a while. When his breathing was completely calm, I stopped drumming, and sat up. He rolled over and rose up on his feet in a single fluid movement.

He needs me more now, and trusts me more. I can finally give him pedicures. I stand at the foot of the stairs to reassure him when he doesn't think he can climb down. I help him get in the car when we go out by lifting his right hind leg over the threshold. He stands on the back seat, and watches me walk around to the driver's side, as he's always done.

I finally twigged to the fact that he's making sure I get in safely.

Some people are slow.

Chapter 101   Too Hot

At the park one evening, a woman asked about the ace bandage and baby sock. I told her what was going on, and she told me about a veterinary physical therapy clinic in Menlo Park that had everything, and would probably be able to fit Magnus with the right kind of footwear. We went the next day, and they put him into the same brand of boot I'd bought online, but in a smaller size and a stiffer material. And those boots worked. He still got tangled up on the grass, but that was not a problem. We stayed on the trails.

On our morning walk—Susan S. had instructed me that at twelve, a walk was fifteen minutes out of doors with me, several times a day—we'd go two blocks, then sit on the nice patch of grass under the tree until he stopped panting, and then walk the two blocks home. In the evening, we'd do the same thing in the park—walk to the end of the greensward, and sit for a while, then walk on until he slowed, turn back and sit on the green again before heading back to the car. No more drinks at the creek, though. I was afraid he'd be unable to get back up, and I certainly couldn't carry him. This way we managed about a mile and a half a day, and he started getting stronger again.

Then came a severe heat wave. My dear friend Lalana was in town for a conference, and had come a day early so she could meet Magnus. And see me, of course.

Lalana lived with me for a summer, years ago. When I interviewed her on the telephone, I asked the usual questions—what are your hours, what do you like to eat, and so on—and she gave me very strange answers. "My hours are terrible. I stay up all night and go to work very late. I eat junk food, mostly. Sausage, potato pancakes, pork, chicken, whatever." I thought she was way too weird, and it wasn't because she spoke with a thick Indian accent. I told her I'd think about it, called her back and told her that we might not be a good fit.

Two weeks later, she called me again. "I've been in this crazy woman's house for one weekend, and I've been cleaning the bathroom the whole time. I still can't bear to shower in it."

A clean girl? That was a good sign. I hadn't chosen a roommate yet. I said, "You'd better come over," and gave her directions. Half an hour later, this tall, willowy, creature with long black hair, huge almond eyes, high cheekbones, and a generous smile came to my door. We talked for a few minutes, and I was utterly charmed. She moved in that evening.

And spent the first weekend cleaning the bathroom.

I asked her later why she'd given me such odd answers to my interview questions. She said, "I didn't want you to think I was some kind of Hindu vegetarian weirdo."

"Why would I think that?"

"I get the impression that Americans don't like Indians."

"Why?"

"Because, in India, as soon as you meet someone you like, you invite them to your home. No American has ever invited me to their home."

I laughed. "That's just America," I said. "Our homes are our castles, and we don't invite people home until we know them well."

"Really?"

"Really. We like our privacy." She didn't really believe me, but she pretended to.

I liked sharing my place with Lalana. I was very grateful for the messy lady with the filthy bathroom who drove her to my house.

We'd talk all evening at the dining table, with Hammett stretched between us so we could stroke and pet him at both ends. We told each other all about our lives, our families, and our homes. She adored the kids. She told me about having adopted every stray she came across when she was a child. "My mother would say, 'Not another one, Lalana. Please!' But I couldn't help it. They were so sweet."

I ate potato pancakes and Indian pickles with her for breakfast—happy, greasy, salty junk food. I cooked for her, and she loved my food. We went to an Indian buffet for dinner once a week. I gained ten pounds. She stayed as slim as ever, the beast.

At the end of the summer, her fiancée came out to visit. Saroosh was a short, stocky, sarcastic, loud guy, as unlike Lalana as a person could be. They teased each other mercilessly—a side of her that I hadn't seen. They're an extraordinarily mismatched, but devoted, couple.

It was Renaissance Faire season, which Kathy and Mike love. They've been going to it for years. The five of us went in full costume, courtesy of their Ren' Fair costume trunk. Lalana and Saroosh were adorable in their peasant getups, making elaborate jokes about how a couple of Indians made it to Renaissance England. The photo I took of them that day is on display in their living room at their new home in Boston.

Lalana has a post-doc from MIT in Internet security, but she's completely without geek pretension. The conference was, not surprisingly, on Internet security. When she "reached"—her term for arrival—she called from her hotel and told me she couldn't wait to meet my man, so I loaded him into the car, cranked the AC up full blast aimed the vents upward so the cool air could sink into the back seat, and drove to Sunnyvale.

We got out of the car, and in the 100° heat, Magnus collapsed almost immediately. I couldn't put him back in the car. I couldn't leave him in the sun. I had to walk him into the hotel, a few steps at a time. As soon as we found some shade, I let him lie on the grass to recover. People started to gather around to praise his beauty and pet him, as usual. I took advantage of this to give him as much rest as I could. When he was recovered, we went in.

I hadn't checked to see if the hotel allowed dogs, but the staff just smiled at us as he struggled up the stairs. Wandering the corridors to find Lalana's room, we came on some people cleaning, and a woman asked, "Agua? Does he need water?"

"Yes, thanks so much." She bustled about to find a bowl, filled it, and set it before him. He looked at her, looked at the bowl.

Nice try. I'm on duty.

We finally made it to the room. Lalana's eyes went round in alarm at his state, and we got water for him, turned up the AC, and washed his face with a hand towel, but he kept panting harshly.

It took him over an hour to cool down. I was going to drive her to the beach, but she said we'd better stay in the room for his sake. So we sat and talked, and ordered takeout Indian food, and ate, and after a while Magnus came back to life. When the temperature went down enough to take him outside, she said, "Can we go to your house so I can see the kitties?"

We did. She fawned over them, took photos of them, and when she had gotten her kitty fix we sat in the patio in the dark with just a candle to see by and talked, drinking the sweet, milky tea she'd taught me to make (with lactose-free milk).

Magnus was listless in the heat the next two days. On Friday afternoon, Lalana called. "The conference is done, and my flight isn't until seven. Can I come over and hang out with you?"

"Please do. I'd never turn down Lalana time." So we sat in the living room talking, watching Magnus suffer. I mentioned that the physical therapy people had tried to sell me a special jacket called a swamp cooler, which you soak in water and strap to your dog's back. The evaporation draws off the heat. She said, "A towel would do just as well. Let's try it."

We did, and the results were wonderful. Magnus was soon breathing quietly, dozing, with his head on his crossed paws, and a beatific look on his face.

Lesson 11: Sometimes low-tech solutions are just fine.

Chapter 102 — More Bad Judgment

The plumbers came in the first week of August to re-pipe my condo (six months after the flood). Magnus restrained himself, but he didn't appreciate the intrusion. We retreated upstairs to the hottest room in the place to avoid them—there are no trees at that corner of the building, and the roof is just a few feet above the ceiling. From time to time Magnus would go downstairs to get some cooler air and check on the workmen.

At one point I went downstairs, and he was gone. One of the men told me he was sleeping behind the next building, and led me to the spot. No Magnus. I said, angrily, "You let a sick old dog wander off?" and ran around the complex looking for him, thinking that he'd gone away out of resentment of the workers. No Magnus. I ran to the car, and drove around the neighborhood, hoping to find him under a tree, seeing mental images of him lying in the street, prostrate with heatstroke. Reason returned: he never walks in the sun if he can help it; he's not capable of walking very far in any case; it might be time to call the police. He had no collar on, and no tags…

Walking back to my door, I noticed a big, yellow post-it on Dan's door: "Magnus is with me." I rang the bell. Dan said, "I saw him lying in the sun. He looked hot, so I brought him inside."

I bent down and cradled my beloved's head, and sobbed and kissed him on the nose and said, as quietly as I could, "I wish you'd told me."

What's up, honey? Did those men hurt you?.

"I didn't know you were home," Dan said.

"I'm always home. Thank you for taking care of him, though. You've been such a great help to us."

It took the workmen five days to complete the replumbing project. Magnus got a little weaker every day under the stress.

The heat didn't let up.

Magnus stopped eating.

I tried everything—doping his food with treats, adding other yummy things, such as milk—but eventually all he would eat was fresh-cooked chicken. This was problematic because I mixed his meds and supplements into his food, so he wasn't getting what he needed to stay healthy and comfortable. At the grocery store, it occurred to me that I could wrap his pills in cheap American cheese. This worked, but his skin and coat supplement was powdered, not pilled, so he went without it for a week. That was enough to bring on another case of hot spots. I called Dr. Paul, and got more antibiotics. Magnus got better, but he was still off his food.

Dan brought some commercial canned stuff over. Magnus loved it. If doggy junk food was what it was going to take to get nutrition into him, doggy junk food it would be.

Though his energy was better, we had to stop taking walks beyond the basic out-in-the-yard duties run. We gave up going to the park again. Magnus stopped barging around begging to go out at sundown. It was so hot.

CHAPTER 103 — GAMING NANCY

When we went out for duties in the evening, Magnus got as far as the redwoods, and then flopped on his side so hard he bounced. I sat behind his head, and lifted it into my lap. He let it drop nervelessly and lay limp, inert except for some spasmodic leg jerking. I thought he was having another fit, and stroked him and wept, and told him if it was time to go he could go. People passed. No one stopped. I wanted to get him back inside, but couldn't carry him, didn't want to leave him lying out there, and just sat helplessly for fifteen minutes or so, rubbing and massaging and trying to comfort my old man through my tears and half-stifled sobs. I finally got up, and said, "Come on, boy," experimentally.

Sure thing, sweetheart. Thanks for the extra-long rubs.

He trotted back to the front door.

Jean got it faster than I did. When I told her the story, as soon as I got to the part about him flopping on the ground, she started laughing. "You trained him to lie down for massage, Nancy. He's got your number."

The men went away. The weather got cooler. My man got his appetite back. We started playing again. He invented new bunny-hop steps with the hind legs to compensate for the neuropathy, and used head gestures and body twists instead of footwork, butting me with his shoulder, and leaning on me and gently wagging his tail. I made a big batch of stew.

Then my contractor started restoration work on the living room.

Chapter 104 — Bad Judgment, Round Three

Five new men came to the condo. Two inspected the work to be done, three brought tools for pulling up the floor, and they all swarmed around, talking, playing Mexican polkas on radios and moving all my furniture, pictures, and books outside to a pile that filled the patio.

Magnus hovered around, eying them.

Get those men out of here, young lady.

I didn't try to calm him down, because I wanted to show him that this was no big deal. But this time the workmen were at the house off and on for over a month.

We retreated back upstairs. We stifled as the workmen levered up glued-down wood flooring. Screech, creak, bang, snap, tubas, guitars, ringtones, grind, screech, crack. Magnus parked himself between me and the door to my office and followed me with his eyes whenever I left the room.

As long as you're up, why don't you go down and make those people get out?

The contractor, Ray, is a good friend. His main business is running restaurants on the Stanford campus. I write menus and ads and business proposals for him, and he's the easiest client in the world to please. "Anyone can write 'soft drinks and juice'," he says. "Only you would come up with 'cool fizzies'." His employees listen to him with respect and affection, because that's how he listens to them. He's a jolly, bald, Jewish hobbit who is dog-crazy and embarrassingly generous.

He does renovations for fun. "I'm over seventy now, so I only work seven days a week," he says. "I'm going to give you more than you expect because you're good people. You deserve it," he says. "Look how you take care of your poor old dog."

"The association isn't going to pay for anything but absolute basics, Ray. I don't want you to be out of pocket on this."

"You're getting a wood floor. It isn't right to destroy your wood floor and refuse to replace it. You're getting a granite countertop." (The association never replaced the countertop when the cabinet was ruined a few years ago.) "I think cove moldings would look nice in this room."

"Ray, there is no way they're going to pay for that."

"We'll work it out in trade. Now, you keep track, because I don't want to take advantage of you."

I laughed. "Okay. Let's just say you have a writer for life."

The old wood, when they pulled it up, was black with mold on the underside. No wonder Magnus had been having trouble breathing—his laryngeal paralysis eased up as soon as that stuff was out of the condo.

Every day the men were here, the stress took its toll on my man. After a week, he couldn't walk as far as the yard. After two weeks, he couldn't take more than a step or two before he collapsed. He had to lay down to poop and pee because he couldn't squat. Finally he stopped peeing altogether. I called Dr. Paul, who said stress would do that. But I wondered.

"Dan, is it time?"

"Give it a few days."

The men left.

Magnus recovered.

He started volunteering to walk out in the neighborhood again.

The men came back and started painting the downstairs in a cool gray-green color Ray chose. He asked if I liked the color. I took him upstairs and showed him that my bedroom was painted in a darker tone of the same hue. This was quieter work, and there was only one man, so Magnus wasn't too disturbed by it.

With new paint, I needed new switch covers—I'd painted the old ones to match the walls—and I went out to buy them, leaving Magnus home because of the heat. I had several other errands to run, but decided to go back home, put the switch plates up, and get this one chore finished. When I pulled up to the complex, there was a police car and an animal control truck parked on the opposite side of the street. I glanced over, and saw my love prostrate on the sidewalk.

I'd left the main door open and let the air circulate through the screen door so Alejandro wouldn't have to choke on the fumes as he painted, figuring Magnus couldn't go anywhere anyway.

He could if he was motivated. Being separated from me motivated him. The woman who found him said, "He was walking down the middle of the street looking lost." One of my neighbors was telling the animal control officer, "She never lets him out. I've never seen him without her." This woman was deathly afraid of dogs and had never come near Magnus, but there she was trying to keep the officer from taking my man away.

I said, "I left him inside when I went out. A contractor's working at my place and must have let him out." The officer said, "What kind of contractor?" I kind of wondered why that was relevant. We dithered for a while, as if they couldn't understand that I hadn't let him out on purpose, and eventually the animal control guy said, "Let's call it a wash. It's a good thing you showed up when you did. I was just about to put him in the truck. No collar, no license, no microchip."

I said, "I take his collar off when he's home so he won't get caught up in it. I didn't know he'd get loose."

He handed me a giveaway leash. I put it on. Magnus looked at me sweetly.

I can't get up in this heat. That was it for me today, I'm afraid.
"Officer, he can't do it."

"Bring your car over. We'll load him into it."

I did, and that man picked Magnus up in his arms and deposited him in the back seat as easily as a sack of groceries. Jesus from next door helped me carry him from the car to the door. I took his hindquarters, because the poor old dear had soiled himself.

I deserved the poopy end anyway, for disappearing on him.

Chapter 105

I hadn't been going out, even to choir, because of a flareup in my foot that stubbornly resisted treatment. When you can't stand or walk, it's tough to socialize. So, we were largely housebound again.

Since we never go anyplace good anymore—i.e., the park—Magnus balks at getting into the car. He gets awfully stiff and sore if he has to lie on that cramped seat for more than ten or fifteen minutes. So I'm leaving him home when I go out. Some days he's home alone for hours at a time. When I get back, his food is untouched. His eyes are dim. He approaches me slowly, clearly worried.

What if I fall, and can't get up? What if I make a mess? I need you, lady. You know this.

All the dog people say not to fuss when you leave or return home because that encourages separation anxiety, so I wait a bit before greeting him. I feel guilty every time, of course.

When we go to Jean's or Susan A's or some equally reprehensible place, he lets me know that sharing me is completely off his agenda. He settles in front of the door and waits for me to take him home. Or he gets between me and the other people and whines. The only good part is when Jean's daughters cluster around him and rub him all over and hug him and praise him. When they're done, he goes straight to the door and sulks.

At Susan A's, he whimpers and backs up when Blue greets him and asks for a romp. Where he used to circulate in the dining room and greet everyone, now he retreats to the living room. If I go to see him, he gets right up and heads for the door.

My diplomat is retired.

You can't blame him, really. For months, since all the downstairs furniture got piled into the patio, we've been cooped up in the computer room without other company.

Being home alone together has become routine.

I'm starting to find that company tires me, and am making excuses to turn down the few invitations I receive—except Jean's. We still go out on Saturday nights, and she is very accommodating about my limitations, such as needing an extra chair to put the bad foot up on, and not being able to walk more than a few blocks.

Our limitations. Me and my man are cripples in company now.

Chapter 106 — Gift Season

I did try to go back to choir, but couldn't stand long enough to sing the whole Mass. Making the attempt set me back, and I broke down and wept angrily when Jean asked me about it. Soaking the bum foot in Epsom salts, stretching, getting ugly shoes with large toe boxes, using insoles, using a night splint—nothing seemed to serve. It was a good thing that all Magnus could manage was to go out for duties, because that was all I could manage myself. Except I did my duties indoors.

Watching Magnus slowly get weaker wasn't particularly cheering, either. When we went out, he'd sit down with his hind legs stretched out in front of him and look at me. I'd come over, pick his legs up behind the knees, and put him back up on his feet. In November, this would happen once or twice as we went around the buildings. In December, he started falling more and more often, reeling like a drunken sailor between falls.

I'd have put him down at that point, except for the fact that from the waist up he was fine. Alert, happy, being nice to the kids—and still able to climb the stairs.

Right. Could barely walk but could climb the stairs. Slowly, but he'd move one leg at a time, picking the hind legs up exactly as high as he needed to clear the riser. Go figure.

You should know by now that I'm not a quitter.

Coming downstairs was harder. I started standing at the foot of the stairs when I heard him start down, to catch him if he slipped. When he reached the foot of the stairs, sometimes his feet would slide out from under him, because the new hardwood didn't offer enough traction. I'd go get his boots, and put them on for him, and he'd get up and walk to the food and water bowls, or to his bed.

Magnus became more incontinent—not fully incontinent, but occasionally he'd extrude one on the floor. The first time, I reassured him, told him it was okay, and flushed the offending material. When I reported this to Susan S., she said, "Don't say anything. Just act like nothing out of the ordinary has happened."

After the next extrusion, Magnus watched anxiously around a corner of the wall while I cleaned it up. After subsequent extrusions he started trying to hide the evidence by rolling it under something, but of course the poopy nose and the stink gave the game away. Finally he accepted his situation, and when I cleaned up he'd wag his tail faintly in gratitude for my forbearance.

Outside, he stopped being able to squat for duties. He quickly adapted to this by simply lying down for solids, but kept trying to squat for fluids, with the predictable result that he'd drag himself through the pee and wet his feet and generally make a mess of his beautiful white fur. He hated baths, but I hated him being soiled, so that was that. I started giving him spot baths with a big bucket of warm water and gentle soap and a wash cloth. That was okay.

Then good things suddenly started to happen. A series of high-paying jobs came in. My client informed me that I'd have steady work for about ten months from just one of their clients. Jean insisted on buying me a Christmas tree and having the girls come over to decorate. I figured out that one particular ligament was causing my foot pain, and started massaging it, with immediate positive results.

And a complete stranger saw us in the parking lot one evening, stopped her car, and rolled down the window.

"Is that a Great Pyr?"

"Close. He's a kuvasz."

"Oh! He's only the second kuvasz I've ever seen! How old is he?"

"Twelve and a half."

"You know, my Akita had that problem when she got older. She was about his size. I still have her cart. Do you want it?"

I'd looked into that. "They cost $500!"

"I know. My family bought it for us. I was going to recycle it—the company takes them back and resells them at a cut rate—but I knew that someday I'd meet a dog who needed it. If he can learn how to use it, it will give him back his life."

"Magnus doesn't tolerate interference very well, but we can give it a try."

"You may as well, right? Otherwise…"

"I know. I have to put him down."

I didn't cry. The facts were obvious, incontrovertible, and inescapable. I didn't know how long I could give him so much care, either. But if this worked, it might be worth it. So we made a date for the transfer.

Jen is a tall, big-boned, blonde, breezy sort of gal with a round pink face and a cheery manner. She took the cart out of the back of her station wagon and dusted it off, saying, "I hope I remember how this thing works."

The cart is a part steam-punk, part Tim Burton prop, and part Rube Goldberg contraption, but clearly sturdy and stable. It looked something like the kind of sulky my stepfather used in horse racing. It's made of metal dowels, bent at various angles to form a basically rectangular frame held together with dozens of chunky u-bolts and Allen-key clamps. In the rear it supports a kind of saddle made of two oval padded rings designed to go around the tops of the thighs and hold them steady. The top rails extend forward like the shafts of a cart, at shoulder level. One padded strap goes under the chest, another goes over the back, and a third goes across the breast. The whole thing rides on twelve-inch pneumatic tires.

Jen pulled it up behind Magnus, slipped her hands under his knees, lifted him into the rings and strapped him in. He looked at her, looked at me, looked at her, struggled to get out, and gave up.

I have no idea what you girls are up to, but for now I'll play along.

Jen praised him effusively, and encouraged him. He took a few steps. The tires were flat, which didn't help, and he wasn't sure what to do with his hind legs, but he managed to go a few yards, and Jen praised him effusively again, using baby-talk.

I didn't tell her that we don't baby-talk the kuvasz. That might have been less than gracious under the circumstances.

"That's enough for the first try." She showed me how to release him and how to tow the cart around. I tried it. It must have weighed 15 pounds.

"I think he'll figure it out in no time. Just put him in it for a few minutes at a time, and gradually extend the sessions. That's what I did. At first we only got to the end of the driveway. Then it was down the block, and after a while she'd go all the way to the park. I'd take her out of the cart, and let her sit on the grass and socialize with the dogs. She got so that when she saw the cart, she'd get right into position for me, and as soon as she was harnessed, she'd take off like a shot. She'd bounce over curbs and whatever just as fast as she could go. She didn't have his breathing problem, though, so he may not be able to do as much."

"If he can do anything, that's enough." I started to cry. Jen said, "I know. But if this gives him even a few months, or even weeks, of quality time, it's worth it."

"Yes." I stifled the sobs.

The next day, I brought Magnus and the cart outside, and struggled to put him in it. I picked up each hind leg, and tried to thread it through the loops of the saddle. Magnus was recalcitrant. He stiffened his legs, squirmed around, and made it as difficult as possible for me to saddle him. The cart kept rolling out of reach.

It's bad enough that you let that lady do this to me, but you? How could you? Whatever are you punishing me for?

The only other time I ever saw that look on his face was on the beach the day after the slime-the-pup leash-punishment incident. Still, I coaxed him with chicken and praised him lavishly, got him to go a few feet, and then pulled him out of the cart. He staggered away from me as fast as he could go, heading for the street and refusing to come back. I caught him, held him, and waited for him to calm down, quietly reassuring him.

For the next few days, I just left the cart by his bed, so he'd get used to seeing and smelling it. Our second try was indoors. I put him in the cart, gave him treats and praise, only asked him to take a few steps, and took him right out of the thing. He stood and looked at me, giving me the gentle tail wag of dawning comprehension.

On Christmas day, Dan saw us outside with what he calls the contraption, and said, "That ought to help."

"I have to adjust it, make it higher for him, and inflate the tires. Can I borrow some tools?"

He disappeared inside, and came out with an adjustable crescent wrench and some Allen wrenches. "A socket wrench would work better, but I don't feel like looking for it." A frustrating, sweaty half hour followed—none of his Allen wrenches quite fit—but eventually we got the height where we thought it should be. I went inside to get meat-motivators before putting my sweetie into the cart again, and when I came out, Dan was blowing up the tires to proper pressure. "That'll reduce the drag a lot," he said.

I felt silly letting him do all the work. I don't really need the help, but I've learned (too late) that sometimes a girl just has to smile and say thank you and let the man be useful. I managed to get Magnus in the traces without too much fumbling, and Dan led us down the walkway in front of the townhouses. My old man's progress was dodgy, but motivators helped, and we got walked a few more yards before I relented.

Over the next few days, we went a bit further on every try until I felt we were ready to go down the block. This took a lot of encouragement and praise and motivators. But when we got to the end of the parking lot and started to turn into the neighborhood, Magnus perked up.

This is what it's for. It's not punishment—it's freedom. Look out ladies, here I come.

The next day, we went out again, and when we were about two blocks out, I noticed my man's hind feet were dragging on the pavement and getting scraped. Two blocks was far enough anyway, so I took him home and bathed his feet. The next day I put his boots on to protect his toes.

Fully armed with boots and cart, Magnus was able to sniff around, greet people, and be outside again, so each day was better than the last. On our third spin through the neighborhood, a man we'd met months ago walked out of his complex with his nervous little Bedlington terrier, a mid-sized white dog that looks like a city-bred lamb with a pompadour.

While Ballou barked at Magnus, David said, "That cart is way too low for him. I can fix it."

"Are you sure you don't mind?"

"Of course not. It'll make a world of difference to him."

David's a dog person.

Ballou the Bedlington was circling Magnus, barking furiously. Magnus was shying back and holding his head up in the way that indicates the imminent onset of disciplinary behavior, but he wasn't sure he could do it in the cart. Ballou darted in and out and all around Magnus while David opened his garage, displaying an impressive array of shiny bicycles and workbenches.

"Ballou, don't bark." David went calmly about making his preparations. "Ballou, don't bark."

"Wow. You have a lot of bikes. How many kids do you have?" He had the comfortable, settled look of a family man, with a smooth, round, slightly freckled face, short hair beginning to go to gray, and a slim, sturdy frame. The Bedlington seemed an odd little breed for someone with such a down-to-earth personality, but with dog people, you never know. A breed apart.

"No kids." He said. "One of those is my road bike, one is my mountain bike, one is the girlfriend's, and those two belong to my neighbor. She has a big car. Not enough space in her garage. Ballou, don't bark."

He came out with measuring tape, a set of socket wrenches, and a set of Allen wrenches. "You certainly have all the right tools," I said.

"I'm pretty handy. I build bikes for myself and my friends. When I spend ten hours building a bike for myself, it's one thing. But I have to admit, when I spend ten hours building a bike for a friend, it can wind up taking weeks."

I'd unharnessed Magnus as soon as we got to the garage, and he was calmly lying down, extruding poop. This seemed to upset David. "Ballou, don't bark. Do you want something to clean him up with?"

"No, that's okay. We do a lot of spot baths these days. I'll bathe him tonight." I scooped the poop, and went across the lot to the dumpster. Magnus tried to struggle to his feet to follow me. David said, "It's okay, she's coming right back."

You say that, but you don't know how slippery she can be. She disappears on me all the time now.

Meanwhile, David started measuring the frame and my man. He also examined Magnus's weak leg, and recommended massage. "That muscle is very tight. Muscles work by contracting, and since that muscle is already contracted, it can't do any work. If you massage him two or three times a day, he may recover enough use to get around the house."

David raised the saddle an inch and a half. He had to undo sixteen bolts and sixteen Allen-screws to do it, and retighten them when the bars were realigned. I put Magnus in the cart, and David wasn't satisfied. "It needs to go up another inch. If I do that, I'm going to have to adjust the front rails or the cart will be out of true." That took about 32 more u-bolts and Allen keys and lots of very studied, careful measurements.

I asked, "How do you know about the muscles?"

He said, "I do push therapy. Mostly for people, but also for animals. Ballou, don't bark."

"Do you have a card?"

He didn't answer. I let him work.

When David was done, I put Magnus in again, and David quietly said, "Well maybe that's too high. You want his feet to just touch the ground so he can choose whether to walk on them or just let them hang." I wondered how he knew this, but trusted his judgment.

He calmly undid all the nuts and Allen keys, took more measurements, made more adjustments, and tightened everything down again. Then he went into the garage, put away his tools, and came out holding a fanny pack. He dug around in that for a while, and pulled out a card. I said, "When I'm in funds again, I'll give you a call. Maybe you can help me as well as Magnus. Meanwhile, I'll massage him whenever I can get to his right leg. Unfortunately, that's the side he likes to lie on, so I'll have to seize my chances."

"You want to rub across the grain of the muscle. Use as much pressure as you're comfortable with, as long as it doesn't seem to hurt him. If you feel knots, press on them."

"I will. Thanks so much."

I did try this, and even learned how to roll Magnus over to reach the right leg, but it didn't seem to help.

When David was done making adjustments, I put Magnus into his taller, squared-up cart, and he took off. We walked around for a bit, and Magnus was willing to go on, but it had been so long since he'd had any real exercise, I figured it was wiser to head for home.

Lesson 12: You're not alone in this.

Ballou never did stop barking while we were in sight, by the way.

Magnus took a few weeks to learn how to use the cart, and to gain enough strength to be stable in it. He got hung up on signposts and such. He fell down sideways a few times, hitting the pavement with a heartbreaking whump. I'd slide him out of the cart, comfort and soothe him for a bit, and ask him to get up. I'd get my hands behind his knees and resaddle him. The first time I expected him to refuse, but he didn't, He let me hoist his legs into the hoops without demur, and walked on perfectly at ease. Once, two city workmen saw this happen, and ran across the street to help us. They were amazed to see him get up, let himself be put right back in the cart, and walk on calmly.

I'm game for anything that lets me go out again, Nan. Do we have to go back home so soon?

I bought area rugs to help him keep his footing on the new floor. I tried exercising his legs by standing him up, moving his feet for him, and getting him to use that set of muscles, but it didn't do much good. I bought one of those hind-end leashes that help hold your dog up, but by that time he was used to the cart, and let all his weight fall on the leash, which didn't do much good either. I wasn't strong enough to hold him up.

I kept trying to make it work, to keep him walking. I let him out and tried to help him walk to Dan's morning cookies, but he kept falling, and the sound of his hip hitting the concrete was sickening. He tried to drag himself, and wouldn't stop trying, and the weaker right hip was the one that went down and I was afraid he'd tear the skin off the bone, and I'd stay behind him and try to keep him upright or at least catch him, but he'd pull away.

He wasn't being disobedient, just indomitable. Impervious to pain. Still ready to take on all comers and tackle all challenges.

Eventually I accepted his condition and stopped taking him out without the wheelchair.

He could still climb the stairs, though, so he could stay with me at night.

Chapter 107

Cyndi's 3rd Visit

The week before Cyndi was due to arrive, I made an appointment with a canine chiropractor who Jen had told me was a miracle worker. The day before the appointment, Magnus ceased being able to walk at all.

I wept. I cursed inwardly. I wept some more.

We're still together. I still love you. You shouldn't waste our time with tears, dear heart.

That day, I accepted that new options weren't going to reverse his condition, but I kept the appointment anyway.

By California law, canine chiro's have to work under the supervision of a veterinarian, so Dr. Thompson and I agreed to meet at Dr. Paul's. Magnus and I saddled up, walked to the car, unsaddled, and I hoisted Magnus's butt into the back seat. Then I tried to get the cart into the car. It's a small car. The cart is large. I twisted the thing this way and that, turned it upside down and backwards, banged up my hands, snapped the rearview mirror off the windshield, knocked a plastic panel off the dashboard, and finally shoved the thing in by main force. (It didn't occur to me for some weeks to simply push the seat back for more room.)

This did not improve my mood, which was already dark.

When we reached Dr. Paul's and got out of the car, I was thinking, "Just go in, get Dr. Paul, and have him put Magnus out of his misery."

Cyndi was coming the next day. I imagined her sitting with me and watching me cry all weekend, and decided to spare her. As I was thinking this, Magnus headed for the street in his cart. It was a busy street. He headed off with great speed and determination. He did not respond when I called him. A man on the sidewalk moved to block his progress. I ran over and grabbed him.

He still had enough determination to run away from the clinic.

Dr. Thompson drove up in a big black truck with a crew cab that was filled with a large brown and black dog, who ignored Magnus. Magnus returned the favor. Dr. Thompson climbed out, and proved to be a stocky man of 45 or so with sandy hair and a pleasant face and manner. He was holding a camp stool and a big black bag.

"Magnus hates the vet. He doesn't want to go in."

"I saw him try to run away. Let me ask Dr. Paul if we can do the manipulation in the parking lot. A lot of vets do that."

Dr. Paul appeared at the window and gave us a nod waving his hand towards the lot. Permission granted.

Kelly—he asked me to use his first name—set his camp stool next to Magnus and said, "Let's have him stay right in the cart. I can work on him more easily that way," and proceeded to adjust my anxious darling. He took the treatment well, but made it clear he didn't like it. After ten or fifteen minutes of this, Kelly took out something that looked like a short flashlight and started running it slowly up and down Magnus's spine.

"This is called cold laser therapy. A doctor in Hungary discovered, completely by accident, that exposing surgical scars to cold laser caused them to heal faster and more completely. He thought he was using hot laser to combat cancer, but he'd gotten hold of the wrong equipment. Another team in Israel has done research with rats showing that exposure to cold laser can regenerate nerve tissue. I've had very good results, but don't expect any real improvement until he's had three to six sessions."

Kelly also told me that the arthritis medicine can cause neuropathy if it's used too long, and advised me to try stopping it. He examined Magnus's sore eye and the cysts along his upper lip (We'd done another round of antibiotics for those the week before) and said, "I'll make you some acid water for that. Just spray it into the nose and on the skin. It'll clear that right up."

"Can I make it myself with vinegar?"

He looked shocked. "No, I make it using electricity. I won't charge you anything for it. Just bring a spray bottle to our next appointment."

He charges a ridiculously low fee. He's in it for the dogs.

When Cyndi arrived the next day, I didn't tell her I was thinking we'd reached the end. She said, "You know, except for the hind legs, he looks very well. He's alert, engaged, and happy."

"He's eating well, too. Last summer he refused to eat for a while. I hate to put him down when all that's wrong is the legs" Except of course for going blind, having growths in his eye and cysts on his lip and fatty tumors on his butt and difficulty breathing, but hey. If he were human he'd be about 87. "He's still climbing stairs."

"That's amazing. Does he haul himself up on his front legs?"

"No. He climbs the stairs."

"He wants to be with you."

"You think?"

"I know."

Magnus leaked a little. Cyndi watched me follow him around with a sponge and bucket. She said nothing.

"He's not really incontinent, he just leaks a little."

"That's what incontinence is, Nancy."

I was kind of embarrassed about the stink. Cyndi is fastidious. I have become very non-fastidious. You have to be, with three animals in the house. Why even bother trying to keep up with all they shed and drop and track in?

"Wait till you see him in his cart. Without it…"

"I understand, dear."

So we took him out. By this point getting him into the cart was a smooth process, up to and including *not* trapping his tail in the frame. I let Cyndi help by holding the cart still as I slipped his legs into the saddle. And out we went.

"He loves this, Nancy. It's wonderful. He's still very much alive."

"Yes, he is."

"Nancy, he's trying to walk with his bad leg."

I went behind to watch. He was. He was moving the right hind leg in a clear alternating rhythm with the left."

"Since we've had the cart, he's just held his legs out stiff as a board." I pantomimed with my arms. "He's moving them."

"He's moving them."

"He's only had the one treatment."

"He's moving the leg."

"That gives me some hope."

"It should."

Cyndi made some helpful suggestions. "Take him out first thing so he can pee. If he's empty, he won't dribble, and you won't have to clean up all the time. Besides, the cart is what makes life worth living. Take him out again later in the day."

Before she left, I confessed that I had been about to end it, and decided not to for her sake. She said, "Thanks for that. But that's what friends are for. You will call me if you need me, right?"

"Okay."

"And meanwhile, the chiropractic stuff may have good results."

"All I need is for him to get around the house on his own."

"Right. That's all you need."

"There's still the breathing problem."

"You're not going to let him suffer. But look, he's not suffering now. He's still enjoying himself."

"I'm glad you think so. That makes me feel better. But oddly, after all the weeping and worrying I did last year, I'm much calmer about his state now that it's definite."

"That's good."

"Yes, it is."

"And you made the right decision on Friday. If there's something non-invasive you can do to keep him comfortable and functional, you should at least try it."

"You don't think I'm going too far?"

"No, I don't."

Okay, then. If my friend, the self-described anti-sentimentalist, says it's okay, then it's okay.

She also suggested that I trim the fur on his belly to reduce the amount of urine it would soak up. I did.

Chapter 108 — Out and About

As we walked around the neighborhood in the cart the Magnus conversation evolved.

"What happened to him?"

"He got old."

"I hope I have as good an attitude when I'm his age. He looks so happy."

"This is literally the difference between life and death for him."

"I've never seen anything like it. Did you make it?"

"No, it's a commercial product."

"A doggie wheelchair! Wonderful."

"A complete stranger gave it to us." I tell the story. I take advantage of their interest to give Magnus a breather. They love the story. "The woman who gave it to me wants me to pass it on when Magnus is done, on condition that the next person pass it on and the next and the next. I'm going to make a name tag with Magnus's name, breed, and the year he used the cart, and hang it from the frame. I'll ask all the people to add their dog's tags to the frame. I'll make a scroll people can enter their dog's name and dates on. I'm going to ask them to email me their dog's stories."

"What a great idea."

Caresses ensue. The old flirt gazes into people's eyes and tries to kiss the women. Some of them let him.

"He's still a beautiful dog."

"He's so sweet."

"He's a very good boy."

"What kind of dog is he?"

"He's a Hungarian kuvasz."

"How do you spell that?"

And so on.

An elderly lady stopped her car when we were crossing the street, rolled down her window, and in a thick Russian accent said, "What a sweet dog! What a sweet dog!" and then watched reverently until we passed out of sight.

A Sikh couple walked up to us with their faces glowing. The man said, "He's a prince."

City maintenance men waved to us from their van and gave us a thumbs up.

An old lady in a sari toddling down the street with a walker stopped, placed her hands around Magnus's head, and breathed life into his face.

A young Indian mother in modern clothes stopped to say all the usual things, praising the wonder dog and the wonder Mom. Her son and daughter were fascinated, but cautious.

A lady we've often seen tending the grounds of a nearby condo said, "He's looking stronger and happier now."

A woman leaned out of a second story window and called out, "God bless you. You're a wonderful mother. He's so beautiful. God bless you. That's the most wonderful thing I've ever seen." She had a heavy MittelEuropean accent.

An Anglo couple said, "It's good to see him out again."

A Mexican family stopped on the sidewalk and waited for us to catch up with them. The young son asked what happened to Magnus.

"He got old."

The son translated. They asked where I got the cart, and I gave them the story. I said, "Es un bueno regalo," The father said, "Si, un mucho bueno regalo." Buenos tardes all around, and they walked off feeling good. So did we.

A white boy on a bike said, "I feel kind of sorry for him."

I said, "Don't be. He's happier than he's been in months."

Chapter 109   Facing Facts

Okay, he's incontinent. They make dog diapers and pee pads, right? I went to PetCo and picked out the biggest pee pads they had they had for his beds. I got an extra-large diaper in a fine, manly denim lined with plaid flannel. They had little packages of absorbent pads for the diaper that looked as though they'd soak up about a tablespoon of liquid. Magnus doesn't deal in tablespoons. I went to the drug store for maxi pads to line the diaper with.

    Got all this stuff home, and started spreading it around. Magnus looked sheepish when I covered his beds with the pee pads. He looked resigned when I cut a hole in the back of the diaper for his tail and strapped it on him. I looked like an idiot when I saw that the diaper ended about 3 inches from where his unit began, which explained why there was something called a male wrap on the same display at the pet store. I'd forgotten that male dogs aren't built like male people, with all the junk between the legs.

    I went back and bought a male wrap. The package had a retro design, and promised that it would "suit his masculine contours." I started laughing, and was still laughing when I got to the check stand, showed the package to the young male clerk and said, "Suits his masculine contours!" The kid went red for a second, and then started laughing. "Suits his masculine contours!" he said.

    Alternative alliterative phrases sped through our heads. A female clerk came up to find out what was so funny. I showed her the package. Thought bubbles went up over her head, too.

At first, I only used the wraps at night. As the incontinence worsened, I tried keeping Magnus in a wrap during the day, but he quickly developed an angry rash. I cleaned his skin and put triple antibiotic on the sores, which cleared up promptly. Jean advised more frequent cleaning and zinc oxide ointment—she'd had babies, so she knew the drill. I put fresh pee pads on his bed and bathed him there with face cloths, a bucket of warm water, and avocado dog shampoo. I soothed ointment on his skin. I stopped using wraps in daytime so his skin could breathe and heal, relying on pee pads instead. We went through a lot of pee pads. Out of eco-guilt, I bought a brand that was made of recycled materials, but we were still creating a lot of trash. Even so, I was washing my love's beds, stuffing and all, every other day because of the leakage. Wash bed one and leave him on bed two until it dried; wash bed two, and so on. It was okay. The laundry room was right outside my door.

Dealing with poo was harder, because it got into his fur and required a trip to the tub. This was misery for him, and induced massive remorse in me, but it had to be done. When I'd get him out of the tub at last, and dry him off and rub him down with the avocado stuff, he'd turn round and wag at me, with his old smile.

I forgive you. I know you have to clean me up, and it does feel better.

A few days later, someone on the kuvasz list posted a message saying "I washed three dogs yesterday afternoon in less than an hour with my new HydroSurge dog-washing tool." I immediately found the website and ordered one. It's a hand-held shower attachment that delivers a strong stream of shampoo and water right down to the skin, with a little switch to turn the soap off for rinsing. You can attach it to your shower head or garden hose. Given our recent history of tub battles, I chose the garden hose. He's not crazy about it, but with coaxing and treats he lets me wash him every day as he stands in his cart. When solids are involved it takes a while, but even as I'm scrubbing out his tail, he wags for me. It probably doesn't hurt that a walk follows immediately after the bath.

Chapter 110 — The New Normal

The chiropractic and cold laser treatment came too late in the game. Magnus's hind legs had atrophied, so although his neurological performance improved he didn't have the strength to stand for more than a moment. If I'd had the money in the fall…but I hadn't.

It became normal to listen for the sound of him dragging his butt across the mercifully smooth floor, and going to help him get where he wanted to go—to the other bed, or to lie in front of the sink or the door. I simply held his hind end while he worked his forefeet. His rear end was a rag, weighed almost nothing by then.

It became normal to bring him his food and water bowls. To sit by him and tease him and let him set his head on my leg and reach up for kisses and ask for a rub. To lift his butt to lay down a fresh pee pad. To put him in the cart, take him outside, and bathe him. When he stopped being able to climb the stairs, it became normal to hold him around the waist and help him get up so he could spend the night in my room. I couldn't bear the thought of leaving him downstairs.

Chapter 111 — The Price of Love

With Mrs. James, Susan A. had already been through what I was going through. The endless decline, the constant care, the worry, the sorrow. Not being able to go away for a week or a weekend because your loved one needs your care. Not wanting to be away for even a few hours, in case something happens. Questioning your every decision, praying you're doing the right thing, and never being completely sure.

Everyone goes through this. It's part of life—the long goodbye.

Watching your parent or husband or sister be put through endless invasive procedures, and finally be imprisoned in a clinical place, is brutal. But watching the personality erode, the judgment fail along with the body is the hardest part.

I didn't have to go through that with Magnus. I wasn't forced to keep him alive at all costs. His personality and judgment never eroded. He let me care for him gracefully, and never expressed shame or humiliation. All we needed was to be together.

The hardest part was knowing that I would have to choose the day of his death. I would have to administer it, or be the agent of its administration. I looked into his eyes every day, and every day I saw life. Every day I made the decision to live, with him. Every day I made a new commitment to love.

Jean says it's a sacrificial offering.

I say it's love, just love, in all its glory.

Chapter 112   The Cart in The Park

Every day, when I put his boots on, Magnus is ecstatic, licking my face and wriggling. When I pull his cart to the door, he's already there, waiting for me to pick him up and slide his legs through the hoops. As soon as I snap the harness on, he dashes out the door and trots to Dan's for the cookies.

Pretty soon he was strong enough to pull through bushes, to yank the cart over roots and cracks and ledges in the sidewalk, and to bounce off the curb into the street without losing his balance. He was putting on muscle, showing positive energy, enthusiasm and, frankly, courage. He still had no cartilage in the right elbow, of course, but pain wasn't going to stop him.

"You amaze me, Magnus."

Hey, I love this. Have I told you lately that I love you, too?

By this point all our walks were off-leash, even in the street. He wouldn't leave my side for more than a few moments, and always had me under his eye. No one, not one neighbor or passerby or even patrolman, ever found fault with us for this—or even commented on it. Magnus followed me so closely that I could steer him around obstacles. If I saw danger ahead, all I had to do was touch him and he'd stop, even if he was excited by the prospect of greeting another dog.

Having become accustomed to the idea that he was disabled, I suddenly realized that we were walking well over a mile every day, Magnus was handling the cart beautifully, and it was time to go back to the park. We were lucky in the weather, which stayed cool, and the spring flowers were holding out and the leaves were fresh and green and our friends were there, astonished at seeing us.

Pulling up the coppice-crowned hill one evening, I saw a man leaning forward and staring at us, with his mouth open. I saw a woman following his gaze in our direction. It was TimDad and TimMom. Without Timmy.

"It's you!" TimDad said. "Look at him!"

Magnus raised his face to TimDad, who held his head in both hands and nuzzled him. His wife joined us and said, "We thought, when we stopped seeing you…"

"Without the cart, you'd have been right. You've been through it by now, I guess. "

"We lost Timmy at the end of December."

"I'm so sorry. It's amazing he held on so long. Bone cancer is supposed to be very aggressive."

"He was very brave. But we finally had to put him down."

"Will you get another dog?"

TimDad said, "Not yet. It still hurts too much." He kept nuzzling my man Magnus.

We stood there a while, the grasses on the hill silvery in the setting sun, dancing lightly in the soft breeze that ruffled Magnus's fur. We walked together again. It had been almost a year since we'd last done that, soon after Tim was diagnosed.

We walked with them a few more evenings. On one of them TimMom said, "Are you in pain? You're walking very carefully."

"My toe hurts. It's probably arthritis."

"That's terrible."

She has suffered plenty in her time—given her uneven gait, she's probably had polio. A sore toe pales before that, but I've always observed that people who have suffered know when others do, and offer much more compassion than those who haven't. I felt the full force of her compassion that evening. I loved her for it. I loved TimDad for the understanding and admiration in his eyes.

"You need a kuvasz," I said. He turned and grinned at me.

"Maybe. After a while."

"I know where I'd go."

"You do?"

"You ask me when you're ready. I know a kennel in Montana that breeds dogs who look just like Magnus, and who grow up in the natural way, in the mountains and fields, driving off bears and moose and coyotes."

TimDad's eyes were twinkling like a Christmas tree.

"You'd have to promise to train him. But living here, he'd socialize beautifully."

More twinkling.

We saw Dolly a few times. At first, she didn't seem to remember Magnus. He remembered her. He held his head up proudly and circled her, smiling broadly until she responded, which she did with a start. Half her life had passed since she'd seen us, and the recognition was gratifying.

We saw the Bernese mountain dog man, who'd advised me three years before to use meat for recall, after Magnus had run off to court the little white dog. He was with the Lab ladies and some other friends, who ran up to Magnus and swarmed him.

"He looks so happy!"

"He looks wonderful.'

"You're doing a great job with him. You always did."

"Where'd you get the wheelchair?"

As the Lab ladies expostulated, the Bernese man knelt next to my man and examined his muscles, running his hands over that great white body and looking closely into my eyes.

"Don't feel guilty if you can't take it," he said softly.

I started to weep. "I don't want to put him down because he's inconvenient for me."

"Don't think of it like that."

"Do you think he looks happy?"

"He does. He should be. You've done more for him than most people would. More than I'd do, probably."

"I can't not do it. I love him so."

He didn't say anything. He didn't try to hug me. He knew.

Every night I plaited wildflowers into my man's harness. Kids would ask why I did that, and I'd say, "All old gentlemen should have a nice boutonniere." The kids seemed to get it, though I doubt they knew the old-fashioned word. We walked with strangers. We kissed little girls. An Indian man approached us one night with his two children and asked me all about the breed. He was considering getting a dog for his family. I advised against a kuvasz unless he was prepared to have everyone in the house take obedience training with their dog. This did not seem to deter him. He couldn't take his eyes off my prince.

We saw the great blue heron. We finally saw him raise his head with his catch and stretch his neck to wiggle a furry beast down his throat. We saw small birds defending their nests spectacularly from attacking crows, and driving them away. We saw the sparrows diving like fighter planes to catch flying insects. We saw the huge faces of gilded by the sun, their branches hanging like clusters of grapes. We saw each other bathed in sunset glow.

When we got back to the street, I'd lay the wilting flowers at the base of a great old oak in offering to whatever nymph or dryad rules the park, and to say a quiet thank you to God for another gorgeous evening with my man.

CHAPTER 113 — I'M A GENIUS.

Why did it take me four months to figure out that I didn't have to wash the stuffing in Magus's beds? I took the covers off, stored them, put the padding in double plastic bags, and wrapped them in canvas drop cloths and old beach towels and sheets. I kept a big bucket in the bathroom for soiled bedclothes, and a gallon of cheap vinegar to pour on them between washes to neutralize the ammonia.

To keep the upstairs carpet clean, I learned to pour rubbing alcohol on poo stains and scrub them out with a stiff brush. For the hardwood floor downstairs, five minutes with a big sponge and a bucket of vinegared water every evening was not a problem. Every few days I'd go over the floor with oil soap to protect the wood. Since at this point Magus only wanted to lie in front of the door or in front of the sink, the area involved was small.

Incontinence became a non-issue.

I started to like having clean floors again.

Magnus turned 13. He'd been a successful wheelchair dog for seven months. And I went down with pain in my foot again. Some weeks later, a cortisone shot and a pair of hideous shoes put me back on my feet.

Jean inherited all my pretty shoes.

Because I hadn't been able to walk him, Magnus lost almost all the strength he'd gained.

Imagine one toe taking both of us down.

Chapter 114 — Happy Feet

The first time I put Magnus back in the cart, he could barely stand in it—its weight pulled him backwards—but he could walk in it once we got going. So it was back to square one and seeing if he could still recover some strength.

We started going around the block, which was actually pretty far for him at that point. He fell a few times, but in a week he recovered his stability. In two weeks, I added another block, and though it seemed to be heavy going, it was do-able. Which is about when I found the annual hot spots. I hadn't been checking, because he'd had a urinary tract infection, and I'd figured that the antibiotics for that would forestall the hotspots. They didn't. I put him on a fresh course of antibiotics, which then gave him diarrhea, naturally.

So I put him back on simmered chicken, rice cooked in the broth, and the steamed winter squash and sweet potatoes people on the kuvasz list always bring up when a dog has elimination issues. A few days of that, and he suddenly got lively and strong. Six blocks—over half a mile—was no problem, no sir, and when we got back home he was far from spent. Knowing that he needed more muscle to hold the arthritic bones in place, I didn't want to push it, so planned to add just one block a week.

We were back at the park in a month.

Children flocked around him, petting and praising him in the midsummer twilight. Dog people exclaimed over him. Some dog people looked at the worn spot on his right hip, and his limp legs, and got tight lipped. I didn't bother to tell them how excited he got at walk time, or how eagerly he whimpered when we pulled up to the park, or how impatient he was to get in the cart and take off. I'd just say, "I'd never get him in that cart if he didn't want to go." They'd shake their heads.

Forget it, Nan. We know what's really going on. We don't want to be parted, and we're doing everything we can to stay together.

One night, a man watched me pull the cart out of the car and position it so Magnus could get in it. He stood still as Magnus poked his head out of the car and got his front feet on the ground. I slipped behind him, got my hands under his knees, turned him around, slid him into the saddle, and did up the straps. The man said, "You've got that down pat." I laughed. "It took a while to figure it out, but now it's routine."

"It's a wonderful thing. Good for both of you."

Having wheels made it easy for Magnus to turn and circle, so he started playing with other dogs. I was surprised that the dogs weren't taken aback by the cart, but they don't seem to be as hung up on such things as we are. If a dog is out, and ready to go, it's all good.

A woman walked up to us, saying, "This must be Magnus, the brave, amazing wheelchair dog."

"I'm sorry, I don't remember meeting you."

"We haven't met. Magnus is the talk of the neighborhood—I heard all about him about him at the store today." She fondled him, and he worked her, giving her the love eyes and the kisses.

Ah, I love the ladies and the ladies love me. Isn't life grand?

We kept going to the park every night, all that summer.

And into the fall.

Chapter 115   Goodnight, My Love

At the end of September, we had a late heat wave. It was too hot to go to the park, even at sunset, so I waited until well after dark and took Magnus out for a neighborhood walk. He was so restless and uncomfortable, stopping, looking at me pleadingly, that I turned back after about a block, and helped him upstairs to sleep beside my bed. The next day he whimpered for me to come to him every hour or so, needing reassurance and comfort. He'd rallied so many times before that I decided to give him a day or two, but the following evening and day were much the same.

On the third morning, I found him at the foot of the stairs, straining to get away from a nasty mess. I helped him into the kitchen, and set him up on his bed. I bathed my love as thoroughly as I could, combed the filth out of his fur, and knew it was time. His legs were dying.

I made the call. Doctor Paul said he'd be at the condo at four.

To rinse Magnus off completely, I had to put him in the cart. He eagerly got up on his front legs and slid himself to the door when I pulled it down the hall. Outside, I rinsed him off and dried him, and as soon as he was clean he headed out toward the neighborhood, and looked over his shoulder at me.

It's a fine day. Let's go out.

I dropped the towel on the doormat, and followed. We walked around the neighborhood, enjoying the sunbeams and breezes, the people and dogs, the flowers and scents, Magnus thoroughly in his element, full of gentle pride. His final gift to me.

A woman was coming outside as we passed with a good-looking female German shepherd on leash. Not one to miss an opportunity, Magnus wheeled over and greeted her through the picket fence.

Good day, madam.

And a good day to you.
It's always a pleasure to meet such a fine young lady.
I've scented you before, but now at last we meet. You're every bit the gentleman I thought you'd be.

"Oh, look at your beautiful dog. What is he?"

"A flirt, it seems. Your dog is gorgeous."

"I'm not actually the owner. I'm the dog walker. I usually come about this time—we could have play dates with them."

I started to cry, and said, "I don't think so."

"Is it time?"

I nodded.

"I'm so sorry. I'm so sorry we never met before."

"Yes. Thanks."

The next few hours were hard. I put Magnus on a clean bed and stroked him for a while, but I couldn't sit still and was trying desperately not to cry. I fussed. I cried.

Ah, she's weeping again. Come here, you, let me make it better.

I went to him. He kissed my hands and my face. I wrapped my arms around his neck. He leaned happily against me, sighing. I got up again. I called on Dan, who came over to lavish treats on Magnus and say goodbye. Other neighbors came over to do the same.

I don't know what this is about, but I'll take it.

I gave Magnus an extra bowl of stew, which he devoured. I started cleaning, breaking off from time to time to give Magnus more love. I called Susan S. She said I was doing the right thing.

People say you know when it's time because the light goes out of your loved one's eyes. All that long, cool, sunny afternoon, the light was bright and strong in Magnus' eyes. He watched me, smiling gently, willing me to calm myself. His hindquarters were dying, but his heart and spirit were very much alive.

Doctor Paul came at five. I sat on Magnus's bed, and gently pulled his head into my lap, stroking him and talking to him softly.

When Doctor Paul gave the injection, Hammett, watching from the patio, howled deep in his throat.

I willed myself to stay calm, embracing and stroking my man. He struggled to get up. Dr. Paul said, "He's fighting it. That's unusual."

You're taking me away from my beloved. Please don't. Please.

And then the breath left his body. And then I broke down. Hammett came in, approached Magnus, sniffed him, let out his own high, keening cry, and ran away in grief. I made the sign of the cross over that beautiful head and silently blessed him.

He was free. There was no more pain, no more disability, no more baths or vet visits. I saw him through my tears, in full coat, with no marks of illness or weakness, cantering in top form, tail up and waving, bathed in golden light. I saw him gathering on a sun-silvered, windswept hill with Raven and Rodney and the other cats I've lost to time and place, telling stories at my expense and laughing at my foibles.

Did you ever go swimming with her?

Not intentionally. She let me fall into a pond once, though.

She left the island without me when I was seven, so I dove in and swam after her. I was swimming around the bay for hours before she came home and rescued me.

She left me alone so often that I had to leave her a pile of poo on the mat in front of the sink. She got the message. You should have seen her weep.

She wept a lot. It worried me at first, but I realized she was just a born weeper, and did what I could to keep her spirits up.

She only wept over me once, the time I made her fall off her bike and she got so angry with me. She kept saying, "I'm sorry, I'm sorry," as if she thought I wouldn't forgive her.

There were a few times when I wasn't sure I would forgive her. She did some amazingly stupid things, such as walking into the ocean.

But she did a lot of nice things, too, didn't she?

Yes.

There was that stew she made.

There was chasing sticks.
There was sleeping together, wrapped up in her arms.
Yes.
I loved that.
So did I.
Me, too.
I'm glad she had your love.
I'm glad she had yours.
I hope she has a lot more.
She will.

I buried my beloved's ashes in the park. His spirit will roam there, where he was so happy. Maybe I'll come upon him some night—a shimmering in the air, a sense of grace, a certainty that I am being watched over and loved. Goodnight, my sweet, my brave, my inimitable prince.

Wait for me.

GRACIAS   ACKNOWLEDGEMENTS

Many, many thanks to my faithful readers, Susan Altstatt, Cynthia Baron, and Jean Doten. Your comments, suggestions, persistence and encouragement helped me polish, refine, improve, and ultimately believe in this book during its early drafts. Thanks also to Susan Weisberg, who wrote my first review, and Barbara Amiel Black, for her ongoing personal and literary support. And thanks to David and Mary Dohrmann for their great advice on strengthening the narrative of redemption through love.

APPENDIX A MAGNUS MEALZ

This recipe provides food that is not only higher quality and fresher than commercial food, but also costs less. A month's worth of canned food can cost over $90, and that's not for a healthy, premium brand. A month's worth of homemade Magnus Mealz costs about $65. Magnus did extremely well on this diet, even though he tends to have allergies (which proteins from mixed sources tend to aggravate). Let's start with the meat.

> 10 – 12 lbs. chicken (99 cents a pound at the wholesale club)
> 5 lbs. ground beef (2.50 per pound at the wholesale club)
> 1 lb. chicken or beef liver
> 1 lb. tripe or chicken gizzards
> (You may have to go to a traditional butcher for organ meats)
> 1 lb. cottage cheese (for D vitamins and calcium)
> I dozen eggs scrambled in healthy oil (for skin and coat)
> 4 tbs salt (aids digestion.)

Sauté the beef on medium low heat.

Sauté the liver in the beef juices.

Put the chicken into a big pot and cover with water. Add the salt.

Simmer on low heat until it begins to fall apart.

Take the chicken out, and reserve the broth.

Take the meat off the bones, put the bones and skin back into the stock pot, and simmer on low for an hour or more to capture the bone nutrients.

Simmer the gizzards or tripe in the broth for at least 45 minutes.

While the meats are cooking, you can prepare the vegetables. Notice that every vegetable family is included: root, leaf, and legume, as well as fruit. Wash and chop (big chunks are fine):

3 large carrots
2 beets with greens
1 acorn or other winter squash, such as a small pumpkin (for fiber: don't use pumpkin pie filling)
1 sweet potato or yam (for fiber)
Large bag of spinach
2 bunches of parsley (to sweeten breath and stomach)
Big handful of string beans
1 medium sized eggplant
2 apples or other non-citrus fruit
Small bag of frozen cranberries (for urinary health)

Put a little stock in the bottom of a large pot, then put the hard vegetables on the bottom and the leafy stuff on top. Steam on low heat until the hard chunks are soft. Puree the lot in a food processor.

While the vegetables are cooking, chop the meats, etc., and mix them together. I use a large canning pot for this (plus every bowl in the house). When the vegetables are ready, mix them in with the meat.

When your super-rich broth is ready—you should have 3-4 quarts—put 1 qt in a separate pan, and use it to cook:
1 cup lentils
on medium low heat until all the liquid is absorbed

In a large stock pan, use the remaining broth to cook:
1.5 cups oatmeal, steel cut or flaked
1.5 cups rice (I use white)
1.5 cups other grain, such as barley or quinoa

Bring to a boil, then cook at low heat until all the broth is absorbed. It's best to add the grains to your meat when they're still warm. Mixing in cold grains is too hard.

When you're done, pack it up in quart boxes, and freeze whatever you can't use in three days. I fed Magnus about 1½ cups of stew with one cup of high-quality kibble twice a day. For his teeth, he got whatever hard chews are on sale, but you could also use raw meaty bones.

If you think this is insane (and it probably is), some people say dogs can live on ground turkey, carrots, and rice. Some also say dogs can live on dry kibbles alone. But who would want to?

APPENDIX B   SUSAN'S CHAMPIONS

Susan entered her dogs in two sets of shows: The Kuvasz Club of America, and the American Kennel Club. Her very first litter produced four champions. She bred many more.

Kuvasz Club of America Championships

1992
Gwyndura's Noble Belvedere
Gwyndura's Noble Melchizedek
Gwyndura's Ladislaus
MAGNUS'S GRANDSIRE
Gwyndura's Debutante Frayda

1993
Gwyndura's Diamond Victoria
Gwyndura's Cyclone Silver

1994
Gwyndura's Dandy Daimon

1995
Gwyndura's Pallas Resounding
Gwyndura's Perpetual Motion
Gwynduras Phylarac Leucocyon
Gwyndura's Chariots Of Fire
Gwyndura's Ritten In The Stars
Gwyndura's Borealis Delight
MAGNUS'S MOTHER

1997

CH Gwyndura's Chariots Of Fire

1998
Gwyndura's Feher Betyar
Gwyndura's Gaia Celeste
Gwyndura's Granted A Wish
Gwyndura Quest Bravissima
National Title Winner
Gwyndura's Sovereign Quest
Best Champion

1999
Gwyndura's Quest's Charlemagne
MAGNUS
Gwyndura's Quest's Major Promise
MAGNUS'S SISTER

American Kennel Club Championships

1992
Gwyndura's Noble Belvedere
Gwyndura's Noble Melchizedek
Gwyndura's Ladislaus
MAGNUS'S GRANDSIRE
 Gwyndura's Debutante Frayda

1993
Gwyndura's Diamond Victoria
Gwyndura's Mira Bella
Gwyndura's Cyclone Silver

1994
Gwyndura's Dandy Daimon

1995

Gwyndura's Pallas Resounding
Gwyndura's Perpetual Motion
Gwynduras Phylarac Leucocyon
Gwyndura's Chariots Of Fire
Gwyndura's Ritten In The Stars
Gwyndura's Borealis Delight
MAGNUS'S MOTHER

1997

Gwyndura's Chariots Of Fire
Companion Dog

1998

Gwyndura's Feher Betyar
Gwyndura's Gaia Celeste
Gwyndura's Granted a Wish
Gwyndura's Quest's Bravissima
Gwyndura's Red Cloud Peak
Gwyndura's Sovereign Quest

1999

Gwyndura's Quest's Charlemagne
MAGNUS
Gwyndura's Quest's Major Promise
MAGNUS'S SISTER

www.ingramcontent.com/pod-product-compliance
Lightning Source LLC
LaVergne TN
LVHW011909080426
835508LV00007BA/312